AF516587

Sri Aurobindo
& the Literary Renaissance of India

Sri Aurobindo
& the Literary Renaissance of India

Pariksith Singh, MD

kāli

Title: Sri Aurobindo & the Literary Renaissance of India
Author: Pariksith Singh, MD

ISBN: 978-81-949547-8-1
Edition: I

Published by:
BluOne India LLP

Publisher's Address:
306, Tower-I, Assotech Business Cresterra,
Plot No. 22, Sector 135, Noida.
Website – www.bluone.ink
Email – publisher@bluone.ink

Copyright © 2021 Pariksith Singh, MD
All rights reserved under the copyright conventions.
Printed in India at Thomson Press (India) Ltd.

kāli

Contents

Dedication *1*

Foreword *5*

Preface *15*

Section I: Sri Aurobindo, the Philosopher

1. Sri Aurobindo and Wittgenstein 35
2. Sri Aurobindo and Husserl 44
3. Sri Aurobindo and Nietzsche 48
4. Sri Aurobindo and Sartre 53
5. Sri Aurobindo and Heraclitus 61
6. Sri Aurobindo and Plato 66
7. Sri Aurobindo and Kant 71
8. Sri Aurobindo and Schopenhauer 76
9. Sri Aurobindo and Spinoza 80
10. Sri Aurobindo and Hegel 85
11. Sri Aurobindo and Parmenides 90
12. Sri Aurobindo and Derrida 95
13. Sri Aurobindo and Heidegger 101
14. Sri Aurobindo and Huxley 106

15. Sri Aurobindo and Buber 113

Section II: The Poet & the Playwright

1. Sri Aurobindo, the Kavi 121
2. A God's Labor 125
3. Nirvana 130
4. Despair on the Staircase 134
5. The Self's Infinity 136
6. Shiva: The Inconscient Creator 139
7. The Divine Hearing 142
8. Descent 147
9. Jivanmukta 153
10. An Image 156
11. In the Moonlight 159
12. Ilion 163
13. Thought the Paraclete 170
14. Baji Prabhou 174
15. Urvasie 179
16. The Vigil of Thaliard 183
17. Rose of God 187

18. Sri Aurobindo and Milton 195

19. Sri Aurobindo and Shakespeare 217

20. Sri Aurobindo and Herbert 224

21. Sri Aurobindo and Yeats 231

22. Sri Aurobindo and Tagore 243

23. The Viziers of Bassora 249

24. Perseus the Deliverer 257

25. Savitri as Play 261

26. What is the Mantra? 264

Section III: Sri Aurobindo, the Aphorist

1. Sri Aurobindo's Aphorisms 271

Section IV: Sri Aurobindo, the First Post-Modernist Translator Before Modernism

1. Essays on the Gita: A Bhashya as Primary Text 283

2. Sri Aurobindo: An Approach to "the Impossibility of Translation" 287

3. Sri Aurobindo: The Scandal of the Vedas 294

4. Vikramorvasie or the Hero and the Nymph 303

Section V: Sri Aurobindo, the First Literary Critic of Modern India

1. The Future Poetry 309

2. Letters on Poetry, Literature and Art 318

3. Indian Literature 321

Section VI: The Poetry of Sri Aurobindo

1. On Quantitative Meter 327

Section VII: The Prose of Sri Aurobindo

1. The Prose of Sri Aurobindo 345

2. The Story of an Artist as a Young Man 351

Section VIII: Sri Aurobindo, the Future of India

1. The Uttarpara Speech 357

2. Sri Aurobindo and the Indian Literary Awakening 366

Dedication

This book is dedicated to one of the greatest teachers of our time who, to my mind, represents the genius of India in its multifarious achievements, to the extent that an individual can represent a civilization as vast and as multi-dimensional. One of its greatest guardians and protectors, its proof to our skeptical mind that the hoary past of India was not only dynamic and real, but also that it may return in new forms and with greater puissance, to help lead mankind out of its present imbroglio. To him, my immense debt as a student of literature and as an Indian. He taught me how not to think and how not to write. And how, finally, to let go of myself and have the courage to write about him. *Sri Aurobindo.*

And then, to the greatest non-living sage of our age, the living repository of all knowledge at our fingertips, the best library I always dreamed of but never had. Who allowed me to access arcane essays written in the 19th century by obscure academics I did not know existed. Who made available many of the quotes in this book and the worldview of the philosophers studied. *Rishi*[1] *Google.*

---

[1] Seer or sage

Along with his able *shishyas*[2], Wikipedia *Muni*[1] and the Encyclopedias of Philosophy. And the hundreds of unknown writers who contributed to the discussions in this book. I apologize for any omissions in acknowledging the assistance of many an anonymous writer in helping build and strengthen my thesis.

But I take comfort in the old maxim: To steal ideas from one person is plagiarism; to steal from many is research.

To my friend and mentor, who introduced me to Sri Aurobindo more than 35 years ago. Who critiqued this book and has matured significantly under my menteeship. Whose purity of vision and utter impracticality gives me faith in a better future for mankind. *Partho.*

To my parents, who allowed me to explore the world at the age of eighteen, on my own for weeks. Searching for the Truth in the Himalayas or in obscure places when there was no cellphone, no texting, no Ola or Oyo. Searching for the Truth that was always at hand. Without them I would have never learnt how to hide my fears as a parent. *Srimati Nirmala* and *Sri Satya Narain Singh.*

To my better two-third. Or shall I say three-fourth? Whose incredible tolerance for my explorations makes me state this unequivocally. That she may not have penned this book but is an equal author. *Maria.*

To my children who make me feel unworthy as a parent. But allow me not to regret it. *Sarina, Shaan, Lenora, Nathan.*

To our puppy, Swami Mochananda, who makes me feel that somehow Darwin and Bergson missed it. That the next

---

[2] Sanksrit for disciple

evolutionary step for mankind is *Canis lupus familiaris*. *Mochi*.

Foreword

By Makarand R Paranjape

I

It is difficult to write a Foreword to this unusual and extraordinary book. That is because it is unusual in an extraordinary way and extraordinary in an unusual way.

It is extraordinary because it proposes a new, exciting, and wide-ranging, if not comprehensive, engagement with the vast oeuvre of Sri Aurobindo (1872-1950). In doing so, it broadens the scope of our understanding and appreciation of the latter's genius in a manner that few books have in the past or are likely to in the future.

It is unusual in the manner in which it seeks to do so, through short, intensely personal, at times eccentric, reflections, rather than scholarly expositions and well-researched explanations. In short and energetic bursts, the author draws our attention to key aspects of Sri Aurobindo's literary masterworks as well as to the crucial ideas that inform his lifework.

Besides offering his own intensely personal readings of well-loved texts such as "A God's Labour," "Nirvana," "Despair on the Staircase," "Descent," "Jivanmukta," and

"Thought the Paraclete," the author, Dr Pariksith Singh, also gives us his uniquely unconventional analyses of not so well-known works such as "The Self's Infinity," "Shiva," "The Inconscient Creator," "The Divine Hearing," "An Image", "In the Moonlight," "Baji Prabhou," and "Ilion." The last, particularly, is a text few Aurobindo scholars and aficionados have attended to properly. This may also be said of Sri Aurobindo's verse plays that the author deals with at some length.

But before he goes to the literary works, Dr Singh spends a lot of time on the foundations of Sri Aurobindo's thought. He does so by bringing Sri Aurobindo into a trans-historic and trans-civilisational, albeit non-chronological, dialogue with some of the leading philosophers of the Western world. These include Wittgenstein, Husserl, Nietzsche, Sartre, Heraclitus, Plato, Kant, Schopenhauer, Spinoza, Hegel, Parmenides, Derrida, Heidegger, Huxley, and Buber.

I cannot think of any comparable attempt after Sisir Kumar Maitra's *Meeting of East and West in Sri Aurobindo's Philosophy* (1956) published some 65 years back. Started as far back as 1942 in a series of articles in *Advent*, Maitra's list of Sri Aurobindo's interlocuters is impressive. It includes Bergson, Plotinus, Nicolai Hartmann, Hegel, Plato, Goethe, and Whitehead.

But Dr Singh's range is even wider than Maitra's if not as rigorously analysed from the point of view of the academic discipline of philosophy. But Sri Aurobindo himself famously said, "Let me tell you in confidence that I never, never, never was a philosopher – although I have written philosophy which is another story altogether. I knew precious little about philosophy before I did the yoga and came to Pondicherry – I was a poet and a politician, not a philosopher."

In that sense, Dr Singh is in exalted company.

II

When we try to find a context for Dr Singh's astonishing achievement in this book, we find ourselves at a loss for a comparable context. Indeed, there are many books which are extraordinary in a much more normal, somewhat anticipated, way. Their achievements and brilliance are to be expected, given the prodigious talents of their authors. They are considered pathbreaking and great for their content, theme, style, organisation, structure, imagery, ideas, contribution to the field, engagement with the past, or even prophesies of the future.

Such books may be considered as great books in the great mode. From Homer to Eliot or Ramayana to Tagore, they form the backbone of any significant literary tradition or civilisation.

It is books such as these which are glorified as canonical in studies such as *The Great Tradition* is by F R Leavis (1948). Even after the canon has been debunked if not destroyed by concerted efforts to democratise literature and criticism, some notion of great works still persists.

This is brilliantly justified by celebrity critic and scholar Harold Bloom in *The Western Canon: The Books and School of the Ages* (1994). Arguing against five prominent "schools of resentment" such as Marxist literary theory and criticism, African-American studies, New Historicism, feminism, and post-structuralism, Bloom makes a passionate plea to restore the primacy of the aesthetic and moral function of literature. In so doing, he identifies twenty-six all-time greats, from Shakespeare to Beckett, whom he sees as defining and constituting the Western canon.

If we were to leave aside canonical writers or great books, there are, besides, major books in a minor mode, such a Kafka's *Metamorphosis* or Kiran Nagarkar's *Cuckold.* Or even one-off great books, like Melville's *Moby Dick*, which is a whale of a book. Works such as the latter have no predecessors, peers, or successors. In the world of literary criticism Auerbach's *Mimesis* comes to mind as one example. Naturally, none of these authors or books make it to lists such as Bloom's.

In engaging with a polymath and literary genius such as Sri Aurobindo, we encounter the problem that he transcends all the above modes and categories. He is not properly a part of the Western canon nor, indeed, of the Indian. No wonder he is more or less ignored in both.

Sri Aurobindo wrote mostly in English, which as an Indian in the colonial era, he had mastered to a degree almost unprecedented. But, unlike Naipaul or Rushdie, he was never part of the mainstream of global English literature.

Even when it came to Indian literature, he was somewhat a solitary colossus. Unlike his contemporary fellow-Bengali, Nobel laureate, Rabindranath Tagore, Sri Aurobindo never composed songs sung by the common people of India. Rather, his poetic and philosophical works are notoriously difficult to grasp. He remains a niche author.

Even so, I cannot think of any other contemporary writer whose books are regarded as sacred scriptures to be read daily by thousands of his followers. *Savitri,* a modern epic of 24,000 lines, one of the longest poems in the English language, is monumental literary achievement, unparalleled in the history of English literature.

In addition, the large body of poetry in every conceivable genre and metre, from dozens of sonnets to epics in quantitative metre such as *Ahana,* Sri Aurobindo wrote plays in blank verse, even a couple of short stories.

Similarly, *The Life Divine,* as a work that expounds a new philosophy, literally a *darsana* or perspective on life, is one of the longest and most complicated compositions of its kind, easily rivalling works of similar scope and ambition by English philosophers of the stature of Russel, who was another contemporary of Sri Aurobindo.

Sri Aurobindo's others philosophical works, ranging from the more accessible *Essays on the Gita* and *Synthesis of Yoga,* to more socially and historically oriented works such as *The Human Cycle* and *Ideal of Human Unity,* to the deeply reflective and esoteric *Records of Yoga* and *Secret of the Veda,* not to mention his vast array of translations, constitute a vast and complex corpus, to come to terms with which requires almost superhuman erudition and effort.

What is extraordinary about Dr Singh's book is that he meets this challenge with such unusual unpretentiousness and obvious sincerity as to make it seem simple and easy. The most demanding and complicated ideas are made familiar and friendly without reduction in meaning or integrity. Each chapter becomes an introduction to the master's work because it is at the same time an invitation, reflection, and meditation.

III

Speaking of the reflective and meditative quality of Dr Singh's intense tryst with Sri Aurobindo, I cannot help feeling that Dr. Singh's book seems to have come in inspired torrents from the Master himself. There is a flawless facility in the prose, a limpidity in both ideas and sentences, which is both rare and consistent. It is almost as if the words were received by the author from a higher plane.

That is what makes me venture to remember Sri Aurobindo's statement about the composition of Savitri, that he used it as "a means of ascension". In this case, Dr Singh, too, has used the writing of this book as a means of his own *sadhana*, spiritual endeavour.

More, if I may be permitted a disclosure, invoking, reading, and writing about Sri Aurobindo meant much more to Dr Singh than what might at first appear at the surface level. Though himself one of the leading medical practitioners and health entrepreneurs in Tampa Bay area, Florida, Dr Singh got very sick with Covid19 in 2020.

Some weeks were almost touch and go for him. It was as if he was seeing death face to face like Savitri in Sri Aurobindo's eponymous epic. Did he actually have a glimpse of the other side? We cannot be sure, but he did come close to what in popular imagination is called a "near death experience," entering, so to speak, the tunnel with the white light that leads to the other side before coming back to our side once again.

It was during this arduously, testing time, that Dr Singh devoted himself to cleansing himself, surrendering to the higher force, and writing this book on his beloved Guru and spiritual master almost as a means to claw his way out of the deep pit of the Covid19 infection that had afflicted him.

The result is here for all to see.

It would not be an exaggeration to assert that this book literally saved the author's life, that he dodged and dredged his way out of disease and death in and by writing it.

As to us readers, I am certain that it can save our lives too, at least metaphorically and symbolically. Its wisdom and commitment to higher consciousness is reflected on every page although its subject is largely literary. But by bringing us into close contact and proximity to Sri Aurobindo, it is bound to uplift us also.

I would like to end on personal note. I have known Dr Singh for nearly three decades. I met him in the early 1990s, when he was a young medical student at the All Indian Institute of Medical Sciences. In those days, I was an Associate Professor at the Indian Institute of Technology, Delhi, which was across the road from Sri Aurobindo Ashram – Delhi Branch.

It was there that I met Pariksith-ji, before he finished medical school in India and went on for his postgraduate studies in the United States. At one of my Sunday talks at the Ashram, he walked up to me, introduced himself with disarming humility, and thrust a sheaf of poems in my hands.

I remember well what I told him then. He had to wait for some years before his literary talents would blossom. I thought he would be disheartened. But on the contrary, he smiled and said, "I know. Thanks for your encouragement, Sir."

Now that he is a writer of international repute and stature, I feel that it is my privilege to introduce his work of criticism as I did his first collection of poems a couple of years back. I think readers will agree with me that the literary world has found an original and ambitious new voice.

I began by heralding this book as both unusual and extraordinary. I can only underscore and reiterate this in conclusion, although for reasons quite different and somewhat less serious than I have suggested earlier.

Tell me, have you ever come across a book with such an uncommon dedication? Apart from Sri Aurobindo, his mentor, his parents, wife, and children, this book is also dedicated to:

> the greatest non-living sage of our age, the living repository of all knowledge at our fingertips, the best library I always dreamt of but never had. Who allowed me to access arcane essays written in the 19th century by obscure academics I did not know existed. Who made available many of the quotes in this book and the world-view of the philosophers studied.

Lest the reader wonders who the object of such grand and lofty praise is, I should clarify that it is "*Rishi* Google along with his able *shishyas* [disciples], Wikipedia *Muni*, and the Encyclopaedias of Philosophy."

Wait, here's more. The book is also dedicated "To our puppy, Swami Mochananda, who makes me feel that somehow Darwin and Bergson missed it. That the next evolutionary step for mankind is Canis lupus familiaris. Mochi."

The sheer chutzpah of such a dedication is sure to stick in our minds as will the much more moving and motivating interpretation of Sri Aurobindo's literary genius.

Need I say more? I rest my case.

All that remains for me is to offer this book as well as my Foreword as a humble tribute to Sri Aurobindo at the start of his 150th birth anniversary on August 15, 2021.

Preface

The literary landscape of India stretches as far back as 6,000 years. At least as far as we know. And these last 6,000 years have been like the Himalayas, range after range of great heights, peak after peak of splendor, the entire width, breadth and height of their massive accomplishment representative of a resilient yet vital civilization and culture. India is a vision vast and profuse and diverse, an achievement equaling the greatest realizations of humanity in any realm of human activity, especially its *sahitya*[3] and *kavya*[4].

This stretch of the Himalayan literary landscape of India comprises of the majestic revelations of the *kavis*[5]and *rishis*[6] of our Vedic times, and those of the Upanishads, the Ramayana, the Mahabharata and Puranas. In addition to this national corpus, let us not forget the regional literatures of its thousand dialects and national languages, and those of the saints of the *bhakti-marga*[7], the Bauls[8] from the East and bards of the South. The resonances and harmonies of the land as of an interminable orchestra rising from the genius of its

---

[3] *Sahitya* means literature in Sanskrit.

[4] *Kavya* means poetry in Sanskrit.

[5] *Kavi* is literally one who can see afar and see through and reveals the Truth, the term used for visionary poets.

[6] Saints

[7] A spiritual path or spiritual practice within Hinduism focused on loving devotion towards any personal deity. (Taken from Wikipedia)

[8] The Baul or Bauls are a group of mystic minstrels or bards of mixed elements of Sufism and Sahaja from Bengal region, comprising Bangladesh and the Indian states of West Bengal, Tripura and Barak Valley of Assam. (Taken from Wikipedia)

innumerable people created the macrocosm we call Bharatavarsha.

Putting together a canon of Indic literature might someday be a worthwhile encyclopedic task for a motivated and dedicated team of researchers, scholars, translators, curators and littérateurs. For the literature of a nation is its subtle body that tells us of its deeper movements, its wide-ranging ideas, and eventually, tells us of its soul. It is critical to acknowledge, honor and study its greatest exponents and ensure that the populace does not forget them due to lethargy or superficial distractions. For if we forget our best writers and poets, we have consigned our future to mediocrity and a slow deterioration into barbarism and crudeness.

It is my realization that Indians have done poorly in ensuring that our national treasures, the most creative minds and spirits of our land, are widely circulated and studied with utmost focus and attention. One among our greatest poets, philosophers, essayists, literary critics, playwrights and visionary global leaders was Sri Aurobindo, who not only defined modern India but is also defining our modern world every day with his far-reaching and prophetic insights.

He is perhaps the greatest literary figure that India has produced in the last hundred years; yet, it is only in India that we can forget our best and highest in such a perfunctory manner. I have recently watched movies made on James Joyce, W.B. Yeats, Samuel Beckett, among others that detail their entire life from birth to their creative excursions, their challenges and development and final literary denouement with what they wanted to realize in their art. And all this is presented with extensive research and analysis. Their places of birth and work are sites of pilgrimage for the faithful. The

Hemingway House in Florida Keys is a place we go to with an almost religious fervor to hear of Ernest Hemingway's stories, his personal life, and absorb every possible vibe of that place. And yet, one of the greatest essayists, poets, and philosophers that the world has produced to date, in any language, is known only to a faithful few in Pondicherry, India.

Sri Aurobindo's prose, lucid and crystalline, intense and poetic, can easily take its place among the best prose writers such as Michel de Montaigne, Samuel Johnson, George Bernard Shaw and Albert Camus. His style, at once classical, yet dynamic and modern, is unique in that it takes a vast scale in its sweep easily, and in the clearest possible language gives us a lapidary experience of reading complex and intricate concepts with utmost simplicity.

His books *The Life Divine*, *Essays on the Gita*, and *The Synthesis of Yoga* have transformed spiritual and yogic literature in a manner that even a secular reading of these books does not take away from their value and significance, and sometimes even enhances it. This is an achievement not too easily realized today. Sri Aurobindo did for Indian philosophy what William Shakespeare did for drama or what Geoffery Chaucer did for English verse.

He made spiritual philosophy secular and secular philosophy spiritual. Removing the artificial separation between the two, Sri Aurobindo integrated Indian philosophy into a coherent whole and made it available to the world in a simple, direct manner, eliminating all the knotty abstractions and "vague Asiatic immensities" that Yeats alluded to in his poem 'The Statues.' He gave us the key to the apparently infantile and barbaric Vedas, showing us how the literary device of the *shlesha*[9] was used in a masterly manner by the ancient *rishis* to keep the esoteric safe from the exoteric, and from a general incomprehension and misunderstanding, even misuse, among the uneducated populace. He unlocked the Vedas for all posterity and made these solutions available to anyone who can read English. He made ancient Indian spirituality available to the entire world, explaining all its essentials and opening the way for further research and investigation. He did this with linguistic and etymological precision and a keen understanding of the psychology and sensibility of our *rishis* who sang of the spirit more than 6,000 years ago and found secrets there that had been lost and forgotten by even the cognoscenti of Indian spirituality.

As a philosopher, rather a *darshanik*[10] in the Indian mold, who does not speculate or play with abstractions, but beholds matters of great import and truth with clear eyes, he gave us far-reaching perspectives that, if paid attention to, can transform, and are transforming, the future of mankind. His philosophy was not theoretical but pragmatic and grounded. *The Life Divine*, his 'word' to his beloved people that Rabindranath Tagore beseeched him for, is a towering accomplishment for anyone who has the slightest understanding of Vedanta and Indian *darshanas*[11].

Vedanta as a worldview is non-dualistic and unitary and has always been integral in its essence. However, in its practical applications, there appears a tremendous confusion. The traditional Indian response to a spiritual calling over the

---

[9] Pun or wordplay.

[10] The *darshanik* is a philosopher; literally, one who sees, from the Sanskrit *darshan*, to see.

[11] Philosophies or schools of thought.

last couple of millennia has been to take *sannyasa*[12]: to drop the world with its attachments and illusions and withdraw into a quietistic monastic nirvanic cloister when confronted with the non-unity of the real world. This withdrawal from community, while deemed spiritual and sanctioned by society, has been immensely harmful to the nation's mind and life since it has robbed India of the best and most industrious minds, the vigor that makes it dynamic and strong, and the creativity without which no spirituality can truly become muscular and athletic in the social, financial, cultural and political activities of a people. Thus, to say that Sri Aurobindo made Vedanta *poorna*[13] or integral appears redundant since Vedanta is always integrally complete. But he laid a new emphasis on the integrality of Vedanta, which can be transformational for the destiny of the entire nation if we consider the practical applications of the ancient *darshana*.

Sri Krishna explicitly states in the Bhagavad Gita that withdrawal from one's responsibilities in the world was not prescribed and was *adharmik*[14]. Yet, somehow the Indian mind forgot this important lesson and got distracted into seeing the world as *dukkha samsara*[15] or as maya. Even the concept of maya was not truly understood and it became simply equated as illusion in a strange perversion of understanding. Vedanta, in popular understanding, degenerated into an effete spirituality unable to master the world and forces which were inimical to the light or harmony that a nation needs as its foundation. Adverse forces began to

---

[12] In this context, formal renunciation and/or taking vows of monkhood.

[13] *Poorna* means complete, integral

[14] Literally, not-*dharmik*, not following or aligned with *Dharma*.

[15] Literally, *dukkha* is sorrow, *samsara* is world.

conquer the Indic narrative, thought and worldview and began to take control of India's material and physical *shakti*[16]. In short, India had forgotten its *dharma* like Arjuna at the battlefield and relapsed into foreign rule, self-forgetfulness, a crippling inferiority complex, a dark inertia, and a slow and steady breaking up of its unity.

It was Sri Ramakrishna Paramahansa who brought about a spiritual and cultural renaissance in Bengal in the 19th century, which exemplified in his person to the world what Indian spirituality truly was, his work ably carried on by Swami Vivekananda and the Ramakrishna Mission. Sri Aurobindo gave a coherent and comprehensive body to the philosophic basis of this renaissance and continued the programmatic development of the nation along these lines. But the philosophic basis, unifying at once Vedanta and Tantra, Sankhya and Yoga, Buddhism and Advaita and other lines of Indian *darshanas*, was established in a masterly synthesis in *The Life Divine*. At once, the confusion of what Vedanta is in its integrality was removed and India was once again capable of speaking in one voice for all its *darshanas*—at least in principle.

Similarly, he accomplished another synthesis of action, devotion and knowledge in his masterly work, *The Synthesis of Yoga*, where he delineated a practical basis for the unification of our philosophies and systems, of a comprehensive and methodical personal, psychological and psycho-spiritual development that we term as yoga. The celebrated clarion call, "All life is yoga," eliminated in one stroke centuries of accretions that had grown over our

---

[16] Force, vitality.

understanding and brought us back to the ancient Indian insight that all movements and energies of life were living vehicles to reach, experience, attain, and establish the Divine in our life, individually and as a community. This acceptance of life in all its multitudinous and expansive expressions by ancient India was what made it truly great and an example to the world, not only as a strong secure nation, but one that was prosperous materially, culturally, in sciences and arts and humanities, and in her greatest flights, fearless experimentations, self-actualization and self-transcendence. His *teeka*[17] on the Bhagavad Gita, itself a work of remarkable philosophic synthesis reflecting a mind that perhaps represented the highest accomplishment of Indian spirituality in the person of Sri Krishna, is a 'magisterial' and unique work. It is perhaps for the first time that one of the greatest philosophers and poets of a nation built on the vast articulation of an equally great visionary, each matching the other in realization. Sri Aurobindo acknowledged with gratitude his own immense debt to Sri Krishna. *The Essays on the Gita* again makes accessible the sometimes complex and knotted concepts of the scripture, and is perhaps greater in value than Sankara's *bhashya*[18] on the same theme, because it is more accessible, and more steadfast in its adherence to the original script.

If there is one work that can awaken the soul of India to its true *dharma*, it is the Bhagavad Gita since it encompasses the wisdom of the Vedas and Upanishads, and exemplifies it in the living example of its personages, who are still accepted by the general mind of India as our best and brightest. Even

---

[17] Expert commentary or exegesis.

[18] Commentary or exposition.

India with its plethora of great and abounding literature has only produced one Bhagavad Gita and it is obvious to me that the stamp of Sri Aurobindo, the Guru of our age, makes it even more effective in its action and power. It is a tragedy that every child in our country does not grow with its *shlokas*[19] flowing in its veins but perhaps that too will be corrected once the real value of the Bhagavad Gita and the contribution of Sri Aurobindo to our national literary heritage is fully comprehended.

Parallels in western and eastern worldviews have been studied extensively over the last few decades, whether it is between quantum physics and eastern paradigms by Fritjof Capra or Gary Zukav or in ecology and economics by E.F. Schumacher. Sri Aurobindo's description of "being" and Martin Heidegger's attempts at an ontological approach in *Being and Time* have been compared by Rhoda P. le Cocq[20]. It is obvious to me that several such parallels exist, between the western philosophies of existentialism, deconstruction, Schopenhauer and Kant, among others, and eastern philosophies. These have only to be investigated so that the artificial demarcation of the Orient and Occident too is eliminated once and for all. Even the study of Sankhya or ancient philosophers such as Heraclitus commented on by Sri Aurobindo with penetrative incisiveness is another opening into the study of mysticism and pre-Socratic philosophies of Greece in concert with that of ancient and modern India. Plotinus is another great Greek philosopher whose study may be undertaken to discover commonalities in perspectives with

---

[19] Verse or couplet.

[20] The *Radical Thinkers: Heidegger and Sri Aurobindo*. Published by California Institute of Asian Studies (1972)

the ancient Indians and applications of this unity in an increasingly global world.

Sri Aurobindo's aphorisms, a work of art in themselves, are equal in significance to the greatest epigrams of Marcus Tullius Cicero, Bhartrihari and Roger Bacon. These abbreviations pack the whole Universe in just a few lines and are perhaps the best introduction to anyone who wants to steep himself in his conciseness, humor, visionary thought and insights about the human condition. There is much to imbibe from them, much to emulate, and much to construct on.

As a literary critic, Sri Aurobindo in *The Future Poetry* presented a coherent, comprehensive and deeply insightful history of English verse and its highest possibilities. He traced the entire 600 years of English poetry with particular attention to its developing psychology and expression with extensive examples and predicted its future direction as one of the representative languages and literatures of humanity. Within the ambit of his worldview about the future of mankind, he encompassed the evolution of English right from Chaucer to the advent of modernist poetry. And he could pick up trends and movements within the larger frame of reference of English literary development and hint which way they would be moving further on. His description of the mantra as the highest achievement of inspired poetry brought an ancient ideal of Indian seerhood closer home and made it accessible to any poet aspiring to write lines that are inevitable, luminous and alchemic, while transforming his or her life in doing so. His sensitive reviews and assessments of other poets and writers such as Sarojini Naidu, Toru Dutt, Manmohan Ghosh, Harindranath Chattopadhyaya, Bal Gangadhar Tilak and AE (George William Russell), are a study in incisive and acute clarity, sensitivity and justness.

The ideal of great poetry, thus spelled out clearly, is at once a liberation and an opening into the vistas of greatness for any aspiring poet. To realize, as D.H. Lawrence declaimed in his *Studies in Classic American Literature* while discussing Walt Whitman that the goal of art is to change one's blood. This transformation of the blood-consciousness happens not only in the reader but the writer too. How to accomplish it with a focused energizing of one's ability to dream and imagine, and then to actualize it: this is the function of all great art. "You must change your life," says Rainer Maria Rilke at the end of his great poem 'Archaic Torso of Apollo,' as if it is only natural for art and personal evolution to move as one. Sri Aurobindo gave us a high ideal that not only sustains the fledgling writer and poet, but also opens possibilities in their hearts and minds, and turns the pursuit of beauty and delight in art as one's own *sadhana*[21], a journey of exploration and self-development. This was the aspiration of art and poetry in ancient Greece and Rome, in ancient India and all societies that saw poetry, and finally all art, as a journey towards the Divine, as a sacred calling and avocation, fit to be that for the oracle and the priest, the seer and the visionary.

Sri Aurobindo also attempted a few plays and stories but it was obvious that these were more fields of experimentation and exploration for him than a serious pursuit. His only complete story, *The Phantom Hour*, is a Borgesian story much before Jorge Borges attempted magic realism, with a

---

[21] In this context, spiritual practice.

tremendous buildup of atmosphere—labyrinthine and recurring, occult and uncanny. It is intriguing to speculate what could have been had he written a dozen or so stories in the same vein. Even now, some of his plays are eminently stageable and enjoyable. He was also a social and political commentator par excellence and it seems that his works, *The Foundations of Indian Culture*, *The Human Cycle*, *The Ideal of Human Unity* and *War and Self-Determination* is yet to be understood fully in all its ramifications by his researchers and scholars. It was Sri Aurobindo who secretly introduced the aspiration for *swarajya*[22] in the Indian freedom struggle and forced the Congress to adopt the resolution of complete independence from the British eventually. And it was he who supported the British against the Nazis and extended a warm hand to Cripps when he came to India with the British proposal for dominion status. It was he too who saw through the Domino Theory of Communist Russia and advised a plan for India to align with the United States to be able to create new lines of engagement as a free nation without compromising its self-respect or freedom.

Sri Aurobindo's voluminous letters on a wide range of subjects including literature, psychology, history, anthropology, art, medicine, yoga, spirituality, war and strategy make him a *letterateur* par excellence, if we may coin such a *shlesha*. In this, he may be ranked with other well-known men of letters such as D.H. Lawrence, Thomas Carlyle, John Ruskin, John Henry Newman, Mathew Arnold, John Stuart Mill, Aldous Huxley, William Morris and Samuel Butler. These letters show a side of him that is not usually visible through his writings—his empathy, humor, eclecticism, and

---

[22] *swa-* 'self', *raj-* 'rule', can mean self-governance, self-rule

mastery of diverse fields of human interests. There is only one phrase I can think of that describes him with some justice – what was appropriately once used for Leonardo Da Vinci, for "he held all the possibilities of an age within himself" – that Sri Aurobindo is the Renaissance Man of modern Indian literature. He is the *sangam*[23] of the Ganges, Yamuna, and Sarasvati rivers of mythic India, the place where the East and the West truly meet and become one river there onward.

As a translator of Sanskrit poetry, especially the Vedas and Upanishads, Kalidasa and Bhartrihari, Sri Aurobindo attempted to give us translations that captured the resonances and sound-significances of Sanskrit poetry. Besides transliterating with accuracy of meaning, he experimented with creating poetic equivalents of Sanskrit lines and often succeeded in catching the note of Sanskrit rhythms and meter. Especially, his translations of the *Rig Veda* and the *Isha Upanishad* along with his masterly commentary on them, create a benchmark in the quality of translations that we need to maintain as our standard. He employed the same approach with few lines of Greek and Latin poetry but it was his emphasis on our national languages, especially Bengali, that is critical to take further in our quest to create world-class translations and catalogues of our canon. He created correspondences among our various languages which already had cognate roots to the extent he could to help create a foundation for the organization and the erection of the future edifice of our literary body. He has hewn a new path for us to travel along further and create new highways and routes of easy navigation. There are thousands of Sanskrit books that

---

[23] Confluence

have not been translated yet after more than 70 years of independence. It is extremely telling of our collective *tamas*[24] and lack of interest "in trying to know what we already know." In this, we need to learn from the West about how to grow a sense of pride about ourselves and respect, conserve, enhance what we have received as legacy. Sri Aurobindo gave us the essence of who we are in the most accessible manner possible; it is our responsibility to build on it now.

Sri Aurobindo created a school of art and literature with his personal leadership and example. His disciples embraced his vision of life and attempted to create a lab for human evolution in Pondicherry, a tiny city in South India, but they did not divorce life. Rather, they embraced it in all its dimensions to the extent possible from their distant outpost. Sri Aurobindo made poets, playwrights, critics, philosophers, linguists, historians, scholars, and critics out of men and women and several of them grew to create remarkable works of art and literature in that secluded ashram that was yet an inseparable part of the Indian landscape. Poets such as Arjava (J.A. Chadwick), Amal Kiran, D.K. Roy, and Harin Chattopadhyaya became their own minor peaks in the Himalayas of the Indian English canon—and no low peaks either, for their work can yet be read with joy and appreciation of their technical and creative prowess.

But it is as a poet that Sri Aurobindo's greatest contribution to the world of literature needs to be seen. Contemporary critics were not ready for Sri Aurobindo, despite their professions to be objective and fair-minded in their review and appraisal. As an experimenter of avant-garde verse forms and meter, as a singer and seer of a new kind of

---

[24] Lethargy or indolence, in this context.

blank verse, as the epic poet of a metamorphic human drama that is at once symbolic, mythological and actual, he has broken the new wood for us, to paraphrase Ezra Pound's encomium for Walt Whitman.

When we look at the occultism of Yeats and the Agrarian-Formalism of Allen Tate we realize how incomplete and impractical their vision for humanity was, though still well-meaning. We also begin to appreciate how vast and coherent Sri Aurobindo is. And we reach a summation and fulfillment of vision, aspiration, knowledge, method and application such that we have seldom seen in any one person in human history.

One may question if and how Sri Aurobindo did inspire an Indian renaissance. If we look at the 19th century, India's literary output was perhaps on par with its GDP: dropping incessantly due to a systematic looting of all its resources, élan, creativity and self-confidence by Britain. The only authors of note were Bankim Chandra Chatterjee and Rabindranath Tagore. Bankim was not well-known outside Bengal until the *swarajya* movement when Tagore set his invocation 'Vande Mataram' to music. Tagore began publishing in the last couple of decades of the century. But he was not known outside Bengal until he won the Nobel Prize in 1913. Who could inspire the country, unite it and set its vision among the stars? That man of destiny was Sri Aurobindo.

Sri Aurobindo's great contribution to awakening a national literature in the various languages was several-fold:

> Being a well-known nationalist and revolutionary who instigated the announcement of *swarajya* or Independence as the goal by the Indian National Congress in 1905, he was well-known and respected across the country

especially after the Alipore Bomb case in 1909. Most significantly, he injected spirituality, religion, nationalism, culture and literature into public discourse with his masterly Uttarpara speech with which he established the inseparable unity of Indian nationalism and Sanatana Dharma.

He discovered the original significance of the Vedas and their secret message and shared it nation-wide, awakening the self-respect and confidence of the Indians, albeit slowly.

He made Vedanta practical and muscular once again and like Sri Krishna absorbed all the *darshanas* of Sanatana Dharma including tantra into an integral or *poorna* philosophy. He reinvigorated India's *tamasic* social, cultural and political life with his quiet presence and clear articulation of our true *dharma* and greatness.

He mentored other poets both inside and outside his ashram and created the Aurobindonian school of arts and poetry. He critiqued the work of other writers and poets and encouraged them. Tagore, who himself was one of the forerunners of the Bengal renaissance, publicly acknowledged and honored the genius of Sri Aurobindo. Sri Aurobindo responded in kind calling him "a wayfarer towards the same goal as ours." This synergy of two great stalwarts crystallized in the national mind what our renaissance men and women and public figures of the future could be.

He began perhaps the first journal of literature, arts, culture and philosophy from India that was distributed worldwide, the *Arya* in 1914. Even now, the influence of his writings in the journal can be felt in the blood-stream of our creativity. It is difficult to contemplate where the impact of this voluminous and intense output ends in our analog and digital life today.

He wrote in English, Sanskrit and Bengali, translated from Greek, Latin, Sanskrit, Bengali and Tamil, wrote the best *teeka* on the Gita and the first book of literary criticism by an Indian in modern times. With his mastery of English and acceptance as an intellectual giant even by the British (albeit a dangerous one), he brought prominence to Indian literature and made it acceptable, and even a high vocation, to write and to poetize.

An educational platform melding the most modern sciences with our ancient wisdom and advancements was attempted by both the giants, Sri Aurobindo and Tagore, revolutionizing our atrophic system which had become servile to the Macaulays of the west. Auroville, though it came 18 years after he left his body, is only a concretization of Sri Aurobindo's vision of our shared future.

Above all, he synthetized Indian *darshanas*, sciences, arts, culture, nationalism, *dharma*, languages, linguistics and wisdom into a singular corpus that, to this date, is unique and representative of India. This self-confidence and assertion, in my opinion, was the shot heard around the world that announced India's ascendancy once again in the comity of nations.

We can see today that even his detractors are his children. Indo-English poets from Nissim Ezekiel onwards, even as they rebelled against him, persisted with writing about the Indian experience and narrative, something that he began in full earnest in the early 20th century. They may disagree with his style but their insistence to write about Indian motifs and themes was his singular achievement. To make the Indian writer and poet free of the suffocating self-awareness and desire to play to the European gallery, something that had crippled several poets in the past such as Henry Derozio, Toru Dutt, Michael Madhusudan Dutt, Sarojini Naidu, among others, was his aspiration and he accomplished it.

The true revolution that Sri Aurobindo brought besides instilling confidence among Indians that they could gain *swarajya* was the awakening of India to its *svadharma*[25], without which no great literature is possible to any people or language. And he did this by making us aware of our great heritage, inspiring the youth to take up literature as a sacred activity, writing in multiple genres himself, initiating lines of development in several fields such as philosophy, criticism and translation and giving us the faith that we can be masters of our own fate and explore and discover our own way. Our own way.

—Pariksith Singh, MD
Spring Hill, June 2021

---

[25] *Sva* in Sanskrit means 'self ', and *dharma*, translates roughly into 'upholding principle', or 'law'. *Svadharma* would then be the upholding and sustaining principle and law of one's being.

I.

Sri Aurobindo, the Philosopher

1.

Sri Aurobindo and Wittgenstein

Perhaps the best way to introduce Sri Aurobindo as a philosopher would be to compare him with Ludwig Wittgenstein, considered by some to be the greatest philosopher of the last century. And this allows us to see their similarities, parallels, discoveries and significant differences. It is interesting to note at the outset that Sri Aurobindo did not consider himself a philosopher. He protested when D.K. Roy requested him for an article on metaphysics requested by S. Radhakrishnan, the future President of independent India.

> Look here!… Let me tell you in confidence that I never, never, never was a philosopher – although I have written philosophy which is another story altogether. I knew precious little about philosophy before I did the Yoga and came to Pondicherry – I was a poet and a politician, not a philosopher!… I had only to write down in the terms of the intellect all that I had observed and come to know in practicing Yoga daily and the philosophy was there, automatically. But that is not being a philosopher!

On the other hand, according to The Duty of Genius by Ray Monk, Wittgenstein saw his task as the destruction of the metaphysics and logical systems that create linguistic games and cause confusion due to bad grammar and attribution of meaning. He considered philosophy as "a battle against the bewitchment of our intelligence by means of language." And this is a crucial point.

Sri Aurobindo saw philosophy as an intellectual, rational exercise while he affirmed the greater validity of the ancient Indian approach of *darshana,* which means to see. And what kind of seeing is this? This seeing is revelation of truth, a direct perception without the screen of language and thought, a beholding that penetrates the screens of mind and perceives without any instrument the Self as Existence, the only thing that is.

In the precise phrase of the *Kena Upanishad*, the seer is described as "the ear of the ear, the eye of the eye, the speech of the speech and the mind of the mind."[26] And whom does the seer behold? His own radiant being, not captured or capturable in words or concepts, thoughts or formulations. *Darshana* goes beyond mentalizing or learning or even the love of wisdom that the term 'philosophy' literally means. *Darshana* is awareness growing cognizant of itself, direct, without any intermediaries of logic or belief. It is not a physical but a total seeing with the heart, deep as the marrow, down to the toes to one's feet. And this beholding is transformative, no longer as the subject observing the object, but both seen as fundamental unity by That which one is.

This *darshana* or sight is silent, where the mind is only a passive and mute instrument. Sight becomes a higher faculty than thinking, so does hearing and all perception. How similar in outlook – though in domains and ability to see quite apart for in case of *darshana*, outlook is also inlook – as

---

[26] *Kena Upaniṣad* 1.2 - श्रोत्रस्य श्रोत्रं मनसो मनो यद्, वाचो ह वाचं स उ प्राणस्य प्राणः।

when Wittgenstein exclaims to his students, "Don't think but look! Only describe, don't explain!"

In the early stage of his revolutionary years (Sri Aurobindo was an ardent leader of India's struggle for independence), Sri Aurobindo had a yogic experience which is quite instructive to understand the Indian approach to *darshana*. Let us hear him describe it for us:

> It was my great debt to Yogi Lele that he showed me this. "Sit in meditation," he said, "but do not think, look only at your mind; you will see thoughts coming into it: before they can enter throw these away from your mind till your mind is capable of entire silence." I had never heard before of thoughts coming visibly into the mind from outside, but I did not think either of questioning the truth or the possibility, I simply sat down and did it. In a moment my mind became silent as a windless air on a high mountain summit and then I saw one thought and then another coming in a concrete way from outside; I flung them away before they could enter and take hold of the brain and in three days I was free. From that moment, in principle, the mental being in me became a free Intelligence, a universal Mind, not limited to the narrow circle of personal thought as a laborer in a thought factory, but a receiver of knowledge from all the hundred realms of being and free to choose what it willed in this vast sight-empire and thought-empire.

In another letter, he writes about his experience thus:

> We sat together and I followed with an absolute fidelity what he instructed me to do, not myself in the least understanding where he was leading me or where I was myself going. The first result was a series of tremendously powerful experiences and radical changes of consciousness

> which he had never intended for they were Advaitic and Vedantic and he was against Advaita Vedanta and which were quite contrary to my own ideas, for they made me see with a stupendous intensity the world as a cinematographic play of vacant forms in the impersonal universality of the Absolute Brahman.[27]

And he further denotes this awareness in this manner:

> I myself had my experience of Nirvana and silence in the Brahman, etc. long before there was any knowledge of the overhead spiritual planes; it came first simply by an absolute stillness and blotting out as it were of all mental, emotional and other inner activities—the body continued indeed to see, walk, speak and do its other business, but as an empty automatic machine and nothing more. I did not become aware of any pure "I" nor even of any self, impersonal or other, there was only an awareness of That as the sole Reality, all else being quite unsubstantial, void, non-real. As to what realized that Reality, it was a nameless consciousness which was not other than That; one could perhaps say this, though hardly even so much as this, since there was no mental concept of it, but not more. Neither was I aware of any lower soul or outer self called by such and such a personal name that was performing this feat of arriving at the consciousness of Nirvana....
>
> Mark that I did not think these things, there were no thoughts or concepts nor did they present themselves like that to any Me; it simply just was so or was self-apparently so ... [28]

And his poem 'Nirvana' captures this state with fidelity,

---

[27] Collected Works of Sri Aurobindo (CWSA), *Letters on Himself*, p. 239

[28] CWSA, *Letters on Himself*, p. 257

All is abolished but the mute Alone.
The mind from thought released, the heart from grief
Grow inexistent now beyond belief;
There is no I, no Nature, known-unknown...

I have treated this wordless thoughtless state in detail since it seems crucial to me to understand where Wittgenstein with his brilliant analysis ends and where Sri Aurobindo begins. Wittgenstein, the genius that he was, knew about the attempts to create perfectly logical systems by his mentor Bertrand Russell and G.E. Moore, Georg Cantor and David Hilbert, and saw the fatal flaw in their paradigms. He pointed out how language is used to create propositions that the logician attempts to resolve in the same language; but the language itself is the barrier and the hole.

"The limits of my language are the limits of my world," Wittgenstein announced famously. "Language disguises thought," he explained. It is a picture that "held us captive." And in addition, "We could not get outside it, for it lay in our language and language seemed to repeat it to us inexorably." Kurt Gödel's "incompleteness theorems" proved mathematically that "arithmetic, and thus, also any system based on it is of necessity incomplete." Thus, language cannot prove what it sets forth to establish in terms of its own grammar and rules.

And, thus, Wittgenstein and Gödel brought down the entire edifice on which western philosophy and mathematics were based. The hope that a perfectly logical system can be created was shown as an illusion. "To imagine a language is to imagine a form of life," added Wittgenstein to this predicament of logic, set theories and systems.

Essentially, metaphysics and philosophy had no way to escape its own death-trap. Wittgenstein only hastened the demise with his brilliant and incisive clarity that saw through the circular logic of all systems based on language, whether specialized like mathematics or the general one used daily for communication among humans. And so, he ended his *Tractatus Logico-Philsophicus* with this axiom of axioms:

> Whereof one cannot speak, thereof one must be silent.[29]

Further developments in western thought such as deconstruction and structuralism only confirm this insight that philosophy as practiced is a "disease, a word-game," and to cure oneself of its perniciousness remains the highest function of the philosopher. Where do we go from here, once we realize, that "at the core of all well-founded axioms is an axiom that is unfounded"? Eastern philosophy or, rather, *darshana* shows the way.

Thus, to be at the center of the silence that Wittgenstein speaks of, or rather, "does not speak of," and write from there or, even, let the silence write itself, from a deeper wisdom than the one known to mind or seizable by thought, is the objective of the *drishta*[30], the *darshanik*, the eastern philosopher. Not through words or thought or the games of interaction is truth known, but from the stillness that transcends them. As the *drishta* or the seer becomes the *kavi*, who not only can see but also reveals through the self-articulated wisdom of the *sruti*[31], truths that transcend our limited landscape.

---

[29] Tractatus 7

[30] *Driṣhta* means the one who sees.

[31] *Sruti* means that which is heard or revelation.

In ancient Vedanta, one of the first trainings of the mind is to see that words are not the object they seem to refer to. That words are the tags given to form and movement that the consciousness perceives. Identifying the object with its tag creates huge misunderstandings. Nor is the world of words the real world. And then, the next realization that the mind and ego too are born of naming. For 'I' *too* is a word that creates further concepts around it. Only direct perception can transform the significance we give to the labels we place on each thing; the perception that the world we live in is an artifact and only when we no longer see it through the screen of the names we have given to it, does awareness become free of its self-created dungeon. Nor can thoughts or intellectual complexes be described or cured by words.

The ultimate reality according to Vedanta is indescribable, *anirvacaniya*[32]. It cannot be talked about but it can be lived and realized. The world of words comes to an end and reality peeks in. And thought, only words connecting to each other in a linear temporal movement, comes to an end.

Wittgenstein showed us the limits of thought because its vehicle of words is itself limited. Sri Aurobindo taught us that to understand we do not need words, rather, we are better off without them. This is the beginning of a new journey of mind and consciousness towards a deeper exploration that does not depend on the mind but finds other faculties such as intuition and direct knowing for the discovery of its truths.

The other breakthrough made by Wittgenstein, in my opinion, was his understanding of time and eternity. He explained, "If we take eternity to mean not infinite temporal

---

[32] *Anirvacaniya* means that which cannot be spoken about.

duration but timelessness, then eternal life belongs to those who live in the present." Modern writers like Eckhart Tolle insist that living in the 'now' is our existential need and is curative. But it is an ancient Yogic concept. The eternal present is the understanding that the only time we live in is the present and the only time we can live in is the present. There is no other time; the past is memory and the future is projection. Living in the present is the way to be sensitive, aware, free of mental anxieties, fear and ambition, free of thought and its trappings. As T.S. Eliot was to say, at the beginning of his first quartet 'Burnt Norton' in 1936,

> Time present and time past
> Are both perhaps present in time future,
> And time future contained in time past.
> If all time is eternally present
> All time is unredeemable...

Wittgenstein was not to know the value of his sagacity and its sacred roots in Indian wisdom. He considered ethics and aesthetics as one, according to *Ludwig Wittgenstein, The Duty of Genius* by Ray Monk. Perhaps he should have added, like Sri Aurobindo, that psychology, epistemology, ontology, cosmology, theology and soteriology are also one. A new way of thinking, about the tools used by thinking itself, a new way of seeing at one's own assumptions and finding flaws in how matters are stated, communicated, conceived and debated, this was Wittgenstein greatest contribution to modern thought. How far had he moved western philosophy from the Socratic dialogue and reason? We appreciate this only when we realize how effectively he undermined the foundations of all metaphysical and dialectical systems, to such an extent that within the few decades after his demise, the death knell of western philosophy had been sounded and widely accepted as inevitable.

2.

Sri Aurobindo and Husserl

If Wittgenstein was a bulldozer ripping apart the edifice of western philosophy from one direction, there was another busy with sticks of dynamite at the other end. He was Edmund Husserl, who discovered a new philosophy, or shall we say, a method to approach philosophy and that method was phenomenology.

Husserl's approach was simple. He brushed aside all concepts, belief-systems, logicisms and metaphysics. And insisted on describing appearances as they are. In detail, with precision, clearly, without any obfuscation of psychological tendencies or biases. And with one wave of hand, he had swept away the great philosophies of the west, including those of Plato, Emmanuel Kant, Arthur Schopenhauer and Georg Hegel. Plato's doctrine of the 'ideal' world behind the world of appearances had been made immaterial. Kant could no longer bring out epistemology as a concern since it became irrelevant. Schopenhauer's *The World as Will and Representation* was relegated to the history of concepts. And Hegel's thesis and antithesis were resolved in a flash of insight.

The German philosopher went straight for life as he experienced it, moment to moment. As Sarah Bakewell points out in her book *At the Existentialist Café* all old puzzles were put into brackets, 'epoche,' and set aside. As the Encyclopedia Britannica describes it, *zu den Zachen selbst*—"To the things themselves," became his rallying cry. Husserl insisted that "a new way of looking at things is necessary." In his terminology, a phenomenon is any object as it presents itself to our experience. In such an approach, the old dichotomy of object and subject was restructured into the duality of consciousness and appearance and all abstract suppositions and intrusive psychological associations cast aside.

We have already seen how Sri Aurobindo describes his experience of watching even his own thoughts, thus turning even his psychological movements into 'phenomena.' The ancient meditation called Vipassana is a method where the practitioner only watches everything as it becomes 'available and present' to the awareness. Even sensations, thoughts, feelings, emotions and one's sense of ego are seen outside awareness in the true phenomenology that Husserl could never discover in his further investigations. And it is my opinion that this is where he fell short. He could not persist with his method to its end, i.e., he could not continue observing until his own subjective states and movements became phenomena to the awareness that solely observed. If he had done so he would have discovered the same dialectic of pure awareness and constant mobility, termed the Purusha and Prakriti in Sankhya philosophy of ancient India.

"To study the structure of consciousness, one would have to distinguish between the act of consciousness and the phenomena at which it is directed"—so said Husserl in his *Logical Investigations* of descriptive phenomenology. Unfortunately, he could proceed no deeper in his pursuit to study consciousness even as he grappled with Descartes and

Kant, while maintaining "it is my conviction that intentional phenomenology has for the first time made spirit as spirit the field of systematic scientific experience, thus effecting a total transformation of the task of knowledge." Perhaps he did not know that the Indic civilization had studied this subject for centuries and had reached an extremely sophisticated understanding of consciousness and how it related to phenomena, the world of appearance and manifestation, in the investigations of Sage Kapila, the founder of Sankhya, and later, the integral approach of Sri Krishna in the Bhagavad Gita.

To an Indian yogi, such an understanding that Husserl reached is taken as a beginning point for investigations into the nature of *Chitta,* Consciousness, and *Sat*, Existence and Truth. As Sri Aurobindo grew in his practice or *sadhana*, he synthetized the *darshanas* of Sankhya, Vedanta, Advaita, Vaishnava devotionalism, Tantra and Yoga into an integral path as vast and comprehensive as Sri Krishna. It would be interesting to compare Sankhya philosophy and Husserl's 'divagations' to see if there is any overlap and what the differences of approach and conclusions might be.

Husserl is important because he changed the direction of western philosophy with his singular and demanding insistence on the new approach. He had a profound influence on Simone de Beauvoir, Jean Paul Sartre, Maurice Merleau-Ponty, Camus, Heidegger and so many others even when they differed with his historical reviews later.

The concept of intentionality that he applied to consciousness is however one that is not accepted in Sankhya and Vedantic systems including Sri Aurobindo's integral philosophy. Consciousness, according to Husserl, is intentional, or always directed to an appearance. But in the eastern *darshanas*, consciousness can be directed towards itself, and this may be one of the most significant turnings in the development of the individual, psychologically and as a philosopher, or rather, as a *darshanik* and a yogi. The first step towards *Samadhi*, the eternal self-absorption of Consciousness within itself, its ultimate liberation and knowledge of Truth is when consciousness is not intentional at all. Or as J. Krishnamurti points out in explaining *dhyana* or meditation that it happens when consciousness has no direction.

As elaborated in *The Essential Husserl* edited by Donn Welton, Husserl brought western philosophy to immediate awareness, without the screen of philosophy or ideas about the nature of the world. He eschewed all theoretical explanations and made philosophy direct and living. Even his subsequent failure in taking his exploration further does not detract from his radical breakthrough that brought modern thought to the doorstep of the East and made a synthesis of the two opposing worldviews possible. Conversely, it makes eastern philosophy or *darshana* intelligible in modern terms to a student of western philosophy.

Husserl, to my mind, is one of the bridges between Sri Aurobindo's *poorna* Vedanta and the partial philosophies of the western hemisphere. For he, in developing phenomenology, did not establish another abstract superstructure but elaborated a method, a way of seeing—in other words, a *darshana*.

3.

Sri Aurobindo and Nietzsche

Friedrich Nietzsche, famous for his popularization of the concept of the Superman, or as he stated, the Overman, became famous for the wrong reasons in the 20th century. Appropriated by the Nazis, even though it does not appear that he was an anti-Semite, his genius is slowly being recognized once it was discovered that his sister selectively edited his works to suit her own ends after his death.

In light of the new research, perhaps it is time to see the parallels of his thought and Sri Aurobindo's vision of the Übermensch. What is this Superman, if one may ask? Sri Aurobindo in a famous aphorism stated that man is a transitional animal. Another being of higher capacity, potential, wisdom and harmony shall replace him. "Evolution is not finished; reason is not the last word nor the reasoning animal the supreme figure of Nature. As man emerged out of the animal, so out of man the Superman emerges."[33] The Superman of his *darshana* shall not work with a diffracted mental or a degenerate vital[34] or discombobulated feelings or

---

[33] CWSA, Vol 12, p. 443

[34] In integral psychology, the emotional being, the seat of our emotions, is called the vital, from the Latin vitalis, vita, meaning life.

degenerating body but will be a being who lives and acts from a highly evolved center where the mind, vital, heart and body are subservient to a Truth-Consciousness. This Truth-Consciousness is unitary, where the will is not separate from its execution, which is global in its outlook and purview, is blissful and *poorna* with Divine love.

If we may attempt to illustrate by using the example of known spiritual luminaries of the past, we might say that the Superman has a heart as open as that of Christ, a vital still and settled as the Buddha, and a mind vast and all-encompassing as Sri Krishna or even more so. Nietzsche's conception of the Supermind seemed to be a will to power that is free of morality as defined by society, religion and state. But newer findings also reveal that he talked about a Creative Love that drives his Overman. If true, his Overman might be a more balanced creature than previously thought.

The Superman becomes a spiritual being of the highest order with Sri Aurobindo, who was careful to distance himself from the Dionysian German. And yet, Sri Aurobindo did acknowledge that Nietzsche deserves credit for casting the concept into the "soil of human growth" in modern times. Rhoda P. le Cocq has pointed out that Nietzsche is important because he boldly tore away the prison that had so far restricted the human mind and vital and that held back man's imagination and willingness to take charge of his condition.

Nietzsche did not accept the Darwinian model of evolution based on chance, coincidence or natural selection. He gave the human will a prominent place as a driver of the upward movement in a new kind of organization of the individual and the society. He brought philosophy back to the psychologic roots it had in pre-Socratic thought and transformed philosophy from a systems-based approach to an individual-centered mode. Psychology was no longer separate from philosophy, ontology or cosmology.

Sartre, Heidegger, Camus, Merleau-Ponty, among others, are all Nietzsche's descendants and even Henri Bergson, Wittgenstein, Shaw and Jacques Derrida were profoundly influenced by him in one way or another. He changed the course of human thought. Without him no Husserl would have been able to set aside all the labors of the past to focus solely on phenomena as perceived by the awareness—Nietzsche had already done that for him. Nor would Creative Evolution be a consideration among intellectuals.

It is interesting that this coming together of psychology and philosophy is a fundamental principle of ancient Indian systems. There is no contradiction between the two; in fact, all philosophy is but the nature of the human psyche.

The second proclamation that God was dead sometimes seems to be a dare—the God of the Abrahamic religions who is little more than a "schoolmaster of souls," and seems to be an irate irascible anthropomorphic Titan consigned to history. No new conception of God is proposed—nor should we expect it from Nietzsche.

Carl Gustav Jung said that our idea of God is outgrown in his book, *The Earth Has a Soul.* Sri Aurobindo's concept of God is the Vedantic description of *Sat-Chit-Ananda*, or Truth-Existence-Bliss, which is transcendental, cosmic and immanent, universal and individual. This new or 'older' God, who was sought by Herman Hesse in his unification of God and Devil, is the understanding of Sanatana Dharma that agrees essentially with the core ideations of the monists, monotheists, pantheists, panentheists, deists, polytheists, even agnostics and atheists in the Indic traditions, and yet suggests that God is not limited by any of these framings. For He/She/It is beyond all concepts and religions and is yet reflected in their picturizations partially.

As J. Krishnamurti once said, we have created a petty God in our own image. Sri Aurobindo elevates our heart, mind and vital so that we can have a wider, higher and deeper realization of the living God who is always integrally us and everything we become and is a God of unconditional Love.

The third important concept, that of Eternal Recurrence, in Nietzsche's philosophy is strange and never fully explained. Is it the repetition of the same circumstances with the same personages? Or is it the understanding that the world evolves in cycles of ascending consciousness? If by the term 'eternal recurrence' we mean the latter, then it coincides with the ancient Hindu concept of *yugas* or ages which follow one another, not as replicas, but in spirals of higher and greater ascents of the manifesting spirit through a helical upward movement.

Man is a spectrum. Nietzsche picked up one shade of color as most philosophers do. But he took the brightest tinge and attempted to make it clearer, more intense, more refined. Walter Kaufman shows in *Nietzsche, Philosopher, Psychologist, Antichrist,* that, unfortunately, Nietzsche could not succeed fully since he had taken up only one band of wavelength and his intellectual powers collapsed prematurely. Sri Aurobindo takes the whole array of colors, the entire range of the rainbow as it were, rejects no hue or frequency, and enhances them all in the true unity before the prism diffracted the rays of the Sun. And this is the most important difference between Sri

Aurobindo and most western philosophers as we have pointed earlier too. That of a one-sided perspective of western mind being absorbed in the holistic and comprehensive eastern vision. And a deeper way of seeing that is harmonious, settled and fulfilling of all the partial and limited occidental viewpoints.

4.

Sri Aurobindo and Sartre

Sartre has the unique distinction of hitting profound home-runs with his philosophical insights and then failing to build his innings by forgetting to touch his base each time. He reminds us of the modern generation with their abundance of Attention Deficit Disorder on a habitual basis. He is unable to follow through his own line of thought. His problem, to my mind, is the inability to hold on the awareness without moving on. He takes the easier path of building a derivative thought and a specious edifice of existentialist philosophy.

For example, when he states that man is condemned to be free, he compromises a fact in his desire for poetic effect. The word 'condemned' gives a negative connotation to a realization that is universal and by yielding to this impulse to be literary, Sartre compromises on the direct and literal. This is an error he keeps repeating and reveling in since, fundamentally, he is a writer, a novelist, a playwright and not a conscientious philosopher or a systematizer.

These non-phenomenologic compromises on his description of phenomena rob him of what would have been a grand achievement in psychology, philosophy, ontology, ethics and sociology. Instead, he became a pamphleteer and a sloganeer, an apologist for Marxism and a compromised institution in his desire to be a celebrity.

He was the first philosopher who became a "sensation" among the youth of the day. And desire for popularity is harmful to a philosopher, as Sri Aurobindo wisely pointed out in a letter to his disciple. He said, in what was a surprising and counterintuitive comment,

> I don't believe in advertisement except for books, etc., and in propaganda except for politics and patent medicines. But for serious work it is a poison. It means either a stunt or a boom – and stunts and booms exhaust the thing they carry on their crest and leave it lifeless and broken high and dry on the shores of nowhere – or it means a movement.
>
> A movement in the case of a work like mine means the founding of a school or a sect or some other damned nonsense. It means that hundreds or thousands of useless people join in and corrupt the work or reduce it to a pompous farce from which the Truth that was coming down recedes into secrecy and silence. It is what has happened to the "religions" and is the reason of their failure.[35]

One may add that this is what happened to the 'philosophy' that Sartre so zealously attempted to espouse.

At the moment of consciousness of appearance without reflection, all residue of past or ideas are put aside according to phenomenology. It was Sartre's insight that this pre-reflective consciousness is utterly free, exactly what Sankhya philosophy had discovered thousands of years ago in the early

---

[35] CWSA, *Letters on Himself and the Ashram*, p. 375

development of Indian thought. This pre-reflective consciousness is the first hint of the Purusha, the pure awareness that is free of all manifestation, according to the ancient *darshana*. But Sartre was unable to build a bedrock of this consciousness as the true existentialism. Instead, he betrayed himself by losing this awareness in reflection and failed to score.

Nor did he build on his insight that the ego is an object of consciousness. He failed to follow up on this brilliant finding. Eckhart Tolle dissects this beautifully in *A New Earth* in this manner,

> Jean-Paul Sartre ... looked at Descartes's statement "I think, therefore I am" very deeply and suddenly realized, in his own words, "The consciousness that says 'I am' is not the consciousness that thinks." What did he mean by that? When you are aware that you are thinking, that awareness is not part of thinking. It is a different dimension of consciousness. And it is that awareness that says "I am." If there were nothing but thought in you, you wouldn't even know you are thinking. You would be like a dreamer who doesn't know he is dreaming. You would be as identified with every thought as the dreamer is with every image in the dream. Many people still live like that, like sleepwalkers, trapped in old dysfunctional mind-sets that continuously re-create the same nightmarish reality. When you know you are dreaming, you are awake within the dream. Another dimension of consciousness has come in.

The implication of Sartre's insight is profound, but he himself was still too identified with thinking to realize the full significance of what he had discovered: "an emerging new dimension of consciousness." For existentialism to be true to its core, the existentialist must realize that Consciousness is the only existence there is; rest all is fluctuation of form and movement, name and shapes, according to ancient Vedanta. And the 'essents' of Greek philosophy, things that are existent, can never be the basis of a sound philosophy. That which does not change, if Sartre had but followed it with single-mindedness, is Consciousness, the *Chitta*. And the existentialist who insists that existence precedes essence – in fact, existence is the only essence, if one might be allowed a fundamental pun – needs to stay grounded in this awareness without leaning on thoughts or concepts or essences to give in to their desire to create a metaphysics.

The system if it must happen shall arise organically out of the nature of *Chitta*—but for this to happen, the existentialist needs to hold on to its thread. In this sense, Camus stayed true and 'absurd' to the end following the methods of existentialism. He could have gone further but he did not take recourse to shallow expedience since awareness without thought can become unbearable. Nor did he bail out but stayed stoic to the end, refusing to capitulate to 'bad faith.'

"Hell is other people," says Sartre. To which Wittgenstein responds, "Hell isn't other people. Hell is yourself." And in stating this, Wittgenstein is more an existentialist than Sartre who focuses more, at times, on the other, the appearance, and loses his 'phenomenological' moorings.

At the end, Sartre's sympathy towards Marxism and calling it "the definitive philosophy of our age," is understandable only partially as a response to his concern for others and against injustice. But, in doing so, he was no longer an existentialist.

And he might have realized had he stayed true to his *dharma*, that compassion only arises if the *Chitta* or Consciousness is truly free of its own inclinations, or *vrittis*[36], and is uncluttered of ego. Then, one helps and cares for others as a Buddha with a compassion that is natural and not an artificial twisting of one's tendencies. J. Krishnamurti calls compassion as having passion for all things—in this *karuna*, or deep empathy for all, one is a true socialist and Marxist without being limited by a partial philosophy.

In some ways, Sartre is a lesson for those who wish to study his work, *Being and Nothingness*. The building blocks of existentialism can only be Consciousness, that is its own Truth, that is the true Existence. The terrifyingly beautiful reality that he had uncovered was soon shrouded in the mist of confusion and unclear identification of things as they are. And his focus soon turned into things as they are not.

And yet, his achievements must be acknowledged. His realization that pre-reflective consciousness is primary consciousness and it is non-personal is a quantum leap in western thought. And also, his realization that the nature of this consciousness is self-consciousness that has its own knowing is another milestone in its historical development.

"We have no alternative but to create our own values," he said. But these values are not arbitrary as Sri Aurobindo shows us; instead, they arise from the harmony and stillness that come when awareness is free, steady and settled. Thus, the self does not live in conflict with the 'other,' as Huxley shows us at the end of his novel *Eyeless in Gaza*, but in unity. And this is so, since the individual's Consciousness is ultimately also

---

[36] *Vrittis* meaning literally whirlpool and signifies the contents of awareness that are a disturbance

the Consciousness of all living beings, transcendent and absolute – *cetanas cetananam* – the One Consciousness in many Consciousnesses, as Sri Aurobindo translates in his masterly essay 'Philosophy of the Upanishads.'

Bryan Magee points out that Sartre had three stages of intellectual development under the influence of Husserl, Heidegger, and finally, Hegel and Karl Marx, respectively. All four are absorbed in the vastness of the integral vision of Sri Aurobindo as he removes the separating line between phenomena and noumena, ontology and psychology, historical dialectic with the spiral evolution of Prakriti and, finally, the self and community.

"Nothingness lies coiled in the heart of being—like a worm," Sartre opines. The first half of the sentence could be taken as a poetic description of *shoonya* in Indian *darshana*. Sartre opens the doors for the future philosopher to delve further, dive deeper and feel greater. This is his mighty accomplishment according to T.Z. Lavine in *From Socrates to Sartre*.

Consciousness is a spectrum, as we have discovered earlier. Our mental awareness is but one band in its spread. There are other tones in this vibgyor. There is the vital awareness more prominent in animals though quite obvious in humans in their moments of anger, ambition, greed, creativity, etc., what D.H. Lawrence poetically calls the blood-consciousness. There is a physical awareness below which there might be the unconscious, and finally, the dense and dark nescience, that is like a block of lead. We may imagine the mental to be layered underneath by the subconscious, as illustrated by Freud. But above the mind are other superconscious planes described in Indian psychology.

Once this is realized, it is easy to appreciate Merleau-Ponty, onetime friend and colleague of Sartre, who insisted that we are physical beings too, neither fully subject, nor fully object, nor both in his book *Phenomenology of Perception.* But something unique, due to the nature of our bodies, which gives us "a perspectival narrowness and incomplete character."

And yet, this body, being an integral shade in the spectrum of Consciousness, has its own awareness unlike that of the mind or the vital, its own subtleties and obscurities, that can grow and widen in a plastic manner just as the mind. And its density of awareness might give it more durability and stability.

It seems to me that Merleau-Ponty breaks the wall between consciousness and object. This was a significant breakthrough in existentialism that has not been fully appreciated yet. The duality of René Descartes' mind and body is breached. Consciousness is no longer intentional as supposed by Husserl but "open-ended and perceptual." Thus, Merleau-Ponty moves from a stance that gives primacy to mental awareness only to an insight that the primordial involvement of the body in the world is a critical element in our awareness and relationship with the world. Here, western philosophy once again begins to approach Sri Aurobindo's rediscovery of the Vedic realizations that the body's awareness or physical *atman* is key to an integral flowering of the human.

This physical awareness might be the bridge between the hidden nescient and the equally hidden superconscious—the secret portal that brings the 'supersolar blaze' face to face with the rocks beneath our feet. The rocks that hide in their absolute unconsciousness the same Sun that shines above in joyous resplendence.

Such was the discovery of the Vedic *rishis* who explored Consciousness scientifically, and in great detail, fearlessly and innocently. Sri Aurobindo discovered the same Truth in his own investigations. He translated the Vedas into the modern lingo showing that the supramental is the same awareness as that of the absolute dark nescience, involved in it, hidden, but slowly evolving out of it in a vast cyclic universal movement we call evolution. This is the secret fire that Sri Aurobindo brought back to the earth from the world of God as a modern Prometheus.

5.

Sri Aurobindo and Heraclitus

Heraclitus of Ephesus is unique among the ancient Greek philosophers in that he is both a mystic and an intellectual. He is a visionary able to see through the blinkers of thought and matter, unrestrained in the articulation of his insights. And yet, he bridges the vision to the intellect so that the intellect may be able to comprehend it. In that he is similar to Sri Aurobindo although the latter is far more comprehensive and goes even further—to the core of existence.

Heraclitus, most famous today for his aphoristic sayings, is considered an unhappy philosopher. That is perhaps because his philosophy concerns itself with Force as a most critical element of the Universe, with an underlying unity, behind it all. But, as Sri Aurobindo pointed out in his brilliant essay, 'Heraclitus', that the Greek pre-Socratic master of aphorism failed to find the third most important aspect of the Universe, that of universal delight, love and beauty. It is possible that Heraclitus did discover this principle but the *Fragments* extant today do not talk about the power "higher than justice, better than harmony, truer than reason, unity and bliss, the ecstasy of our fulfilled existence." Rhoda P. le Cocq mentions the possible lacuna in her book, *The Radical*

Thinkers: Heidegger and Sri Aurobindo, that we have no way of confirming since what is left of Heraclitus' work is nothing but *Fragments*.

The most significant insights of Heraclitus are in his cryptic statements that come to us in his *Fragments* such as, "It is not possible to step into the same river twice." The implication is that everything is in flux and there is nothing stable even for a moment. To this Osho Rajneesh, the Indian mystic, replied that it is not possible to step into the same river even once. To Heraclitus fire is the fundamental constituent of all things in the cosmos, which Sri Aurobindo believes is not an ordinary fire but the "luminous divine energy, the Seer-Will of the universal Godhead active and creative in all things."

Each object is likened to flames and thus, there are no things. They are only processes. The second great insight of Heraclitus is the unity of opposites. Everything is a coming together of opposites as opposing tendencies. Thus, strife and contradiction are not to be avoided and war is an essential characteristic of our world. According to Heidegger though, this struggle is there to reveal the 'being' of cosmos and bring a flowering of the world, the original meaning of the term *physis* in Greek used by Heraclitus.

Heidegger also notes that Logos, according to Heraclitus, is not the 'word' but a steady gathering, "a maintenance of the common bond in the conflicting." And "being is the gathering of this conflict and unrest." If this is true, then we can easily understand the next apothegm of Heraclitus as quoted by Sri Aurobindo in his essay on Heraclitus, "One out of all and all out of one." Sri Aurobindo explains this aphorism as "an essential unity of being, which is many in its becoming."

In this unity of opposites and unity of being, despite the surface multiplicity, "the way up is the way down." And "a hidden connection is stronger than an obvious one." One is reminded of the Buddha who avers that change is the nature of our world although he does not talk at all about the secret unity underlying all this change.

"The thunderbolt that steers all things," in the terms of Heraclitus can then be considered as the underlying wisdom and will that directs all movement. And when he says that the gods are mortals and men immortals, that too can be divined as showing the infinite possibility in each man and the limitations inherent in being a god.

Similarly, when Heraclitus says in the *Fragments* that the dry soul is best but it is a pleasure and satisfaction to souls to become moist, it is possible that he is hinting at some principle other than war that humans might wish to avoid. What is this principle? It is not clear. Is it his allowance for emotion or feeling? In another saying he condemns idol worship, "He who prays to an image is chattering to a stone wall," perhaps as a corollary.

These are remarkable insights the Greeks, as Sri Aurobindo points out with critical incisiveness, failed to go forward with—to that final discrimination that India attributed to Kapila, which is the discovery of pure consciousness or the Purusha. "The Fire of Heraclitus has to do duty at once as the original substance of all matter and also as God and Eternity," Sri Aurobindo elucidates. This fundamental omission was not addressed in western philosophy until existentialism made its appearance in the 20th century and that too, in a manner partial and disfigured.

"Heraclitus is the first and the most consistent teacher of the law of relativity," explains Sri Aurobindo. And yet, the 'weeping philosopher' maintains that there is an absolute which is Fire. And all our concepts of this Fire are partial, limited and relative; "He is named according to the pleasure of each." This is similar to the truth proclaimed by the Vedas, "One existent the sages call by many names." Heraclitus goes beyond the relative standards and avers, "Fed are all human laws by one, the divine."

"Nature loves to hide," says Heraclitus, as he turns his sight from being towards becoming. Sri Aurobindo states that it is a sign that the lore of the early mystics had been lost, the spiritual sense had departed out of their symbols, even as in Vedic India. And he adds, "But there took place in Greece no new and powerful movement which could, as in India, replace them by new symbols, new and more philosophic restatements of their hidden truths, new disciplines,…"

"Greece at last followed the turn given by Heraclitus, developed the cult of the reason and left the remnants of the old occult religion to become a solemn superstition and a conventional pomp," he concludes.

Heraclitus was more a destroyer, not a creator, similar to the Fire that he used as his symbol. But Fire can also be creative according to the Vedas. This, Heraclitus was unable to accomplish. He destroyed the old creeds and superstitions such as animal sacrifice and idol worship among the Greek. But he could not offer "something more profound in its place" as Sri Aurobindo has shown us. Nor could he outline a practical method to attain or share his insights.

"Time," Heraclitus says, "is playing draughts like a child, amusing itself with counters, building castles on the sea-shore only to throw them down again." Sri Aurobindo understands this to imply the Divine Lila that has no purpose except the playing and no end except its own joy. And he defines Logos as the "divine dynamic, the energy and the self-revelation of God." Has Heraclitus touched the Indian conception of *Brahman*, the cause, origin and substance of all things, the *Sat-Chit-Ananda*? Or is this only a fanciful attempt to run parallels between his philosophy and the Vedantic? We will perhaps never know.

Then again, one of his most mysterious sayings is that the kingdom is of the child and that you cannot find the limits of the soul. The first part reminds one of Christ's famous response to the protest of his disciples. The second leaves much room for further exploration and allows us to complete Heraclitus with our own seekings.

6.

Sri Aurobindo and Plato

At the dawn of human reason came a mind limpid and clear, whose lucidity was reflected in his prose, and his love of mathematics and order. He established the first academy for education and was the first professor in western history. He was a bridge between the mysticism and intuitive approach of the past to the reality and rationality of the future. He was Plato, his name in Greek meaning 'wide and broad' quite appropriately.

Plato took the being of Parmenides and the becoming of Heraclitus and affirmed them both. Both eternal stability and eternal change are true, he said. And yet, he was not a Sankhya philosopher or a mystic such as Plotinus who saw the unchanging behind the flux. His eternal, perfect world behind the world of objects is an abstract, not experienced or experienceable, a world not unlike the world of arithmetics made of universals.

One may say that there can be no basis for this paradigm for a hidden world behind all things. But Plato believed in it, the ideal of a perfect place, like a heaven of mathematics and perfect order. Modern thought has moved us away from such a framework—that posits an apparent world of concrete objects known to sense which changes covering up an unchanging and unseen world of Forms or abstract shapes grasped by pure reason only. We may wince at such airy-fairy dreamworlds today but there was a time when it was the predominant philosophy of Europe and remained so for at least two thousand years.

It was only Husserl who bracketed the world of Idea and pushed it aside in an epoche-making radical break from the past—as he developed phenomenology, and brought us back to awareness of appearance as it is in the last hundred years or so. Alfred North Whitehead wisely commented that the safest general characterization of European philosophical tradition is that it consists of a series of footnotes to Plato. After all, he and Bertrand Russel attempted to find a logical system that would need no outside justification or proof for its consistency and completeness as Plato's descendants.

The Upanishads do talk of the subtle worlds behind the gross world—the *manomaya* and the *pranamaya*, the mind and the vital, but they are experienceable to any person with the slightest sensitivity. The ancient Indian *rishis* also talk of the even deeper and perfect *vigyanamaya* and *anandamaya*, and these too are beyond sensual experience, but are known intimately as oneself as one sheds identification with the world of gross and even subtler forms. But the subtle worlds of yoga are not abstractions or arithmetical forms, but felt and known as real and directly influencing the realm of the gross.

Plato's mathematical approach is almost mystical like that of Pythagoras, who perceived all things as numbers and thought that the cosmos came from numerical principles. He also thought that mathematics and abstract thinking is a basis for philosophical thought and any worthwhile thesis in science and ethics. As a manifestation of a mathematical and perfect order, the world has a consistency and perhaps a divine power behind its existence.

This way of thinking was imbibed by Einstein later, and his stance even though grounded in Relativity, was yet Deterministic and Platonic. And when Einstein tried to discover the Unified Field Theory through advanced theoretical physics, he was emulating the same paradigm.

And yet, Plato's achievements are significant not just in philosophy but also in political thought. The concept of a Philosopher King was an important step towards envisioning the politics of the future. Even though he failed as a politician, and his Republic as a community of like-minded people did not take off, the idea of defining an Ideal man and then creating a hierarchy with him at the top is enticing even today. The philosopher who loves the sight of Truth, and establishes justice for each, assigning to each his or her due is unrealistic in the practical affairs of men.

The Indian ideal, that of the Yogi Emperor, is a lineage of kings who are liberated from the world and themselves, who have mastered themselves and thus the world. Sri Aurobindo's solution of a gnostic community of highly evolved beings who bring transformation with their presence is a quantum leap in socio-political thought and is an advance on Plato's Dream and Idea.

The Allegory of the Cave as described in *The Republic* is a classic illustration of the human condition. Tied up and restricted utterly, exposed to stimuli themselves limited and of a partial kind, man does not have the data points to develop a full understanding of his situation. The awareness, taking these conditions as granted, looks at no other alternative explanations and treats the status of bondage as sole reality.

And yet, when a prisoner of this twilit screen of shadows with total inability to move, becomes free of his shackles and experiences the reality of fire or that of the Sun, he is initially blinded and confused. And, when he has become able to face the world of light, if he attempts to share it with his fellow prisoners, they are unwilling to listen to him and incapable of fathoming what he is attempting to describe.

This metaphor of human thralldom is apt and replete with suggestiveness, symbolism and possible hope for the future. Sri Aurobindo, looking at the next dawn of the human cycle, attempts to bring man out of the cave, expose him to the world of light and make it natural for him. He stands too as a bridge but this time in reverse, between the dry stultifying rationality of the past and a luminous metamorphic intuitiveness of the future.

Bernard Shaw said that western philosophy had not progressed since Plato at all and had only been his repetition time and again. Modern thought has shifted from the Socratic dialectic with recent disruptions in philosophy by Husserl and Wittgenstein. And it seems that we have come full circle in returning to the fecundity and boldness of pre-Socratic thinkers.

Plato sees himself becoming free of his cave finally and ascending to stagger into the world of dazzling sunlight. This time it may not be difficult to explain to his fellow humans the radical new world he has seen. For the ground has been prepared and Being and Becoming are no longer irreconcilable as in his immediate past. Sri Aurobindo has given us in his thought a mind as limpid and clear, in prose as lucid and flowing, this time though with a love not for mathematics but of poetry. One of the greatest writers of prose finds completion in another just as great and as crystalline.

7.

Sri Aurobindo and Kant

Sri Aurobindo as a philosopher has been compared to Emmanuel Kant by some critics such as John King-Farlow, Ranjan Ghosh and Haridas Chaudhuri. And that is perhaps because the magnum opuses of both philosophers are so voluminous, some numbering 800 to 900 pages. Both wrote tomes that deal with complex and intricate subjects. The treatment is detailed, considering multiple perspectives, and can sometimes be difficult for the uninitiated. Both wrote works that are immensely ambitious dealing with metaphysics, ethics, theology, epistemology and aesthetics. But there the similarity ends.

Kant attempts to turn back on the mind to solve all his difficulties; he sometimes succeeds, but sometimes also creates a bigger complication. To Sri Aurobindo, mind is only a tool and a mode of cognition and not the highest one either; and his mind is an enlightened one, informed by other faculties and psychological realms that were not available to Kant.

Transcendental Idealism established by Kant took on the skepticism of David Hume but in the process uprooted reason as the foundation of western philosophy. Kant, as his name suggests, gives us "categorical imperatives." Thou shalt do this and thou shalt not do that. As if a new Moses had returned with a set of commandments after seeing the burning bush. This is why Schopenhauer criticized his "theological morals" and "Mosaic Decalogue in disguise." But Kant's categorical imperatives are highly flawed as any man who turns to duty as his highest arbiter often is.

One of the greatest achievements of Kant is the "universal ethical principle stating that one should always respect the humanity in others, and that one should only act in accordance with rules that could hold for everyone." But resorting to "a paradigmatic deontological or duty-based system of morality" may create its own contradictions. If I know that the stranger asking for my friend's address is looking to kill him, should I still speak the truth? Kant's answer is "yes," an obvious absurdity. In Sri Aurobindo's system of supra-ethics, one decides the answer not by a lower consciousness that is ego-based or with a *satvik*[37] pride that does not use discretion, but by a higher consciousness that knows the wider and global ramifications of each word and act.

While Kant always respected the humanity in each person, Sri Aurobindo honored the divinity not only in each human, but also animal and even the so-called inanimate things. And yet, for European society, law and morality, it was a significant step to see the other person not as a means but always as an end.

The other achievement of Kant was to establish that our minds have an innate "a priori" knowledge or way of knowing. Thus, space and time are "forms of intuition"

---

[37] *Satvik* is an adjective used to describe something or someone that has *satva*, which is a Sanskrit word meaning "light," "goodness" and/or "purity." (Taken from Yogapedia)

which shape our experience. He also elaborated how our minds are extremely limited due to the restricted nature of the sensory data that is available to us.

Sri Aurobindo went far deeper into the nature of the mind being a yogi and showed us that what we call the mind is but the thoughts that collide pell-mell in our awareness. That mind is only one level of consciousness just like the physical and vital. But there are other levels too, that are way higher and of which we are hardly aware. And yet, they influence our minds every now and then. These levels higher than the mind are termed by Sri Aurobindo as the 'Higher Mind,' the 'Inspired Mind,' the 'Illuminated Mind,' the 'Overmind' and the 'Supermind.' Each has its own function, quality, reach and dynamis. In higher states of awareness, time and space lose their reality until one moves to the realization of a timeless spaceless reality that swallows time and space in its stillness.

Kant declares that mind is not capable of proving the existence of God; it does not have the ability nor the data to make such a judgment. Paradoxically, reason paves way to faith in his philosophy with a clear realization that our so-called rationality and knowledge is extremely limited. Sri Aurobindo with the advantage of Indian *darshana* behind him, avers that God can be realized by each human being but such an approach would involve silencing the mind and going beyond its limited modes of perceiving.

For not only is the sensory data to mind limited, the nature of mind, flitting, inconsistent, random and easily influenced by the subconscious or supra-conscious, makes it a poor instrument in matters of serious philosophy. This understanding, easily available to even a beginner of yoga, is only now beginning to percolate western thought.

Similarly, realizing that time is in our minds, as memory and as anticipation, as Carlo Rovelli, a quantum physicist, points out in his book *The Order of Time*, makes us come to the present moment, which alone exists. If the a priori knowledge of Time too comes to an end, what happens to the whole Kantian edifice then? As with most of western philosophers, Sri Aurobindo takes off where they end and leads us to "the superconscient realms of motionless Peace where judgment ceases and the word is mute and the Unconceived lies pathless and alone."[38]

Kant's insistence that we have free will is not well-reasoned, it seems, and seems more as an a priori acceptance in itself. Bryan Magee notes that his actual demonstration was not so much that we have free will as that we find it impossible to believe that we do not. Kant, the old fox of Konigsberg who had unlocked John Locke and exhumed Hume, who had undermined the most precious arguments of theology and science equally, had finally hit a wall. He walked away from it fractured and bruised with the help of some specious justifications, but the future of western philosophy had been decided. Questions of such critical import cannot be wished away. They come back with greater vigor to destroy the paradigm that sought to avoid them.

Here again, Sri Aurobindo, with the advantage of Sankhya philosophy at his disposal, could aver that the only free will belongs to the Purusha and not the Prakriti. And the true philosopher goes beyond the three *gunas* to a state where

---

[38] *Savitri*, p. 33

freedom is finally possible and there the will can be called unconditioned and liberated.

Kant created an almost Platonic world of the noumenon, the world not available to our experience, of things-as-they-are, whatever that means. By definition the noumenon is unknowable to us. And the objects of experiences are mere appearance. Western philosophy rid itself of this disease of the world of Idea or non-empirical realms only once Husserl and Wittgenstein, as shown earlier, revolutionized it by categorically eliminating such extrapolations. And once they did, nothing else was left of the edifice that was western philosophy since Kant had already ripped out its entire foundation. Not even a rubble that could be recognized.

It was time perhaps for Sri Aurobindo to appear and bring a synthesis of east and west, in philosophy as well as psychology, ethics as well as aesthetics.

8.

Sri Aurobindo and Schopenhauer

The philosopher closest to Indian *darshana* who brought Kant to his culmination in some ways, is Arthur Schopenhauer. It is said that when Schopenhauer, the pessimist philosopher, read a translation of the Upanishads he began to dance in the streets. That seems quite appropriate since the Upanishads describe the ultimate reality as having a body of bliss.

Schopenhauer disagreed with Kant even as he acknowledged his predecessor's metaphysical framework. He denied that the noumenal world, the world beyond our sensory experience, has particular things as they-are-in-themselves. Space and time are no longer germane to the non-empirical realm of the noumena. It is a world that has no objects or forms and no differentiation. "All must be one and undifferentiated," Schopenhauer insisted. One is reminded of the pre-Socratic Parmenides with his mystical doctrine that "All is One."

Stephen Law in *The Great Philosophers* describes how Schopenhauer also rejected that this undifferentiated something is the cause of the world as we experience it. For causation too, is a concept that applies only within the phenomenal world. The noumenal world is the inner core or nature that is hidden from our senses. For western metaphysics, this was a "phenomenal" step in moving towards the eastern understanding of the world.

Schopenhauer describes the world as "will and representation." This will is not individual, conscious or intentional but "vast, undifferentiated and cosmic, a kind of ceaseless striving for life and existence." And the phenomenal world we see about ourselves is a manifestation of the underlying reality. Even an inanimate rock is a manifestation of this will.

But according to Stephen Law, "Schopenhauer does not view this underlying reality as something positive but something horrific. When we look around us, we see appalling suffering and torment caused by a ceaseless striving of man and nature." This appears similar to the Buddhist view that life is full of suffering, *dukkha*, and this suffering is due to our unsatisfiable willing or thirst, *trishna*. The way to escape suffering, as Bryan Magee in *The Story of Philosophy* notes, is to repudiate desire as such, to abjure willing. And like the Buddhists, he does not believe in permanent selves or in the existence of a personal God.

It is not clear if the ultimate ideas worked out by Schopenhauer were on the basis of Kant's philosophy before discovering Hinduism and Buddhism. He did remark once that his work had become possible only now that Plato, Kant and the Upanishads had all become accessible to a single mind. Magee also suggests that it is possible to see Schopenhauer's philosophy as a more or less seamless fusion of Kantianism and Buddhism expressed in the vocabulary of mainstream western philosophy. When Schopenhauer differs from Kant on essential points, it is usually in the direction of Buddhism.

Magee also makes clear that to someone who compares these two paradigms in this light, eastern philosophy might appear to have been metaphysically more profound and philosophically more advanced than western philosophy until the Kantian revolution. But Magee feels that eastern philosophy lost its advantage at this point, when western philosophy caught up with it in metaphysics, and had itself then the immense advantage of having got there independently of religion, and with a tradition of tighter logical rigor behind it. Also "a symbiotic relationship with both mathematical physics and (newly with Schopenhauer) the arts" gave the western counterpart a more solid grounding.

But Magee makes a few cardinal errors in his comparative analysis. As Sri Aurobindo points out, eastern philosophy – as is clear from his own case – came out of living realizations and transformative experiences and not from speculation. Thus, to Schopenhauer the undifferentiated noumenon is an abstract or a concept but to Sri Aurobindo it is "the ground of his being," to borrow a phrase from Huxley in *The Perennial Philosophy.*

Also, it is not true that eastern philosophy is divorced from mathematics and arts or logical rigor. But the sciences or humanities in the east were always taken as a means to realize the Truth. Magee seems to have conflated the political mastery of imperialist Europe on South-East Asia with a new-found intellectual superiority. Be that as it may, colonialism of geography as well as that of mind is a thing of the past. A greater synergy of the two streams of thought is possible now that the east is finding its own surer footing and this is exemplified remarkably well in the person of Sri Aurobindo.

Western philosophy is beginning only now to reach the subtlety and depths of Indian *darshana.* Husserl, Heidegger, Sartre, Huxley, Wittgenstein, Ken Wilber, among others, have brought new insights to western thought by bringing in elements that were hitherto absent or ignored. And it is interesting that western philosophy was unable to synthetize its isolated discoveries into a larger vision until Huxley and Wilber attempted it in the recent past.

It seems to me that the future *kavi* and *darshanik* will be liberated from the constraints of looking at things in a certain way. He or she will be free of the baggage of the past and will be able to see not as a German or an Indian but as a global citizen, as a human evolving to greater and greater heights in perception and understanding.

9.

Sri Aurobindo and Spinoza

When I read Baruch Spinoza, sometimes I feel like I am reading the *Zohar*, the Book of Splendor from the Kabbalah. He too takes an exoteric thought process such as the Cartesian duality of mind and matter and merges the two against a larger backdrop of glimmering oneness. For Spinoza was a monist, the first one in western thought after Parmenides. While Parmenides is hidden from us mostly due to the loss of his ancient writings, Spinoza bursts forth, "noble and lovable" as Bertrand Russell observes in *A History of Western Philosophy*, in resplendence to save western theology and cosmology from its own reductionism.

At the heart of Spinoza's metaphysics lies his conception of the world as a single unitary substance, notes Stephen Law in *The Great Philosophers*. He rejected Descartes' splitting of the world into two, and insisted that there is only one substance. That substance is the spatio-temporal world and it is God. This God is not an anthropomorphic creature with eyes and ears and a beard who is sitting outside the world he created, and running it like a teacher, handing out pink slips and scorecards for every activity. This God is the totality of the Universe whose essence is its existence.

And having made the natural and the divine one in essence in a single indivisible package, he single-handedly made God omnipotent, omniscient and omnipresent. And from this insight sprang the Romantic movement of William Wordsworth, John Keats and P.B. Shelley, and inspired giants such as Johann Wolfgang von Goethe and George Eliot, Albert Einstein and Sigmund Freud, and Hegel, Schopenhauer and Nietzsche.

He took away our free will with a simple gesture, since our actions are determined by factors outside our control. Since we are, for the most part, unaware of the real causes of what and how we do things. And he finally freed western cosmology and psychology from the shackles of narrow Abrahamic theology.

"God is the cause of all things, which are in him," he enunciated and he was ex-communicated from his faith for this approach. And yet he continued, with a vision at once humane and divine, when he advised us to look at our own lives through the eyes of eternity, *sub specie aeternitatis*[39]. And to begin to see things as they are. And not to be obsessed with our own petty egos but to see our difficulties "occupying a place they actually do in the totality of things."

He spoke for the freedom of speech and the liberty of judgment without which no civilized society is possible. And he spoke up even as he was shunned and ostracized as ungodly by his contemporaries, as he "affirmed the unity of all reality and the divineness of that unity."

When the great critic Gotthold Ephraim Lessing said that there was no other philosophy other than that of Spinoza, he had brought into possibility the final maturation of

[39] In a universal perspective

metaphysics that the West needed. He prepared the world for the advent of the French Revolution, the Romantic Movement in arts and literature and a quantum shift in outlook and inlook among its thinkers and theologians.

Spinoza fell short in his vision, it is true. But perhaps more was not possible in his life and those times. Another 400 years were needed for the West to begin enunciating the relativity of Einstein and the psychology of Freud, the stream of consciousness by Virginia Woolf and James Joyce and the *Tractatus* by Wittgenstein.

And then, of course, the philosophers who tried to bring the east and west together, Huxley, Wilber, Sri Aurobindo: Sri Aurobindo the most, in life, action, word and spirit.

Sri Aurobindo writes in the first chapter of *The Life Divine* words apropos to this debate, "… Spirit is involved in Matter and apparent Nature is secret God … the eternal paradox and eternal truth of a divine life in an animal body, an immortal aspiration or reality inhabiting a mortal tenement, a single and universal consciousness representing itself in limited minds and divided egos, a transcendent, indefinable, timeless and spaceless Being who alone renders time and space and cosmos possible, and in all these the higher truth realizable by the lower term, justify themselves to the deliberate reason as well as to the persistent instinct or intuition of mankind."

For excluding God from his own universe was one of the most serious errors of Abrahamic theology which Spinoza tried to correct. This was never an issue in the east since Vedanta is a monist or Advaitic approach to life and the Universe. And God is not only beyond and outside, untouched, pure, unexperienceable to our senses, but he is also involved and inseparable from our world, universally and individually. The concept of the Holy Trinity remained mostly a concept to the lay clergy and religious practitioners. God as the three-in-one is the secret truth; the Father, the Holy Ghost and the Son to my understanding signify the three aspects of the Divine, that which is transcendental–cosmic–immanent as one reality.

Spinoza asks, can anything be outside God? If yes, it is a God who contradicts his own definition as the Supreme Being. If no, then we need a deeper understanding and a more comprehensive formula. But where Spinoza erred was not to see the various manifestations of God as nature, and as each individual, in their secret reality to be as ethereal and heavenly while appearing gross in matter. Not only pantheism but panentheism, which means to not only see God in everything but God as everything while also as the one who is beyond space and time. Not only a monism of substance but also a panpsychism even though in matter consciousness seems hidden and buried.

Thus, Christ himself is a pantheist, to my mind, when he says that the bread is his flesh and the wine is his blood. The sacrifice of his being of selfless love and psychic in matter is unfortunately turned into a confused and tortured theological explanation. But it can be easily understood if the framework of Vedanta and perhaps Spinoza is applied.

Sri Aurobindo bridges the gap between the spirit and matter with a simple and luminous reconciliation,

> Nor is this, even, enough to guard us against a recoil from life in the body unless, with the Upanishads, perceiving behind their appearances the identity in essence of these two extreme terms of existence, we are able to say in the

> very language of those ancient writings, "Matter also is divine," and to give its full value to the vigorous figure by which the physical universe is described as the external body of the Divine Being. Nor – so far divided apparently are these two extreme terms– is that identification convincing to the rational intellect if we refuse to recognize a series of ascending terms (Life, Mind, Supermind and the grades that link Mind to Supermind) between Spirit and Matter. Otherwise the two must appear as irreconcilable opponents bound together in an unhappy wedlock and their divorce the one reasonable solution. To identify them, to represent each in the terms of the other, becomes an artificial creation of Thought opposed to the logic of facts and possible only by an irrational mysticism. If we assert only pure Spirit and a mechanical unintelligent substance or energy, calling one God or Soul and the other Nature, the inevitable end will be that we shall either deny God or else turn from Nature.[40]

Thus, a true, real and dynamic monism is made possible, one that does not deny the individual, nor his free will, nor the difficulties of the world or the realization of God in man. This, I believe, was the aspiration of Spinoza even as he struggled with the words to articulate this understanding and was misunderstood and ignored by fellow humans he sought to liberate psychologically, spiritually, politically and ethically.

---

[40] CWSA, Vol. 21, p. 8

10.

Sri Aurobindo and Hegel

The most ambitious of western philosophers, with the largest scale of time and reach universally to all the people, Hegel is the first European thinker to study the historical development of human societies and civilizations. Before him, surprisingly, it had never been attempted. This historical awareness influenced the methods of influential scientists, sociologists and economists to follow, prominent among them Charles Darwin and Marx.

Hegel saw the world evolving in a dialectic of thesis and antithesis reaching a resolution in synthesis. Any force or movement creates a reaction or opposite movement and the play of their conflict becomes the human drama on a global scale. Eventually, something that unifies both emerges from the struggle of forces but then becomes a new thesis which creates its own opposition. Thus, the movement of conflict, resolution, synthesis and new conflict is the story of humankind, whether in society or thought or any other field. Such seems to be the import of the rational framework he gave to the entire global scheme of things from time immemorial to the final resolution in the Absolute. It is then, he felt, that human society will reach its ultimate perfection and have "self-realization and self-understanding."

Idealistic as this is, all in the world of mind, is there any truth to this vague philosophy of history? It seems to me that Hegel caught a truth in his analysis of evolving time, what the Indians termed as *kala*. This *kala* is not time as a separate entity, flowing like a perennial river, as physicists thought before Einstein, but is the unfolding of the possibilities already inherent in the Universe. Thus, *kala* is not a separate entity. The seed grows into a tree but already contains the tree in itself in its fullest potential. And *kala* is the becoming seen at various stages with the help of records or memory. Did Hegel fully understand time as the Indians understood it? I do not believe so but I think that his emphasis on studying the unfolding of the *geist*, as the time spirit, shed a new light on changes happening at a universal level.

Another important idea that comes from Hegel is that of alienation. Man becomes separated from the institutions he created and this rift causes strife and creates a disharmony. He blamed Socrates for creating a sense of individualism and personal responsibility among the Greeks which led to the fall of the Greek states. In his opinion, the individualistic conception of liberation was superficial and limited until the individual became an integral part of an organic society. Here too, Hegel considers perfection on the vast scale of the Universe and understands correctly that individual growth is meaningless without an ascent in human consciousness. However, his error was in partitioning individual perfection from universal perfection; the two are an integral part of each other, as Sri Aurobindo later showed, envisioning the establishment of gnostic communities in the future. These communities would have men attaining spiritual mastery over themselves in harmony with mankind with their individual consciousness no longer limited and narrow.

Sri Aurobindo explains in *The Life Divine*,

> The individual must be the instrument and first field of the transformation; but an isolated individual transformation is not enough and may not be wholly feasible. Even when achieved, the individual change will have a permanent and cosmic significance only if the individual becomes a center and a sign for the establishment of the supramental Consciousness-Force as an overtly operative power in the terrestrial workings of Nature, — in the same way in which thinking Mind has been established through the human evolution as an overtly operative power in Life and Matter.[41]

"The finite has no genuine being," says Hegel. But the individual is not finite as Vedanta says. And Sri Aurobindo eloquently describes the infinite that resides in each human, made manifest in the gnostic being:

> The gnosis is the effective principle of the Spirit, a highest dynamis of the spiritual existence. The gnostic individual would be the consummation of the spiritual man; his whole way of being, thinking, living, acting would be governed by the power of a vast universal spirituality. All the trinities of the Spirit would be real to his self-awareness and realized in his inner life. All his existence would be fused into oneness with the transcendent and universal Self and Spirit; all his action would originate from and obey the supreme Self and Spirit's divine governance of

[41] CWSA, Vol. 22, p. 997

> Nature. All life would have to him the sense of the Conscious Being, the Purusha within, finding its self-expression in Nature; his life and all its thoughts, feelings, acts would be filled for him with that significance and built upon that foundation of its reality. He would feel the presence of the Divine in every center of his consciousness, in every vibration of his life-force, in every cell of his body…
>
> All beings would be to him his own selves, all ways and powers of consciousness would be felt as the ways and powers of his own universality. But in that inclusive universality there would be no bondage to inferior forces, no deflection from his own highest truth: for this truth would envelop all truth of things and keep each in its own place, in a relation of diversified harmony…
>
> The gnostic individual would be in the world and of the world, but would also exceed it in his consciousness and live in his self of transcendence above it; he would be universal but free in the universe, individual but not limited by a separative individuality. The true Person is not an isolated entity, his individuality is universal; for he individualizes the universe: it is at the same time divinely emergent in a spiritual air of transcendental infinity, like a high cloud-surpassing summit; for he individualizes the divine Transcendence.[42]

I have quoted this passage in great length only to show the essential difference between the two philosophers. Even as "the evangelist of the absolute," Hegel knew it only in theory. But in Sri Aurobindo's *darshana*, the absolute can be realized by each individual in its fullest resplendence and

---

[42] CWSA, Vol. 22, pp. 1007-8

manifestation. And this evolutionary step would be the ascent of the *geist*, by which term Hegel meant the overarching human mind and cosmic spirit.

Hegel showed that in religion or psychology, an anthropomorphic God who is perfect makes man feel inadequate and lacking, causing alienation. He rejected the schism between the human and the divine by insisting that God and man share the same spiritual existence. And declared that the history of the world is none other than the progress of the consciousness of freedom. The fullest manifestation of the absolute is the perfect society, he claimed.

Wiser words were never said; yet, these are only words. It was left to Sri Aurobindo to complete the dialectic loop in practice and reality. And yet, as one reads the phrases used by Hegel such as "mothered by zeitgeist," the "womb of time" and "existence … the series of revolutions," as ascribed by Will Durant in *The Story of Philosophy*, one cannot but wonder if Hegel was a philosopher or a mystic. "The real is rational," he famously averred. But his own dialectic eventually condemned his thesis to further churning and conflict, not preserving it as the absolute that he thought it was.

Can the absolute appear in time, on a universal scale? Both Hegel and Sri Aurobindo said yes. But one conceptualized this possibility as theory; the other showed us how it works.

11.

Sri Aurobindo and Parmenides

Parmenides of Elea and Heraclitus seem to be the polar opposites of pre-Socratic philosophy. While Heraclitus is known for his emphasis on constant change as the defining characteristic of the Universe, Parmenides sees it as One Eternal and Unchanging. Change is only an illusion. Parmenides sounds as if he accepted the basic postulate of Vedanta which sees reality as One, Uncreated and Indestructible.

Everything must always have existed, says Parmenides in his poem *On Nature*, "nor are there any gaps in reality." Thus, reality is an "enclosed and unchanging system." We know very little about his philosophy other than what we may glean from *On Nature*, of which but fragments survive, putatively written by him. But, whatever remains, including Plato's dramatized dialogue, *Parmenides*, describing the conversation between Parmenides and a young Socrates in Athens, we may reasonably infer at least some of the salient features of his philosophy mentioned above.

Some translated excerpts given below appear to be more a direct beholding than intellectual postulates that make me believe that Parmenides was more a mystic than an intellectual in the tradition of the Vedic *rishis*, Egyptian priests and Delphic Oracles.

> You must needs learn all things,/ both the unshaken heart of well-rounded reality/ and the notions of mortals, in which there is no genuine trustworthiness… the one, that [it] is and that [it] is not not to be,/ is the path of conviction, for it attends upon true reality,/ but the other, that [it] is not and that [it] must not be,/ this, I tell you, is a path wholly without report:/ for neither could you apprehend what is not, for it is not to be accomplished,/ nor could you indicate it…It is necessary to say and to think that What Is is; for it is to be,/ but nothing it is not…[43]

This "It" referenced in the translation above seems like the *Tat* of Vedanta, That, with no other descriptors or qualifiers. What Is must be "ungenerated and deathless":

> …but not ever was it, nor yet will it be, since it is now together entire, / single, continuous; for what birth will you seek of it? / How, whence increased? From not being I shall not allow/ you to say or to think: for not to be said and not to be thought/ is it that it is not. And indeed what need could have aroused it/ later rather than before, beginning from nothing, to grow? / Thus it must either be altogether or not at all.

The being of What Is is "whole and uniform":

[43] Stanford Encyclopedia of Philosophy, https://plato.stanford.edu/entries/parmenides/

> Nor is it divided, since it is all alike;/ and it is not any more there, which would keep it from holding together, / nor any worse, but it is all replete with What Is./ Therefore it is all continuous: for What Is draws to What Is.

It is "still" or motionless:

> And unmoved within the limits of great bonds/ it is unbeginning unending, since generation and destruction/ have wandered quite far away, and genuine conviction has expelled them./ And remaining the same, in the same place, and on its own it rests,/ and thus steadfast right there it remains; for powerful Necessity/ holds it in the bonds of a limit, which encloses it all around,/ wherefore it is right that What Is be not unfulfilled; for it is not lacking: if it were, it would lack everything.

And It is perfect:

> But since there is a furthest limit, it is perfected/ from every side, like the bulk of a well-rounded globe, / from the middle equal every way: for that it be neither any greater/ nor any smaller in this place or in that is necessary;/ for neither is there non-being, which would stop it reaching/ to its like, nor is What Is such that it might be more than What Is/ here and less there. Since it is all inviolate, / for it is equal to itself from every side, it extends uniformly in limits.

Popper considered Parmenides as deterministic but that sense does not convey to me at least from these translations done above by Denis O'Brien, Leonardo Tarán and John Palmer. Perhaps a better way for a western philosopher to understand Parmenides would be to appreciate Sri Aurobindo and Vedanta. For Vedanta founds itself on the understanding of Brahman, the all-pervasive reality that is *Sat-Chit-Ananda*, Truth-Consciousness-Bliss, and is a monistic approach that is experiential and not theoretical.

Thus, Vedanta does not theorize based on this understanding of Brahman, but merely describes the features of the Brahman, how That acts, holds the Universe and each individual together. It seems that western philosophy has taken this revelation of Parmenides and converted it into concepts from which conclusions and logical postulates can be drawn. Perhaps, but the absurd lengths this approach can go to is seen when we have Zeno of Elea's paradoxes and the later attempts by prominent thinkers to wrestle with them intellectually.

Zeno with his paradoxes about Achilles and the tortoise or the arrow shot from a bow has attempted to confuse the issue by stating that movement is not possible. But his paradoxes collapse when we realize that "infinite number of finite distances" is not possible unless we are willing to keep dividing space to sub-atomic levels. And as soon as we reach sub-atomic levels, we realize as quantum physics has shown us, that our Newtonian laws and logic collapse making the paradoxes themselves meaningless and inapplicable.

To paraphrase Wittgenstein, a mixing of paradigms has happened and it is time we disabuse the philosopher of the word-games he is indulging in. And free him of his linguistic confusion. Sri Aurobindo does not attempt to prove the Unity or the One by analysis or dissection but with insight and clarity and the knowing that begins to happen when the mind is still and no longer seeking. Zeno never had the necessity of demonstrating lack of movement through logic.

It is also interesting that Sankhya sees the Universe as the interaction of two principles, the Purusha and the Prakriti; the latter eternally still and indestructible, while the former eternally mobile and causeless. If we place Heraclitus and Parmenides side by side, we see that one philosopher emphasizes one aspect of reality and the other focuses on the second aspect. They seem to be the yin and yang of European mysticism which never came together in one symbiotic understanding as far as we know.

One is reminded of Sri Aurobindo's essay on the *Isha Upanishad* where he discusses the discovery by the Vedic *rishis* of the eternally unchanging principle in the world of constant flow, *nityo nityanam*[44], the One Unchanging within all Change. And their discovery of the principle unifying all the individual consciousnesses and Purushas, *cetanas cetananam*, the One Consciousness within all Purushas. And that these two principles of Purusha and Prakriti that seem to be opposites are in essence one and the same. Here, we come face to face with the true monism of realization of which Parmenides was a unique singer in European thought. Before he too fell into silence and immobility among further developments in western philosophy.

---

[44] *Katha Upanishad*- 2.2.13- नित्योऽनित्यानां चेतनश्चेतनानामेको बहूनां यो विदधाति कामान् ।

12.

Sri Aurobindo and Derrida

Sri Aurobindo's writings are a Derridean's delight. He abounds in what Jacques Derrida would call oppositions, a pair of related terms or concepts that are opposite in meaning. Binaries, as the term is used by Derrida, such as Time and Timelessness, Being and Non-Being, *Sat* and *Asat*, are constantly considered, reconciled and harmonized in Sri Aurobindo's *darshana*, since he is what we might call a constructionist.

Sri Aurobindo is the greatest integrator of disparate lines of philosophy since Sri Krishna. If there can be deemed a monist in modern philosophy, who addresses almost every concern of mankind in his works and brings them all under one super-vision, it is Sri Aurobindo.

Benoit Peters in *Derrida, a Biography* states that Derrida primarily analyzes language, texts and subtexts. Modern linguistic analysis under his influence tells us that the word is not the experience and there is a schizophrenic approach in western philosophy. The schism between oppositions is already loaded and "one of the two terms governs the other."

The Stanford Encyclopedia of Philosophy notes:

> Deconstruction is a criticism of Platonism, which is defined by the belief that existence is structured in terms of oppositions (separate substances or forms) and that the oppositions are hierarchical, with one side of the opposition being more valuable than the other. The first phase of deconstruction attacks this belief by reversing the Platonistic hierarchies: the hierarchies between the invisible or intelligible and the visible or sensible; between essence and appearance…[45]

The second aspect of deconstruction is an incisive study of the present moment as it points out that:

> …every appearance or every experience is temporal. In the experience of the present, there is always a small difference between the moment of now-ness and the past and the future…this infinitesimal difference is not only a difference that is non-dualistic, but also it is a difference that is, as Derrida would say, "undecidable." Although the minuscule difference is virtually unnoticeable in everyday common experience, when we in fact notice it, we cannot decide if we are experiencing a memory or a present perception, if we are experiencing a present perception or an anticipation.

Thus, deconstruction questions the primacy of Platonic essence over the appearance. It also delegitimizes the presentness of present and concludes that the present moment is mixed with memory and anticipation, past and future, which do not let our experience of the present be "pure."

---

[45] https://plato.stanford.edu/entries/derrida/

This segues us into the Aurobindonian approach where abstracts and thoughts are mental formations and of inferior value; the *darshanik* does not speculate but sees reality that is not separable from his own awareness. And the presentness of the present is exactly what the seer experiences, ridding himself of all thought and the need to anticipate.

Derrida separates the meaning of words into synchrony (the meaning they derive from other words in the language) and diachrony (the meaning that arises due to contemporary and historical use and connotations of the word). And we can see how Sri Aurobindo in his detailed study of the etymology of Sanskrit sounds and comparison with cognate words in other languages, brings out meanings and shades that have been forgotten. We also learn from his study of root sounds in Sanskrit that these sounds are not separable from experience and are psychologically evocative of similar feelings they were associated with 6,000 years ago. Thus, in Sri Aurobindo's linguistic and comparative philology, the word is the experience if we go to its *beeja* and its *moola*, the seed and the root. Also, as a poet, he points out in his study of mantra, which we may tentatively explain as poetry that reaches inevitability in all its aspects, that the best poetry goes beyond word-meaning to the sound of meaning that creates its own experience. This advanced study of the psychology of sound might be a subject worthy of the future. And it seems to me that the key has been given to us by Sri Aurobindo already, at least for the Indo-European languages and the principle would likely hold in other languages too.

Sri Aurobindo also adopts the Indic approach of unifying words to avoid binaries, e.g., *Sat-Chit-Ananda* is the triune description of the Supreme Reality, implying Existence-

Consciousness-Bliss although not exactly. The combination of words in this manner suggests that he, like the ancient *rishis*, realized the inherent insufficiency of words in describing any experience. Other unifications like *Satyam-Ritam-Brihat* (the Truth, the Real, the Vast) or *Satyam-Shivam-Sunderam* (the True, the Conscious, the Beautiful) are adoptions of the same approach.

When we come to oppositions, like Time and Timelessness, *Sat* and *Asat* (Truth and Untruth), *Chetan* and *Achetan* (Conscious and Unconscious), Sri Aurobindo explores the underlying unity of each term and synthetizes them all in the Vedantic monism of Brahman. Thus, oppositions that are so crucial to the deconstructionist stance are reconciled into a vision that gives no preference to any one term over the other, nor is there "the desire for immediate access to meaning" or the carrying over of deadwood from the past, present or future. It is possible that the final duality of Vedanta might be the consciousness of duality itself, which might be considered as a binary opposition. Yet, Vedanta insists that the resolution of any duality is never complete conceptually, but as an experience or *anubhava*.

Another opposition that might be considered here is between the intellect and experience. This too is reconciled in the Aurobindonian realization as the partitions between thought, will and act fall away with the psychological evolution of the seer. Moreover, at a certain point, the purified intellect becomes the experience and models and creates *anubhava* just as the experience creates intellect.

The aporia or irresolvable internal contradiction or logical disjunction in text, argument or theory is taken up as a tool to help discover a larger truth that might have been missed by an exclusivist approach.

Deconstruction is not something radical to Indian thought. Vedanta uses deconstruction as a tool for instruction. The student learns to deconstruct word-meanings and learns to separate them from empirical experience. As insight grows, the experiential world is de-identified with names or tags, and the artificial separation of things and identities falls off. Thus, an inherent and organic knowing that is wordless and liberated of time replaces the linguistic and impure subjectivity we live in.

The Buddha attempted a similar deconstruction that is Vedantic in approach. However, the difference is that after every deconstruction, Vedanta points out a deeper paradigm or order that supports or conditions that order that was deconstructed, while the Buddha leaves the mind in *shoonya* or pure absence without offering any alternatives. Nagarjuna developed this *shoonyata* or emptiness further into a metaphysical anti-realism.

J. Krishnamurti in our own times took a similar approach as Nagarjuna in a more modern language and attempted to untag words from our identification of things and free feeling from thought and desire from awareness, in a similar manner. *Neti neti*, not this not this, a process of de-identification, disallowance and negation remains one of the most powerful deconstructive tools in Vedantic psychology.

Modern philosophy in the west has taken yet another step towards a 'synchrony' with Indic *darshanas* with the advent of Derrida and other 'incorruptibles' as described by Benoit Peters in *Derrida, a Biography*. But the truest incorruptible among all of them, to my mind, remains Sri Aurobindo, who to borrow Derrida's words had "an intransigent, even incorruptible, ethos of writing and thinking … without concession even to philosophy, and not letting public opinion, the media, or the phantasm of an intimidating readership frighten or force … into simplifying or repressing. Hence the strict taste for refinement, paradox, and aporia."

13.

Sri Aurobindo and Heidegger

Of all the western philosophers, it is Heidegger who attempts the deepest and most extensive explorations of ontology, the study of being. His failures are many, including the gravest, his association with Nazism. And yet, his achievements too are significant enough to be considered with full awareness of his grievous 'error' in judgment.

But that is the lot of philosophers. They deal with concepts or thoughts, while Hitler's falsehoods preceded thoughts and came from a source that was subliminal and subterranean to most abstractions that intellectuals are capable of. And Heidegger missed the darkness behind Nazism and its *weltanschauung*. Sri Aurobindo on the other picked up on the evil that Hitler incarnated very early. In fact, so clear was his understanding of the anti-evolutionary force behind Hitler that he reversed his lifelong opposition to the British and supported them against the Germans. And that is the difference between an intellectual, no matter how profound he is, and a *darshanik*, who sees things as they are, without the veils of personal preference, name-tags or ideology. Reality, in all its facets, is the only ideology for a seer like Sri Aurobindo.

The same lapse of judgment happened with Ezra Pound. But Ezra Pound was a poet and as Eliot pointed out, his philosophy was immature. But Heidegger was expected to know better. And "it is difficult to forgive him," as Emmanuel Levinas has noted in his essays on Husserl and Heidegger. With this subtext, it is important to know of Heidegger's contributions to modern philosophy and his influence on other philosophers, most notably Derrida who inherited deconstruction via destruction and *abbau* (de-building) from Heidegger.[46]

Heidegger's approach to being, or what he calls Dasein or 'being there,' comes from understanding that the 'essence' of Dasein lies in its existence. In this, he differs from Sartre as he attempts to study something that is a precursor to the essential and existential. In this, he begins to touch the Vedantic method of pursuing "a single thought to its very end as a lifelong pursuit." He astutely critiqued Sartre's statement that "existentialism is the understanding that existence precedes essence" by noting that the reversal of a metaphysical statement is still a metaphysical statement, and thus, an essence.

In rejecting Husserl's intentionality of consciousness, he is again correct to replace it with "the concept of care or Being-in-the-world (a non-intentional, or perhaps pre-intentional, openness to a world)." This is akin to J. Krishnamurti's description of meditation as the state when consciousness has no direction. *Dhyana* begins when the tendencies of awareness or *vrittis* are dropped and it is remarkable that Heidegger had this insight.

---

[46] https://plato.stanford.edu/entries/heidegger/

In his seminal work, *Being and Time*, he says, "Basically, all ontology, no matter how rich and firmly compacted a system of categories it has at its disposal, remains blind and perverted from its ownmost aim, if it has not first adequately clarified the meaning of Being, and conceived this clarification as its fundamental task." Dasein is not to be understood as "the biological human being." Nor is it to be understood as 'the person.' Dasein is distinguished by the fact in its very Being, that Being is an issue for it. And here, he hits upon another significant realization that our awareness is unique because it is capable of self-awareness or awareness of awareness inherently.

Heidegger's otherwise opaque claim in *Being and Time* that Dasein, and indeed only Dasein, exists, where existence is understood (via etymological considerations) as ek-sistence, that is, as a standing out, is another significant step for modern thought. Dasein can stand back or 'out' from its own occurrence in the world and observe itself. It can also imply an openness to and an opening of Being. An extension of this discovery would have been the description by Sri Aurobindo of *Sat-Chit-Ananda* as the highest state of Reality, where Existence or Being is Consciousness and is Bliss.

Phenomenologically speaking, there are no subjects and no objects; there is only the experience of the ongoing task. According to Heidegger, as noted in the Standard Encyclopedia of Philosophy, Descartes presents the world to us "with its skin off" (*Being and Time*), i.e., as a collection of present-at-hand entities to be encountered by subjects. It is no surprise that according to some accounts Heidegger was profoundly impressed by Buddhism and Taoism although this remains unconfirmed. When Heidegger says that "nothingness is something positive," he is as close to Indic roots as any western philosopher has ever been.

When he says in his critique of Hegel in *Being and Time* "So it's clear from whence the history of philosophy is the inner movement of the course of spirit, that is, of absolute subjectivity, towards itself," he hits upon another profound truth. To me, these discoveries are so close to the Vedantic realization that Heidegger seems to be one of the most important bridges to eastern thought among all western thinkers.

Rhoda P. le Cocq in her book, *The Radical Thinkers, Heidegger and Sri Aurobindo*, describes how Heidegger turned to poetry in his later years, especially that of Friedrich Hölderlin and Sophocles. This is perhaps the first time that a western philosopher has dedicated himself to verse. For poetry is one of the best vehicles to describe and sing of Existence and Being. Sri Aurobindo, as we study his literary contributions, too moved more and more to a highly advanced form of poetry, the mantra, and seems to have dropped away all the other forms of literature in his attempt to express the highest reaches of awareness to mankind.

Further comparing the two philosophers in her book, le Cocq describes their approach to verse and says: "Poetry," says Heidegger, "is the establishing of being by means of the word." This is perhaps one of the best descriptions of the mantra. And he adds, "… the highest and the holy are one and the same, the Serene. As the origin of all that is joyous, it remains the Most Joyous … Through the Serene, he (The Joyous One), 'opens' things out to that in their surroundings which causes joy. Through the Joyful Serene, he illumines the spirit of men so that their nature may be open to what is genuine ..."

It is only fitting that Heidegger comes closest to echoing Sri Aurobindo when he sings about poetry, and that too, about joy and serenity, "The Joyous is what has been made into poetry. The Joyous is joy harmonized into poetry. So too it is rejoiced and therefore the enjoying. Itself it can again delight others."

And she describes further, "The highest 'above the light' is the streaming lightning itself. This pure lighnting, which for each 'space' and each 'temporal space' houses (i.e., grants) a vacant place—this we call the Serene." We do not know if Heidegger redeemed himself in such Joy and Light but it is sufficient to know that he came close, digging higher, enough to give us a written document of the "possible that is higher than the actual."

14.

Sri Aurobindo and Huxley

Aldous Huxley is perhaps one of the finest and most astute intellectuals of last century. A brilliant novelist, philosopher, poet and speaker, some of his greatest contributions to English literature consist of his ability to meld the east and the west.

His novel *Eyeless in Gaza* ends with a powerful mystical experience, reconciling all the opposites, dissolving the violence, anger and fear, into a growing stillness and peace. The entire last chapter of the book is a new possibility in language, in feeling and experience expressed in a literary framework but this passage reaches heights not usually seen in the secular world:

> Meanwhile there are love and compassion. Constantly obstructed. But oh, let them be made indefatigable, implacable to surmount all obstacles, the inner sloth, the distaste, the intellectual scorn; and, from without, the other's aversions and suspicions. Affection, compassion—and also, meanwhile, this contemplative approach, this effort to realize the unity of lives and being with the intellect, and at last, perhaps, intuitively in an act of complete understanding. From one argument to another, step by step, towards a consummation where there is no

more discourse, only experience, only unmediated knowledge, as of a color, a perfume, a musical sound. Step by step towards the experience of being no longer wholly separate, but united at the depths with other lives, with the rest of being. United in peace. In peace, he repeated, in peace, in peace. In the depth of every mind, peace. The same peace for all, continuous between mind and mind. At the surface, the separate waves, the whirlpools, the spray; but below them the continuous and undifferentiated expanse of sea, become calmer as it deepens, till at last there is an absolute stillness. Dark peace in the depths. A dark peace that is the same for all who can descend to it. Peace that by a strange paradox is the substance and source of the storm at the surface. Born of peace, the waves yet destroy peace; destroy it, but are necessary; for without the storm on the surface there would be no existence, no knowledge of goodness, no effort to allay the leaping frenzy of evil, no rediscovery of the underlying calm, no realization that the substance of the frenzy is the same as the substance of peace.

Frenzy of evil and separation. In peace there is unity. Unity with other lives. Unity with all being. For beneath all being, beneath the countless identical but separate patterns, beneath the attractions and repulsions, lies peace. The same peace as underlies the frenzy of the mind. Dark peace, immeasurably deep. Peace from pride and hatred and anger, peace from cravings and aversions, peace from all the separating frenzies. Peace through liberation, for peace is achieved freedom…

…For now there is only the darkness expanding and deepening, deepening into light; there is only this final peace, this consciousness of being no more separate, this illumination....[47]

When Sri Aurobindo read this passage, he was entirely impressed. In his conversations with Nirodbaran, he said, "...it is a big yogic experience — a psycho-spiritual one. It shows a going through the psychic down into the vital being and finding there the unitarian principle, the principle of oneness with everybody. Huxley speaks of 'dark peace' because it is down below that he goes and from there opens to the Light above. All the details are quite recognizable, and they cannot be a mental construction. This experience must have changed his life." He recognized immediately that it was "remarkable and significant ... with a remarkable style and a subtle and plastic mind."

Aldous Huxley quoted Sri Aurobindo in *Perennial Philosophy* and considered *The Life Divine* to be "a book not merely of the highest importance in regard to its content, but remarkably fine as a piece of philosophic and religious literature." What is remarkable is that Huxley's novel *Point Counterpoint* explores the opposing tendencies of matter and spirit just as Sri Aurobindo does throughout his *darshana*. But his great reconciliation comes in *Eyeless in Gaza* as mentioned above and his solution to the problems of the world too was a spiritual awakening as was Sri Aurobindo's.

Huxley also influenced Michael Murphy and inspired him to initiate the Human Potential Movement in Essalon, California. Murphy had already been impressed deeply by Sri Aurobindo's vision of the future of humanity and had lived for a short while in Pondicherry at the Sri Aurobindo Ashram. In his book *What Really Matters: Searching for Wisdom in*

---

[47] Excerpted from *Eyeless in Gaza* by Aldous Huxley

America, Tony Schwartz describes how the movement came into being and became one of the significant and influential movements in modern western society.

Huxley contributed enormously to a profounder understanding of eastern *darshana*, especially Vedanta, in the United States. His dialogues with J. Krishnamurti, another remarkable modern figure who influenced artists such as Eugene Ionesco and Henry Miller, show his insights into life's complex problems and their zen-like solutions. Thus, he could write lines such as these, "The Bhagavad Gita is the most systematic statement of spiritual evolution of endowing value to mankind. It is one of the clearest and comprehensive summaries of perennial philosophy ever revealed; hence its enduring value is subject not only to India but to all of humanity."

And when Huxley writes as he does in the last chapter of his novel, *Island*, he touches upon the most intense and clear descriptions of the bliss-existence-awareness that is at the root of all things:

> This Allegro—he knew it by heart. Which meant that he was in the best possible position to realize that he had never really heard it before. To begin with, it was no longer he, William Asquith Farnaby, who was hearing it. The Allegro was revealing itself as an element in the great Present Event, a manifestation at one remove of the luminous bliss. Or perhaps that was putting it too mildly. In another modality this Allegro was the luminous bliss; it was the knowledgeless understanding of everything apprehended through a particular piece of knowledge; it was undifferentiated awareness broken up into notes and phrases and yet still all-comprehendingly itself. And of course all this belonged to nobody. It was at once in here,

out there and nowhere. The music which, as William Asquith Farnaby, he had heard a hundred times before, had been re-born as an unowned awareness. Which was why he was now hearing it for the first time. Unowned, the Fourth Brandenburg had an intensity of beauty, a depth of intrinsic meaning, incomparably greater than anything he had ever found in the same music when it was his private property.

...And tonight's Fourth Brandenburg was not merely an unowned Thing in Itself; it was also, in some impossible way, a Present Event with an infinite duration. Or rather (and still more impossibly, seeing that it had three movements and was being played at its usual speed) it was without duration. The metronome presided over each of its phrases; but the sum of its phrases was not a span of seconds and minutes. There was a tempo but no time.

"...Luminous bliss." From the shallows of his mind the words rose like bubbles, came to the surface and vanished into the infinite spaces of living light that now pulsed and breathed behind his closed eyelids. "Luminous bliss." That was as near as one could come to it. But it — this timeless and yet ever changing Event — was something that words could only caricature and diminish, never convey. It was not only bliss, it was also understanding. Understanding of everything, but without knowledge of anything.

...Knowledge involved a knower... all the infinite diversity of known and knowable things. But here, behind his closed lids, there was neither spectacle nor spectator. There was only this experienced fact of being blissfully one with oneness. In a succession of revelations, the light grew lighter, the understanding deepened, the bliss became more impossibly, more unbearably intense.

It seems to me that the literary world has not fully appreciated Huxley's contributions especially in his final work *The Doors of Perception*, perhaps biased due to his use of mescaline to elevate his awareness. But legitimate or not, whether through mescaline or meditation, he hit upon an experience usually available only to a yogi. And his description, clear and lucid, is a touchstone in western literature. Nor is it my intention to advance Huxley's use of mind-altering drugs. But there is no doubt that a scientific approach to Consciousness is possible.

When one reads Sri Aurobindo's *Records of Yoga*, one realizes with what painstaking and granular detail he described each movement, each experience and how it can be scientifically established as a permanent state. My personal inclination is towards the latter approach to transform consciousness. Whatever is realized is done without any shortcuts, honestly, with clear eyes and understanding which makes the experience more repeatable and less fleeting. But the path of yoga is tough and demanding and it is easy to fall prey to the fast food of spirituality.

Huxley was unique in that he could handle the effects of mescaline and internalize them without losing control. Perhaps through him life explored another avenue of possibility. Needless to say, he brought to light a possibly different approach, alluring and dangerous. But how many can be of his level of mental and emotional sophistication to handle the storm of neurotransmitters such sudden biochemical transitions might bring? It is perhaps better to stay true to the time-tested methods of Vedanta and Yoga, which are radical enough to allow each individual to experiment without compromising their inner and outer balance.

Sri Aurobindo insisted first on developing the foundation of *samata*, equanimity, and forbearance towards the challenges of life as a condition of yoga. *Sthairya* or stillness might take time to develop and progress, may be slow initially but without the necessary investment of time, understanding and energy, further development in yoga might always be risky and vulnerable to downfall. It might be wise to heed his strong admonition.

15.

Sri Aurobindo and Buber

Each of us is defined not as a separate entity but as a relationship, according to Martin Buber. Our individual existence may be categorized as one that sees everything as a thing, an object, in a transactional interaction of the business we call life. Or one that approaches each individual or things as an undefinable, indescribable, illimitable mystery. The former is named by Buber as 'I-It' relationship; the latter as 'I-Thou.'

When we are in an I-It relationship, our I too is an It. Our ego too is a thing, one that can be defined clearly, with obvious borders, needs, requirements, formulations, etc.

When we are in I-Thou relationship, our I too is a Thou, an unspeakable, unnameable unknown that can only be felt and lived in our own wholeness, totality and the complete gestalt.

This was Buber's great insight, perhaps derived from Jewish mysticism. It helps us understand in existential terms what love is, the agape that Christianity talks about, the selflessness and the unconditional nature of the unity we feel with the beloved or with everyone. It also helps us understand what Carl Rogers attempted to develop as patient–provider engagement, an interaction that is deep and breaks through the professional façade that modern psychiatry has created on its practitioners.

Ich and Du (I and Thou), Buber's wonderful book also helps us realize the conundrum of modern medicine. For most doctors, the relationship with patients has become mechanical, distant, part of the disease complex and, if you may excuse my pun, clinical. The wholeness of being together in sharing and giving, without the screens of hierarchy and objective assessments, is a need not only for the patient but also the doctor. That healing (the word is derived from 'holos,' wholeness) is what our allopathic military-industrial complex needs today. Without that healing, disease is a commercial activity and curing a buyable item in the bazaar.

I am reminded of the great teacher, J. Krishnamurti, who used to insist on giving "one's total attention, without any presumptions or prejudices, without the baggage of the past or the anticipation of the future." Krishnamurti brought us back to our own awareness, constantly, insisting that the relationships are the mirror in which we see ourselves as we are. I-Thou takes us away from the mathematics and calculativeness of our approach to others and the world, whether in politics or journalism or daily relationships.

One limitation of Buber is that he talks about I-Thou in an almost mystical manner but does not tell us how to reach it. To him, I-Thou is a product of grace. Indian *darshana* and yoga solved this difficulty by giving us the principles, the methods and the system on how to prepare the instrument, the *adhaar*, i.e., ourselves so that we may begin to experience I-Thou and not know it as a concept or as an It.

The second limitation of Buber is his attempt to bring God into the equation of I-Thou. God the mystery, the unknown, the indescribable, may be understood and lived once we are in an I-Thou relationship. But Buber attempts to extend the mystery of I-Thou into a setting where God becomes a Thou, and therein was his biggest failure. For in attempting to bring the immediacy of God-experience into the I-Thou experience, he turns God into a concept, an It.

He gives God an a priori definition and he then proceeds to twist his paradigm of relationships so that somehow God becomes an end-product, the summum bonum, the ultimate acquisition. And that is the contradiction in terms that he struggles with at the end of the book, *Ich and Du*. Krishnamurti would have had none of this; he would have derided the attempt to experience God the concept and would have rejected any 'experience' of God as a creation of the mind. Krishnamurti and Buddha bring us to the awareness that drops its proclivities and becomes nondirectional which alone can be in an I-Thou relationship. Then whatever happens is within the realm of that which has no borders nor definitions and really cannot and should not be talked about. It is apparent that it is Krishnamurti and the Buddha who practice the I-Thou to its limits since they are not attempting to acquire God. Buber fails to see this limitation of his entire mindset and misunderstands the Buddha.

Buber also sees the Vedantic realization as annihilation, a misreading that even Derrida would have lambasted (if he had understood Vedanta, that is). But this might not be entirely Buber's fault since he had only Max Mueller's translations of the Upanishads to read from, it seems. For Max Mueller is one translator whose skill in creating fancies and fantasies exceeds his skill at translation.

And yet, that cannot be an excuse at this level of dialogic communication that Buber excelled at. For the fulfillment of Vedanta is when the whole Universe and the I are in a non-dual unity. Buber said that such an experience has "nothing in common with lived actuality." This is an utterly ignorant statement but also tells us of the immense but razor-thin gap between the western philosophers and Indian *darshaniks*[48]. It may have been worthwhile for Buber to have read this passage from Sri Aurobindo describing his realization of Thou in Alipore jail:

> I looked at the jail that secluded me from men and it was no longer by its high walls that I was imprisoned; no, it was Vasudeva who surrounded me. I walked under the branches of the tree in front of my cell but it was not the tree, I knew it was Vasudeva, it was Sri Krishna whom I saw standing there and holding over me his shade. I looked at the bars of my cell, the very grating that did duty for a door and again I saw Vasudeva. It was Narayana who was guarding and standing sentry over me. Or I lay on the coarse blankets that were given me for a couch and felt the arms of Sri Krishna around me, the arms of my Friend and Lover. This was the first use of the deeper vision He gave me. I looked at the prisoners in the jail, the thieves, the murderers, the swindlers, and as I looked at them I saw Vasudeva, it was Narayana whom I found in these darkened souls and misused bodies...
>
> When the case opened in the lower court and we were brought before the Magistrate I was followed by the same insight. He said to me, "When you were cast into jail, did not your heart fail and did you not cry out to me, where

[48] Seers, those who behold the Truth

> is Thy protection? Look now at the Magistrate, look now at the Prosecuting Counsel." I looked and it was not the Magistrate whom I saw, it was Vasudeva, it was Narayana who was sitting there on the bench. I looked at the Prosecuting Counsel and it was not the Counsel for the prosecution that I saw; it was Sri Krishna who sat there, it was my Lover and Friend who sat there and smiled.

Buber did not understand that I-Thou, if lived in totality, intensity and purity, leads one to spontaneously experience the Divine. This experience is not mental nor contrived by the mind to fulfill its goals. Buber also failed to understand that the Atman, the self that perhaps described inchoately as the I-Thou, is the Brahman, that the 'soul' is a living spark of the God it is seeking. Perhaps more was not possible to understand and articulate at that time. For to understand that we would need to go far deeper into understanding the mysteries of the Kabbalah and Indian spirituality than Buber could manage.

Martin Luther King though picked up on the core of *Ich and Du* and realized that each of us embodies the inviolable and supreme that we call the Divine. And his greatest understanding, even as a politician, was that until the divinity of the African American is accepted, there will be no true solution to segregation. He said in *A Testament of Hope*, that "man is not a thing. He must be dealt with not as an 'animated tool' but as a person sacred in himself." It is this sacredness that Buber strove for in our daily lives and pointed us to 'the end that is always present.'

II.

The Poet & the Playwright

1.

Sri Aurobindo, the Kavi

It is perhaps time for a reappraisal of Sri Aurobindo as a poet. Critics have not been too kind to him, especially among the Indians. But if every generation needs its own translation, as Pound noted, every generation also needs its own critique.

It is also important for India to come to terms with its own history of arts and literature and someday reach a valuation of the past that is more comprehensive and profounder than what we have seen in the last few decades. For a nation that does not truly appreciate its history—whether it is literary or literal, mythology, philosophy or culture—does not truly mature and become capable of addressing its present.

If literary criticism is a distinctive activity of the civilized mind, as T.S. Eliot proclaims, it is clear that India is lagging way behind. What we habitually see about us in the literary–critical landscape is Eliots in pajamas if not 'Matthew Arnolds in a saree.'

Why should we read Sri Aurobindo's poetry at all? Is it only for a relative valuation or is there something unique here? Perhaps even something for poets to learn? And if so, why do we hesitate to discuss his achievements openly against the uninformed and unrefined opinions of the cognoscenti?

It is perhaps due to the fact that Indian poetry in English is still heavily influenced by T.S. Eliot and the modernists while the world of literature has moved on in most other countries, especially the US and Europe. There is nothing new coming out in anthologies published these days and they seem to me to be compilations made by friends, families and fraternity.

Indian English poetry is in the doldrums and perhaps partly due to the inability and abject failure of its critics to appreciate poetry beyond their narrow tastes. If this is true, then we need to approach newer founts of inspiration and appreciation. Whether it is formalism or post-modernism, such appraisal of the past only brings us to a better understanding of the present and perhaps helps in forming a more just and balanced view of our writers and poets.

To me, the most significant achievements of Sri Aurobindo as a poet have been threefold:

a. He brought an Indian motif, its mythology, culture, *darshana*, and literary traditions, into English poetry. His poetry is that of Indian themes and characters and their unique worldview. This was perhaps the first systematic attempt to encompass these elements in Indian English poetry. Sarojini Naidu and Rabindranath Tagore had written in English before him but Sarojini's talents though unique and Indian in themes stayed restricted to a narrow lyrical strain. And Tagore's English poetry was not original to the language and he stayed within the confines of translating his own Bengali poetry. Sri Aurobindo attempted works on a much larger scale, whether in blank verse or quantitative hexameter, that were steeped in India and its civilization. For this alone, a study of his oeuvre is worthy of serious study.

b. Sri Aurobindo adopted new meters in English poetry, some very successfully and others perhaps not as successfully. His attempts to describe his yogic experiences in sapphics or alcaics or even a blank verse that hews its own path away from the mighty structures of Milton introduce a new sound in English verse that is not artificial or forced but is natural and native to the language.

c. He attempted the first Indian epic in the English language. 'Savitri' remains a difficult work unless one catches the strain of a new kind of word music in its verse, a new harmony and intonation. There are passages in 'Savitri' of sustained and vibrant Upanishadic sound with a mantric quality, an achievement that is unique in English. The fact that he could make an attempt such as this and achieve success, at times more intensely than others, is a remarkable achievement in English poetry.

Sri Aurobindo, if we may use the literary classification of Isaiah Berlin, is not only a hedgehog in his singular persistence with Indian motifs and *darshana*, he is also a fox when it comes to experimentation with various forms and styles, even new meters. He is a classic, if we may use Ezra Pound's definition of a classic as "a certain eternal and irrepressible freshness" in his primer, the *A B C of Reading*.

To me, a poet has value if in his or her best creations, something new is achieved. Something that is capable of giving us a new appreciation and perhaps even of teaching us. There are no poets, whether T.S. Eliot or Wallace Stevens or William Wordsworth or Alfred Tennyson, who have been able to sustain their inspiration consistently all the time. But we can truly judge if their methods are justified only when we study their best and not make opinions based on their experimental failures or not-so-successful outpourings.

I believe that Sri Aurobindo has amply shown us by his achievements what the English language is capable of with new meters or invocations. Over the new few pages, we shall attempt to familiarize ourselves with what I believe are his most representative.

2.

A God's Labor

I have gathered my dreams in a silver air
Between the gold and the blue
And wrapped them softly and left them there,
My jewelled dreams of you.

Every time I read these lines from 'A God's Labor' by Sri Aurobindo, I feel a certain softness enveloping me. It is the gentleness of a love that is discreet and unobtrusive. Unlike the reality shows of today, it does not make a drama of its *bhava*[49]. Nor does it attempt to control or tell you how great the poet is with the unconditional *agape* that he feels towards the future generation, i.e., us.

There are very few lines in English literature that are so quietly sweet and still. Perhaps we can compare it to another similarly gentle poem written by Shelley a couple of centuries ago.

---

[49] Emotion in Sanskrit is *bhava*, which approximates the English phrase, a state of being.

I can give not what men call love,
But wilt thou accept not
The worship the heart lifts above
And the Heavens reject not, —
The desire of the moth for the star,
Of the night for the morrow,
The devotion to something afar
From the sphere of our sorrow?

We do not know whom Shelley was addressing. Perhaps he too felt that silent voice that comes from the depths of heart where one can no longer differentiate between feeling and being. We are used to applying the word 'soul' to all kinds of things in life, even soul-music and soul-food. But if there is an essence of our human existence on earth, a principle that touches selfless love in all its purity and simplicity, that is what we might call our soul. What the ancient Greeks called the 'psyche' or the ancient Indians called the '*chaitya purusha*' or the '*anahata*,' that which can never be injured. The Gita says that fire cannot burn this principle and sword cannot cleave it.

Sri Aurobindo is a unique writer in that he was not only a great poet, he was also a remarkable philosopher whose world-vision was vast, comprehensive and coherent. He was a man of letters and a classicist, who was yet unassuming and simple. These words full of light are not the words of a thinker but someone whose heart is open to the whole world, all-embracing and universal.

A God's Labor is unique in that it is one of the few poems in which Sri Aurobindo talks about his spiritual journey, something he rarely did even with his closest disciples.

I have been digging deep and long
Mid a horror of filth and mire
A bed for the golden river's song,
A home for the deathless fire.
I have labored and suffered in Matter's night
To bring the fire to man;
But the hate of hell and human spite
Are my meed since the world began.

Perhaps someday we shall fully realize what he accomplished for humanity in his personal yogic *sadhana*. Prophets and pioneers are meant to be misunderstood. They hew their way not only through the dense forests of some untested and untried terrain but also have to face our own suspicion and ignorance.

All that was found must again be sought,
Each enemy slain revives,
Each battle for ever is fought and refought
Through vistas of fruitless lives.
My gaping wounds are a thousand and one
And the Titan kings assail,

But I cannot rest till my task is done
And wrought the eternal will.

Without seeking any recognition or acclaim, he sheds these words of light with a generosity and joy that only a select few have been capable of in the history of mankind. This is true spirituality to my mind and this poem is one of the few sustained passages of 'soul' or 'psychic' poetry in English.

I have delved through the dumb Earth's dreadful heart
And heard her black mass' bell.
I have seen the source whence her agonies part
And the inner reason of hell.

Above me the dragon murmurs moan
And the goblin voices flit;
I have pierced the Void where Thought was born,
I have walked in the bottomless pit.

Perhaps we can see such expressions of intense and self-giving love in the poetry of Mirabai or in the paintings of Radha and Krishna. Or perhaps in the love story of Laila and Majnu. Or perhaps in the compassion of the Christ that lifts his intense suffering too into the utmost surrender of spirit. In Sri Aurobindo's words:

Heaven's fire is lit in the breast of the earth
And the undying suns here burn;
Through a wonder cleft in the bounds of birth
The incarnate spirits yearn ...
I shall leave my dreams in their argent air,
For in a raiment of gold and blue
There shall move on the earth embodied and fair
The living truth of you.

3.

Nirvana

'Nirvana' is one of the best sonnets by an Indian poet that I have read so far. Not only because it deals with an entirely Indian motif but also it is completely satisfying technically and displays an extremely competent and sophisticated mastery of the form.

T.S. Eliot has noted that the sonnet is a way of thinking and feeling. If so, the octet and the sestet here create an interesting point and counterpoint. The first eight lines creating the preliminary movement that happens as the yogi begins to detach from the world. The sestet is the 'experience' of Nirvana with its overwhelming 'sense' that surpasses the senses and all experiences. How else could one depict that which surpasses words verbally? I know of no other description with such detail and precision.

The rhyme scheme follows that of ABBA ABBA in the first eight lines and CDE CDE in the next six. Slant rhymes are used in lines ten and fifteen. The rhythm varies from a stressed beginning in lines one, three, six, seven and eight in the octet and lines nine and thirteen in the sestet.

Line one with its dactylic beginning sweeps aside all perception with its forceful but wide impact. If one were to scan it, one would note that it begins with a dactyl followed by three trochees and one stressed syllable. Alternatively, one could say that it begins with a trochee followed by four iambs. I prefer the former scansion since the swing of the rhythm is overwhelming though quiet in its intensity.

> All is abolished but the mute Alone.
>
> The mind from thought released, the heart from grief,
>
> Grow inexistent now beyond belief;
>
> There is no I, no Nature, known-unknown.
>
> The city, a shadow picture without tone,
>
> Floats, quivers unreal; forms without relief
>
> Flow, a cinema's vacant shapes; like a reef
>
> Foundering in shoreless gulfs the world is done.

The first line begins with a stressed syllable and ends with one. It uses the 'a' and 'l' sounds elegantly to give a sense of openness and inclusion. The alliteration of 'al' in the beginning and the end and splitting of 'a' and 'l' in the third word is another subconscious trope that reinforces the sense of gathering and concentration in a vast consciousness.

The second line is iambic but the third line repeats the meter of the first with a dactyl at the beginning followed by three trochees and a stressed syllable. The fourth is iambic again. Line five is iambic and lines six, seven and eight begin with stressed syllables and are predominantly trochaic with a few dactyls. The switch of iambic with trochaic rhythms creates an internal poise and counterpoise subtly, to my mind.

Internal rhymes are used with the deployment of "grow," "now" and "flow" and "nature" and "picture" with subdued prominence creating a hidden unity among the lines that plays under the surface.

The octet prepares the ground with the play of syllables, assonances, consonances and alliterations. The last line of the octet is a powerful close and technically and psychologically prepares for the sestet:

Foundering in shoreless gulfs the world is done

The sestet lifts us into a realm of absoluteness if that were possible linguistically. This is not just a poetically perfect coming together of six lines, it is as perfect a description of the nirvanic experience as is possible with words. Word-meaning fuses with sound-significance and the only image in the last line is that of seas.

Only the illimitable Permanent
Is here. A Peace stupendous, featureless, still,
Replaces all, — what once was I, in It
A Silent unnamed emptiness content
Either to fade in the Unknowable
Or thrill with the luminous seas of the Infinite.

Again, the alliterations and repetitions of sounds create a vibrational sense in the meter. The sound 'ill' recurs in the words "illimitable," "still," "unknowable" and "thrill" and resonates with “all” in line eleven bringing us back to the word with which we began the sonnet. Similarly, the sound ‘it’ reverberates in the last six lines with the words “illimitable” and “It” and “infinite.” The sibilance of ‘s’ and the roll of ‘ll’s is used to manufacture an artifact that yet transcends its own form and meaning into something beyond.

A sweeping comprehensive movement in the last two lines completes the sestet on a ‘high’ note, that of the yogic realization in disappearing completely or embracing the Universe in oneness.

Perhaps this is over-analysis. For the poet lets the inspiration flow and finds words that bear his experience. The critics critique and ponder over every possible nuance. If so, one should forget all that I have noted and just return to the perfection of this sonnet and let its sounds reverberate through one’s inner worlds like a veritable mantra. That is the true nirvana.

4.

Despair on the Staircase

Mute stands she, lonely on the topmost stair,
An image of magnificent despair;
The grandeur of a sorrowful surmise
Wakes in the largeness of her glorious eyes.
In her beauty's dumb significant pose I find
The tragedy of her mysterious mind.
Yet is she stately, grandiose, full of grace.
A musing mask is her immobile face.
Her tail is up like an unconquered flag;
Its dignity knows not the right to wag.
An animal creature wonderfully human,
A charm and miracle of fur-footed Brahman,
Whether she is spirit, woman or a cat,
Is now the problem I am wondering at.

Indians are usually not very good at writing light verse. Perhaps this is because they take themselves too seriously. But here is a delightful work of nonsense poetry, perhaps the first one in English by an Indian.

Writing nonsense verse is not light work. Carrying the flippant, the irreverent, the insouciant, or, most importantly, the meaningless, with poise and to pull it off requires great expertise. We find such success with Edward Lear and Lewis Carroll, and later, with *The Importance of Being Earnest* by Oscar Wilde and *Old Possum's Book of Practical Cats* by T.S. Eliot. Light verse is primarily written for the sheer delight of it and it is written with sheer delight. And yet, it can say things that serious poetry cannot. And give us insights that the ponderous and the inflated never can.

Harold Bloom has pointed out in his book *Genius* that a similar spirit pervades absurd theater as in Beckett's *Waiting for Godot* and plays by Eugene Ionesco. They free us of "ordinary nonsense and take us to a realm at once weirdly light and ultimately unsettling." My only regret is that Sri Aurobindo did not write many more of these for, among our poets, perhaps he most of all was seriously capable of the non-serious genre. *A Dream of Surreal Science* and *Surrealist* are two other works of his in this vein that might inspire more nonsense verse from the present generation.

5.

The Self's Infinity

I have become what before Time I was.
A secret touch has quieted thought and sense:
All things by the agent Mind created pass
Into a void and mute magnificence.

My life is a silence grasped by timeless hands;
The world is drowned in an immortal gaze.
Naked my spirit from its vestures stands;
I am alone with my own self for space.

My heart is a center of infinity,
My body a dot in the soul's vast expanse.
All being's huge abyss wakes under me,
Once screened in a gigantic Ignorance.

A momentless immensity pure and bare,

I stretch to an eternal everywhere.

The sonnet came to us from Italian verse, especially Petrarch. Over the last 600 years it has undergone various experimentations including changes in rhyme scheme and the length of stanzas. What is unique about Sri Aurobindo's sonnets is that he slowly developed the sonnet form to describe his yogic experiences. The more direct he is, the more impactful the sonnet movement in my opinion.

As above, in *The Self's Infinity*, the first three quatrains prepare as in graded steps for the ending couplet. From Petrarch to Shakespeare to Milton, we have finally arrived from a mental–emotional expression to a spiritual 'use' of the sonnet where its structure works very well in preparing the reader for the completion and closing. I do not know of any other Indian poet writing in English who has experimented so much and so well with the sonnet.

The first line is a clear and straightforward statement that to anyone slightly familiar with yoga and spirituality is immensely meaningful and concise. The eighth line is yet another direct description of a yogic realization. The ninth and tenth lines continue this plain depiction without the need for flowery language or metaphors. The eleventh line is problematic unless one takes it to mean the opening of the vast subconscious and unconscious layers of one's awareness.

The couplet at the end is at once the statement of the fulfillment and completion while depicting the expansion of consciousness in a timeless, 'momentless' state.

To the modern mind, a sonnet might seem to be a relic of the past. Yet, in skillful hands, it can accomplish great feats. Shakespeare's sonnets are yet fresh and full of vigor. In our own times, Pablo Neruda has experimented with the form trying to make it unstructured and rhyme-less. But, call me traditional, I prefer the form that stays within the parameters of its structure, yet surprises and delights at the same time.

Sri Aurobindo, in my opinion, has done both in the sonnet above.

6.

Shiva: The Inconscient Creator

A face on the cold dire mountain peaks
Grand and still; its lines white and austere
Match with the unmeasured snowy streaks
Cutting heaven, implacable and sheer.

Above it a mountain of matted hair
Aeon-coiled on that deathless and lone head
In its solitude huge of lifeless air
Round, above illimitably spread.

A moon-ray on the forehead, blue and pale,
Stretched afar its finger of still light
Illumining emptiness. Stern and male
Mask of peace indifferent in might!

But out from some Infinite born now came

Over giant snows and the still face
A quiver and color of crimson flame,
Fire-point in immensities of space.

Light-spear-tips revealed the mighty shape,
Tore the secret veil of the heart's hold;
In that diamond heart the fires undrape,
Living core, a brazier of gold.

This was the closed mute and burning source
Whence were formed the worlds and their star-dance;
Life sprang a self-rapt inconscient Force,
Love, a blazing seed, from that flame-trance.

'Shiva' is a remarkable poem that, to me, is completely satisfying. The beauty of imagery in recreating one of the most enduring of the Indian myths of creation is breathtaking. This poem might be one of Sri Aurobindo's most successful in terms of justifying his theory on quantitative meter.

If one takes a close look at the meter, one notices that the first and third lines of each stanza usually begin with an unstressed foot, except in the third line. The second and fourth lines of each stanza begin with a stressed foot. For a quantitative meter, Sri Aurobindo insisted on following the natural genius of English language and not subjecting it to arbitrary theories. Efforts to force the reader to read the lines with artificial stresses on feet that would naturally be read as unstressed and vice versa would create a false scanning system. 'Shiva' can be read with natural enunciation, its unique sound-scheme enjoyed fully and the quantitative meter appreciated without resorting to the traps of prosody. In other words, I can enjoy the poem fully without the need for scanning it first and learning how to read it.

I am reminded of Karl Popper who famously stated that even one exception disproves a scientific theory. Thus, a theory in empirical sciences can never be proven but it can be falsified, meaning that it can (and should) be scrutinized with decisive experiments. In arts perhaps, the opposite is valid. A single successful validation of a theory of art or prosody is sufficient to justify its value. How commonly it can be applied and on how vast a scale are matters that might need further exploration but a single "proof" is enough to show us that there is merit in a particular theory.

I believe that as our literary criticism of English Literature matures, especially in India, his quantitative theory will be studied with more attention, discussed and analyzed with a truer understanding.

7.

The Divine Hearing

All sounds, all voices have become Thy voice:
Music and thunder and the cry of birds,
Life's babble of her sorrows and her joys,
Cadence of human speech and murmured words,

The laughter of the sea's enormous mirth,
The winged plane purring through the conquered air,
The auto's trumpet-song of speed to earth,
The machine's reluctant drone, the siren's blare

Blowing upon the windy horn of Space
A call of distance and of mystery,
Memories of sun-bright lands and ocean-ways,–
All now are wonder-tones and themes of Thee.

A secret harmony steals through the blind heart

And all grows beautiful because Thou art.

Sri Aurobindo may perhaps be best described as a spiritual poet. By spirituality I mean a non-dogmatic and non-denominational universal sense and realization of the Spirit in us and among us that has been described variously by different religions. This spirituality identifies with the secret and Truth both immanent and transcendental, cosmic and individual. And is achieved via an individual development or opening to what is usually occult and ignored among most of us.

The poet sees the world not only as a manifestation of the Divine but as the Divine—the pantheism which sees all as an expression of God turns into panentheism which means the poet sees all as God. In certain states of mystical ecstasy, we hear many great sages and saints burst into song. We hear of the same experience from Rumi or Tagore or St John of the Cross or Christ himself.

Dr. Samuel Johnson, usually a fine critic and appraiser of poetry, passed fierce strictures against religious verse in a most deprecatory and peremptory manner, especially against those of Edmund Waller. He railed *In the Lives of the Poets* thus:

> Contemplative piety, or the intercourse between God and the human soul, cannot be poetical. Man, admitted to implore the mercy of his Creator, and plead the merits of his Redeemer, is already in a higher state than poetry can confer.
>
> The essence of poetry is invention, such invention as, by producing something unexpected, surprises and delights. The topics of devotion are few, and being few are

> universally known; but, few as they are, they can be made no more; they can receive no grace from novelty of sentiment, and very little from novelty of expression…
>
> From poetry the reader justly expects, and from good poetry always obtains, the enlargement of his comprehension and elevation of his fancy; but this is rarely to be hoped by Christians from metrical devotion. Whatever is great, desirable, or tremendous, is comprised in the name of the Supreme Being. Omnipotence cannot be exalted; infinity cannot be amplified; perfection cannot be improved…
>
> Of sentiments purely religious, it will be found that the most simple expression is the most sublime. Poetry loses its lustre and its power, because it is applied to the decoration of something more excellent than itself. All that pious verse can do is to help the memory and delight the ear, and for these purposes it may be very useful, but it supplies nothing to the mind. The ideas of Christian theology are too simple for eloquence, too sacred for fiction, and too majestic for ornament; to recommend them by tropes and figures, is to magnify by a concave mirror the sidereal hemisphere.

Even the best minds oddly lose their bearing when they confront something beyond their immediate expertise. Perhaps Doctor Johnson did not realize that some of the greatest scriptures and spiritual–religious expressions are set in verse of the highest order. From the Vedas to the Upanishads to the Bhagavad Gita to Vaishnava poets to the Bauls of Bengal and Kabir and Mirabai, we have seen some of the most exquisite and perfect verse sung or written in the

Indian subcontinent over the last few millennia. The Holy Quran is verse of the highest order and can be appreciated even by those who do not understand or speak Arabic. The same goes for the Bible of the gospels and the psalms. In English, we only have to look at the masterly articulations of Donne, Herrick, Vaughan, Herbert, Thompson, Hopkins and even Eliot to know that Dr Johnson erred grievously in his judgment. And what about Dante! And Milton! Such astringent dismissals fail to pass the most basic review and consideration.

In fact, I would turn this around and state that the emotion and sensation of spiritual experience by its very exalted nature may birth some of the most elevated and impassioned verse. We need more of the religious verse to charm the secular and secular verse to captivate the spiritual and disrupt this artificial separation between the two. All great art becomes sacred and sacrosanct and what is most sacred and expressed in a most refined manner may be our greatest art.

Sri Aurobindo avoided metaphor and adornments in spiritual poetry just for the sake of it and advocated describing the realization simply and directly. The poetry is in the bliss and the beholding, if we may paraphrase Wilfred Owen. The human mind, especially in Indic cultures, has accepted religion as a valid subject of artistic expression whether in poetry or painting or sculpture or dance or architecture. Take these away and you leave the history of human culture and civilization way poorer in quality, intensity, expression and excellence by leaving out much that is the best in us.

A clear transcription of the spiritual states, if read receptively and with empathy, can transform the reader's awareness and bring to him a touch of the original experience. That is the function of great literature. To communicate and connect most intimately, though separated by great space and time, the poet and the reader. And to transform one's blood, as D.H. Lawrence proclaimed the function of great literature to be.

Coming back to the sonnet, Sri Aurobindo uses the simple and elegant Shakespearean rhyme scheme of ababcdcdefefgg. A sonnet is not just a verse form but also a reflection of awareness in poetic form. One may add that to Sri Aurobindo the sonnet is also a way of developing and conveying the gestalt of his consciousness. While most of the sonnet above is description one comes across a remarkable phrase "the windy horn of Space" which is a metaphor of a high order, something Donne might have appreciated. The horn is not only a musical instrument but also a shape of land and also a metaphor for space. We are reminded of Einstein denoting space as curved. Even memories in this sonnet are treated as sounds or notes that can be heard in this Divine orchestra or concert.

To the mystic, there is no difference between the hidden and the real, the expressed and the spiritual. The Divine Hearing makes us hear this actually if we only pay close attention.

8.

Descent

An experiment in verse must find a curious balance. It needs to disrupt while finding or creating a new poise. It needs to break a pattern of sound or 'dislocate into meaning' if necessary and yet not create a rupture just for the heck of it. In other words, it should accomplish something. A new way of feeling or seeing or expressing.

Stéphane Mallarmé did unique experiments with French verse, some eminently successful, some clear failures, but through them all, there was an attempt to express something different. Even his failures in that sense are an accomplishment since through the incompleteness of form, one might be able to glimpse something he was trying to say. Thus, the failures of innovators become steppingstones for future poets and give them the space to be even bolder if necessary or calibrate the balance between radical shifts and continuity.

T.S. Eliot attempts to say something new in the Four Quartets in a similar manner. Some passages like "At the still point of the turning world ..." or "In my beginning is my end ..." hew a new path in mystical literature while others create a new musical structure with words.

Other experiments like 'The Cantos' by Pound to my mind are largely a failure since it appears that his desire to write poetry surpassed having something to say. E.E. Cummings broke new ground whenever his lyrical note could bear the weight of innovation, which is done with a clear purpose and not just for the sake of it. Hemingway, Gertrude Stein and Camus are more such examples of disruption that establishes new landmarks in literature and transforms the entire landscape of creative expression.

Sri Aurobindo with his sapphics for the first time has established the form in English poetry and naturalized it since he has fused form and content, verse and feeling, expression and sense in the poem 'Descent.' Not art for art's sake only, nor form for form's sake only, as Algernon Swinburne had attempted with his sapphics in English. But form chosen, adapted, established, and delivered for a clear purpose. Nor sapphics as written by Pound which lose their rhythm with his prosodic patches becoming glaring and obscene. Trying to serve two different masters, rhythm and meaning, can be difficult business.

Sri Aurobindo has used the tremendous metrical force of the dactyl in each line to create a powerful effect in lines such as:

All my cells thrill swept by a surge of splendor

And

Light and still more light like an ocean billows

And

Dire the large descent of the godhead enters

And

Voiceless, thronged, Infinity crowds upon me

Who can write like this today! The whole poem is a success the way it has transposed a celebrated meter from Greek verse upon the natural flow of English. Trochees, spondees, dactyls and cretics are used to show the intensity that the yogi feels when a transformative spiritual experience is happening.

Let us take a look at Gaius Catullus first, the first one to successfully recreate Sappho's meter in Latin:

Ille mi par esse deo videtur,
ille, si fas est, superare divos,
qui sedens adversus identidem te
    spectat et audit
dulce ridentem, misero quod omnes
eripit sensus mihi: nam simul te,
Lesbia, aspexi, nihil est super mi
    vocis in ore…

The first three lines of a Sapphic are hendecasyllables, i.e., made of eleven syllables. The fourth line is composed of five syllables. In each line, there can only be one dactyl. To hear how the meter sounds, one may easily google Catullus 11 and 51 readings, and try to catch the rhythm.

Now, read slowly these lines from 'Descent':

Swiftly, swiftly crossing the golden spaces
Knowledge leaps, a torrent of rapid lightnings;
Thoughts that left the Ineffable's flaming mansions,
Blaze in my spirit.

Slow the heart-beats' rhythm like a giant hammer's;
Missioned voices drive to me from God's doorway
Words that live not save upon Nature's summits,
Ecstasy's chariots.

All the world is changed to a single oneness;
Souls undying, infinite forces, meeting,
Join in God-dance weaving a seamless Nature,
Rhythm of the Deathless.

The lines are forceful and not forced, natural and not specious. The experience itself might appear foreign to most of us but that is the purpose of art, is it not? To express the supernormal or at least the different in a way that it can be felt viscerally even if not understood intellectually.

Let us compare this with the famous sapphics by Swinburne:

All the night sleep came not upon my eyelids,
Shed not dew, nor shook nor unclosed a feather,
Yet with lips shut close and with eyes of iron

Stood and beheld me.
Then to me so lying awake a vision
Came without sleep over the seas and touched me,
Softly touched mine eyelids and lips; and I too,
Full of the vision,
Saw the white implacable Aphrodite,
Saw the hair unbound and the feet unsandalled
Shine as fire of sunset on western waters;
Saw the reluctant…

Swinburne has brilliantly captured the rhythm while sustaining a beauty of imagery. Yet, as Eliot has pointed out there is throughout his poetry a diffuseness of meaning and imagery, such that only the sound is predominant, and the rest remains as a faint echo in the background. Swinburne is a great artist of sound but tends to lose intensity by the end of the poem while Sri Aurobindo is far more satisfying in his inspired fusion of sound, meaning and imagery.

Pound in 'Apparuit' attempted to recreate the sound of Catullus, whom he greatly admired:

Half the graven shoulder, the throat aflash with
strands of light inwoven about it, loveliest
of all things, frail alabaster, ah me!
swift in departing.
Clothed in goldish weft, delicately perfect,

gone as wind ! The cloth of the magical hands!

Thou a slight thing, thou in access of cunning

Dar'dst to assume this?

These lines above have a certain beauty, but we can see how the third line begins with an iamb. No amount of artificial inflexion can save this line from failure. The "ah me!" at the end of the third line is meretricious as padding.

When we look at Sri Aurobindo's sapphics, the power of the metrical structure is unmistakable, even if the spiritual experience is not understood. The fourth line in each stanza brings to a close the impact of the first three in a manner that to quote Shakespeare from 'Hamlet', "brings it smoothness." This is one instant where execution proves the theory. Not only a master versifier is at play here but also a master poet, in my opinion.

9.

Jivanmukta

Alcaics are a difficult meter, especially in our age, where form is no longer at a premium and sound has taken a backseat to sensationalism and image. But if one finds pleasure in structures of sound and its close concordance with meaning, then form poetry still has value. So the sonnet and villanelles in the hands of a great artist may have immense power.

One of the most powerful examples of the intensity and impact that classical forms can create would be the poem 'Do not go gentle into the good night' by Dylan Thomas. Using the refrain and the rhyme with the power of spondees and dactyls in his lines, he has created a poem that is at once deeply touching and expressive of his inner state at the impending loss of his father and a revolt against the reality of this ephemeral world.

We see the same disruption of meaning with Mallarmé's 'Le Cygne' where with the remarkable use of homonyms, symbolism and alliterations, he invests the sonnet form with revelatory and insistent power. Thus, form poems can still create great effects, perhaps more so within their structure than free verse, although as Eliot has pointed out, there is no such thing as free verse for the poet who wants to do a good job.

One of the reasons for the deterioration of modern verse is perhaps this loss of mastery over sound and form, the discarding of beauty and discipline, and the ability to sustain an inspiration on a strong platform. Free verse has become freedom from verse. As Robert Frost once said in an interview, "Free verse was like playing tennis without a net." Without the restrictions there can be no game.

Coming back to alcaics, they are an intriguing form used by the Greeks to wonderful effect. In English, Alfred Tennyson tried to capture their allure in his lines of 'Milton.'

O mighty-mouth'd inventor of harmonies,
O skill'd to sing of Time or Eternity,
  God-gifted organ-voice of England,
    Milton, a name to resound for ages;
Whose Titan angels, Gabriel, Abdiel,
Starr'd from Jehovah's gorgeous armouries,
  Tower, as the deep-domed empyrean
    Rings to the roar of an angel onset—
Me rather all that bowery loneliness,
The brooks of Eden mazily murmuring,
  And bloom profuse and cedar arches
    Charm, as a wanderer out in ocean,
Where some refulgent sunset of India
Streams o'er a rich ambrosial ocean isle,
  And crimson-hued the stately palm-woods

Whisper in odorous heights of even.

The challenge of eleven syllables in first two lines, nine in the third line and ten in the fourth line seems imposing. But the use of dactyls and trochees creates a rhythm, which if managed well, can create new effects in English.

For me these lines from Sri Aurobindo bring great delight:

He who from Time's dull motion escapes and thrills
Rapt thoughtless, wordless in the eternal's breast,
Unrolls the form and sign of being,
Seated above in the omniscient Silence.

The rest of the poem *Jivanmukta* seems to be admirably managed. A master of classical poetry, he is able to wing the meter but truly takes flight only in the lines mentioned above. A new height is reached; a possibility is shown. For future poetry, and for anyone who might deem such explorations worth the challenge.

10.

An Image

Rushing from Troy like a cloud on the plains the Trojans thundered,

Just as a storm comes thundering, thick with the dust of kingdoms,

Edged with the devious dance of the lightning, so all Troas

Loud with the roar of the chariots, loud with the vaunt and the war-cry,

Rushed from Troywards gleaming with spears and rolled on enormous.

Joyous as ever Paris led them glancing in armour,

Brilliant with gold like a bridegroom, playing with death and the battle

Even as apart in his chamber he played with his beautiful Helen,

Touching her body rejoiced with a low and lyrical laughter,

So he laughed as he smote his foemen. Round him the arrows,

Round him the spears of the Argives sang like the voices of maidens

Trilling the anthem of bridal bliss, the chant hymeneal;

Round him the warriors fell like flowers strewn at a bridal

Red with the beauty of blood.

Although called 'An Image,' this phanopoeic fragment is more than an image. It is in the powerful hexameter sustained through fourteen lines, certainly a new rhythm in the English language. Reminiscent of the best of Walt Whitman, it adapts the quantitative hexameter of the Greeks into a foreign tongue. And what a performance! All theories aside, the proof of the prosody is in the reading.

A new sound-music, what Pound called melopoeia, with resonances, an oceanic sound with echoes and multi-layered undertones, is what we hear. Orchestral harmonies as if various instruments were at play, and yet the sound is not diffuse. It is energized in the body of a new language.

I came across a remarkable essay 'English Hexameter Verse with a Specimen' by T.S. Omond published in 1897. It is remarkable that the author, after reviewing English hexameter written by various poets such as Edmund Spenser, Samuel Taylor Coleridge, Swinburne, Arthur Clough, among others, states clearly that this form in English is yet to be written. In my opinion, 'An Image' is the first successful fragment that captures the 'galloping' and 'reverberating' rhythm to its fullest.

Sri Aurobindo had a theory of how to adopt quantitative meters of the Greek and Latin into English and yet keep them natural in the new tongue. One notices that each line except the fifth and the tenth begins with a dactyl. The fifth line begins with a trochee and the tenth line with a spondee. Thus, he is not enslaved to the idea that the quantitative phrase always begins with a dactyl.

Sri Aurobindo gave importance to stress as well as accent, and sometimes even the length of the sound-unit, to trans-create the sounds of a rhythm that does not adapt too easily to the non-quantitative structure of English.

He attempted sapphics and alcaics among other meters using this prosody, while allowing them flexibility and variance in the new dialect. And perhaps, this might be something for new poets to study if they wish to bring new meters into the English language.

All in all, a powerful performance, intense and wide, such that only methodical, systematic and consistent approach to versification can create. But this is not just verse. It is poetry that experiments and yet delights with innovation, surprises with originality of imagery and its deployment.

A mastery of classical forms and yet the ability to soar freely in a new language is at display here and this is why it is one of my most favorite passages in English poetry.

11.

In the Moonlight

If now must pause the bullocks' jingling tune,
Here let it be beneath the dreaming trees
Supine and huge that hang upon the breeze,
Here in the wide eye of the silent moon.

How living a stillness reigns! The night's hushed rules
All things obey but three, the slow wind's sigh
Among the leaves, the cricket's ceaseless cry,
The frog's harsh discord in the ringing pools...

These lines above remind one of Thomas Gray who wrote 'Elegy Written in a Country Churchyard.' It is interesting that both poems begin on a most satisfying note of melody and then veer towards a more intellectual stance. The lyrical feeling is lost or submerged in the poetic discussion. Sri Aurobindo recovers the musical note again as he builds the argument in verse, then returns to the philosophic debate.

Two genii in the dubious heart of man,
Two great unhappy foes together bound
Wrestle and strive to win unhampered ground;
They strive for ever since the race began.
One from his body like a bridge of fire
Mounts upward azure-winged with eager eyes;
One in his brain deep-mansioned labouring lies
And clamps to earth the spirit's high desire.
Here in this moonlight with strange visions rife
I seem to see their vast peripheries
Without me in the sombre mighty trees,
And, hark! their silence turns the wheels of life.

After the near-perfection of the first four stanzas, these stanzas seem to be less spontaneous, though still technically sound.

Stars run their cycle and are quenched; the suns
Born from the night are to the night returned,
When the cold tenebrous spaces have inurned
The listless phantoms of the Shining Ones.

From two dead worlds a burning world arose
Of which the late putrescent fruit is man;
From chill dark space his roll of life began

And shall again in icy quiet close.

Our lives are but a transitory breath:
Mean pismires in the sad and dying age
Of a once glorious planet, on the edge
Of bitter pain we wait eternal death.

"Putrescent" and "pismires" are not words that we hear from Sri Aurobindo's mouth usually. But "The listless phantoms of the Shining Ones" is a line that goes through like a lance with its pungency and metaphysical wit.

Freedom, God, Immortality, the three
Are one and shall be realised at length;
Love, Wisdom, Justice, Joy and utter Strength
Gather into a pure felicity.

It comes at last, the day foreseen of old,
What John in Patmos saw, what Shelley dreamed,
Vision and vain imagination deemed,
The City of Delight, the Age of Gold.

Sri Aurobindo chooses God above science, spirit over matter, and foretells a renaissance of the Divine. It took him many more years of personal development and spiritual realizations to refine his poetry where some lines of his poems begin to embody his vision in form and content boldly and authoritatively. But this poem might be called a foretaste of what was to come. And even the beauty of the first four stanzas, while perfect on its own, was exceeded later in some of the sonnets and his epic, 'Savitri.'

12.

Ilion

'Ilion' is an attempt by Sri Aurobindo to give us epic poetry in quantitative hexameter. It was written based on his theory that the quantitative hexameter cannot be created in English strictly on the basis of quantity, or the length of the syllable, but has to incorporate stress and accent too as equally important factors to create the hexametric intonations of ancient Greek or Latin.

Did he succeed? It is not an easy challenge for the poet to follow the grammarian at the moment when inspiration seizes hold of him. And yet, it seems that there are sections in the poem when Sri Aurobindo has given his verse some naturalness even while attempting to create the quantitative hexameter.

> Calm from his seat Antenor arose as a wrestler arises,
>
> Tamer of beasts in the cage of the lions, eyeing the monsters
>
> Brilliant, tawny of mane, and he knows if his courage waver,
>
> Falter his eye or his nerve be surprised by the gods that are hostile,

> Death will leap on him there in the crowded helpless arena…

It seems to me that there are lines where the hexameter is naturalized to the English language and, on the whole, the passage sustains the meter. Overall, a masterly performance, though not as intense as the fourteen-line fragment *An Image*.

After reading Sri Aurobindo's thesis and his practice, I tend to agree that the dactylic and trochaic intonation can be brought to English more often, whether in the pentameter or hexameter. This may not be entirely radical as a submission. We hear the same swing of the dactyl and trochee in lines from the Bible:

> Hear, O heavens, and give ear, O earth, for the Lord hath spoken.

And then, again,

> God is gone up with a shout—the Lord with the sound of a trumpet.

These rhythms are not isolated either but recur often in the scripture of taste and standards in English poetry. And we see them in Whitman too, as he sings his lament at the death of Lincoln:

> Come lovely and soothing death,
>
> Undulate round the world, serenely arriving, arriving,

In the day, in the night, to all, to each,

Sooner or later delicate death.

Prais'd be the fathomless universe,

For life and joy, and for objects and knowledge curious,

And for love, sweet love—but praise! praise! praise!

For the sure-enwinding arms of cool-enfolding death...[50]

Sri Aurobindo brings in similar sounds and again touches a more sustained intensity as he describes the scene where Paris prepares himself for battle:

Here in a chamber of luminous privacy Paris was arming.

Near him moved Helen, a whiteness divine and intent on her labour

Fastened his cuirass, bound the greaves and settled the hauberk,

Thrilling his limbs with her touch that was heaven to the yearning of mortals,

She with her hands of delight caressing the senseless metal

Pressed her lips to his brilliant armour; she bowed down, she whispered:

"Cuirass, allowed by the gods, protect the beauty of Paris:

Keep for me that for which country was lost and my child and my brothers."

---

[50] Poem: 'When Lilacs Last in the Dooryard Bloom'd' by Walt Whitman

> Yearning she bent to his feet, to the sandal-strings of her lover;...

It seems that the subject matter chosen has to be right for success in sustaining such a difficult meter. T.S. Eliot has examined the challenge of writing long poems in English poetry and the need to change the meter to sustain inspiration and interest in modern times. It might be that the hexameter needs to be juxtaposed with the tetrameter or pentameter in sections to create an impact and sustain the intensity. Eliot himself attempts lines of various lengths in the 'Four Quartets' with success.

Sri Aurobindo, time and again, reaches the epic note in the hexameter. Here, as Cassandra talks of how she tricked Apollo into giving her the vision of the god that can see through the future:

> Give me thy vision sheer, not such as thou giv'st to thy prophets,
>
> Troubled though luminous; clear be the vision and ruthless to error,
>
> Far-darting god who art veiled by the sun and by death thou art shielded.
>
> Then I shall know that thou lovest.' He gave, alarmed and reluctant,
>
> Driven by Fate and his heart; but I mocked him, I broke from my promise;
>
> Courage fatal helping my heart to its ruin with laughter.

> Always now I remember his face that grew tranquil and ruthless,
>
> Hear the voice divine and implacable: 'Since thou deceivest
>
> Even the gods and thou hast not feared to lie to Apollo,
>
> Speak shalt thou henceforth only truth, but none shall believe thee:
>
> Scorned in thy words, rejected yet more for their bitter fulfilment,
>
> Scourged by the gods thou must speak though thy sick heart yearns to be silent....

Yet again, she can bear the weight of the meter in these words, tortured and prophetic. But has the hexameter reached the inevitability that the pentameter of Shakespeare and Milton accomplishes? That is the challenge and the opportunity before the poet of the future who might feel inspired enough to attempt further development along this possible opening.

If we accept the approach advocated by T.S. Omond in his essay 'English Hexameter Verse with a Specimen,' referenced earlier, that "thc truc unit of English verse is not the foot, not even the accent, but simply a period of time," then a new possibility emerges. Some modernist poets have attempted to restrict the length of a line to the time it takes for a single breath. Modernist verse is attempting to find a new principle of unity in rhythm that is at once immediate, colloquial, relevant, precise and appropriate for the emotion or thought expressed. We have seen another attempt at form poetry in the 50s and 60s after the full play of *vers libre* and imagistic poetry by Pound and Eliot in the last century.

It is possible that the experiments with the music of the meter will yield more treasures for our verse. For suddenly, even through the valiant attempt at creating a new swing and snap of the metrical line, Sri Aurobindo finds greater intensity and justifies 'A God's Labor':

> Then in the silent chamber Cassandra seized by Apollo
>
> Staggered erect and tossing her snow-white arms of affliction
>
> Cried to the heavens in her pain; for the fierce god tortured her bosom:
>
> "Woe is me, woe for the guile and the bitter gift of Apollo!
>
> Woe, thrice woe, for my birth in Troy and the lineage of Teucer!...

More effort will be needed to naturalize these sounds to English verse. Perhaps another Shakespeare is needed to make this meter sing. But, one achievement, it seems to me, from all this discussion might be that we might find a new system of cohesion and coherence to bind the rhythms of free verse. "The desire for *vers libre* is due to the sense of quantity reasserting itself," asserted Ezra Pound in his essay 'A Retrospect.'

Sri Aurobindo is thus able to offer a new means in his 'Elegiacs' to measure the lengths of a 'foot' or length and breath 'of periods of time' and is able to give us new rhythms to bear the weight of his spiritual realizations like a Hopkins:

> Wisdom supernal looks down on me, Knowledge mind cannot measure;
>
> Light that no vision can render garments the silence with splendour.[51]

Here, the first line is a hexameter, has a predominantly dactylic ring and the second one is a pentameter with variations introduced from the strict rules of elegiac Greek verse. And this attempt to move from one length to another gives the fluidity that the modern poet is looking for while staying within the framework of a unitary harmony.

And then, he tries free verse with a predominantly dactylic movement and succeeds in giving us an intense fusion of form and content:

> Swan of the supreme and spaceless ether wandering winged through the universe,
>
> Spirit immortal.[52]

Perhaps this is where quantitative hexameter will find its place in English verse. As snatches of the traditional intonations of ancient languages in the Bible or in Whitman and Sri Aurobindo in a passage, a couple of lines or even half a line. Or in free verse which would yet be verse that obeys certain laws of sound.

---

[51] Sri Aurobindo's poem – 'Trance of Waiting'

[52] Sri Aurobindo's poem – 'Beyond the Silence'

13.

Thought the Paraclete

As some bright archangel in vision flies
Plunged in dream-caught spirit immensities,
Past the long green crests of the seas of life,
Past the orange skies of the mystic mind
Flew my thought self-lost in the vasts of God.
Sleepless wide great glimmering wings of wind
Bore the gold-red seeking of feet that trod
Space and Time's mute vanishing ends. The face
Lustred, pale-blue-lined of the hippogriff,
Eremite, sole, daring the bourneless ways,
Over world-bare summits of timeless being
Gleamed; the deep twilights of the world-abyss
Failed below. Sun-realms of supernal seeing,
Crimson-white mooned oceans of pauseless bliss
Drew its vague heart-yearning with voices sweet…

'Thought the Paraclete' is a very interesting and challenging poem. It is akin to seeing a master contortionist fit himself in an awkward and restrictive space, manage to accommodate his body to it and come out of the framework intact and victorious.

The poem is written in hendecasyllables, each line composed of eleven syllables, in the meter of Catullus. It originally had strict requirements of starting and ending with a trochee, with a dactyl following the first trochee. For those of us who have attempted form poems, especially the difficult forms such as sestina, leave aside a sonnet or villanelle, know the challenge of writing a good poem in such a structured verse form.

Swinburne attempted the hendecasyllables in his book of verse, *Poems and Ballads.* He too seems to struggle with the form except in few lines such as these:

> Gazing eagerly where above the sea-mark
>
> Flame as fierce as the fervid eyes of lions
>
> Half divided the eyelids of the sunset;...

Coleridge too could barely maintain the meter in his Catullan Hendecasyllables almost half a century earlier and is indistinguishable from ordinary blank verse:

> Hear, my beloved, an old Milesian story!—
>
> High, and embosomed in congregated laurels,
>
> Glimmered a temple upon a breezy headland;...

Perhaps only Tennyson fared a little better with his attempt thus:

As some rare little rose, a piece of inmost
Horticultural art, or half coquette-like
Maiden, not to be greeted unbenignly.

It is extremely difficult to make each line natural and organic while fulfilling the complex requirements which seemed arbitrary and constrictive. And then, to make each line flow into each other as part of the stanza and the sentences, while honoring the demands of peculiar rhyme, words ending the line, or the number of syllables per each line. Failure is easy, success uncertain. Very few can even appreciate if the poet is able to successfully set the verse form to words and music. It is easy to become artificial if not artefactual. It appears to me that a couple of lines capture a high note in the poem while satisfying fully with meaning and imagery:

Crossing power-swept silences rapture-stunned,
Climbing high far ethers eternal-sunned…

Do we hear the resonances of Catullus here as in these lines:

Multas per gentes et multas per aequora vectus
Advenio has miseras, frater, ad inferias...

So why would anyone subject themselves to such torture and not let the inspiration define the chosen form? It is my opinion that Sri Aurobindo made two major contributions to the world of prosody among others: trying to adapt the classical Greek and Latin forms of poetry to English, and then, attempting to bring Sanskrit meters into English. I would have been curious to know if he had a similar quantitative approach to bring the Sanskrit *chhanda* into English rhythms. Perhaps the principles would have been similar but how to bring the vibrations of Sanskrit verse into the Anglo-Saxon harmonies of English! That would be a research in itself and might be worth pursuing in academic fields.

14.

Baji Prabhou

'Baji Prabhou' is a triumph, literally. Patriotic verse is dangerously difficult to write in English. It either borders on rhetoric or sentimentality, maudlin sloganeering or partisan parochialism. To me, it is one of the most perfect, most satisfying minor works in blank verse. It is perhaps the most modernistic of Sri Aurobindo's poems due to its directness, lack of adornments and rawness.

D.H. Lawrence used to advocate bare rocky poetry that is instantaneous. Well, 'Baji Prabhou' may not be instantaneous, but it is inspired and sustained in intensity, and is definitely bare and rocky. Grim, harsh, showing true heroism in the face of death, without relapsing into false notes, fearless even in the midst of a slaughter of comrades, it shows the character of a true *kshatriya*, a fighter, an Indian samurai, reaching his highest fulfillment.

Using verse that is almost parched and dry on one's lips, depicting a noon in the Deccan, the whole poem displays what Sri Aurobindo called "the psychology of sound." Hemingway with his short staccato sentences would have been proud.

A noon of Deccan with its tyrant glare
Oppressed the earth; the hills stood deep in haze
And sweltering athirst the fields glared up
Longing for water in the courses parched
Of streams long dead. Nature and man alike,
Imprisoned by a bronze and brilliant sky
Sought an escape from that wide trance of heat...

I wish I could quote the whole poem as an example of what possibilities are still held in blank verse. After Milton, it has been extremely difficult for any poet to stand apart from his mighty rhythms that imprison and limit with their restrictive range. Shelley and Keats tried to break through; so did Tennyson. But to write in an epic tone and yet steer clear of the sounds of 'Paradise Lost' and 'Paradise Regained' has been challenging for any post-Miltonic poet. Sri Aurobindo seems to open a line of development that may not be equal in range to Milton but is definitely a refreshing shift into a new soundscape.

...Thou seest this gorge
Narrow and fell and gleaming like the throat
Of some huge tiger, with its rocky fangs
Agrin for food; and though the lower slope
Descends too gently, yet with roots and stones
It is hampered, and the higher prone descent
Impregnably forbids assault; too steep

The sides for any to ascend and shoot
From vantage.

There is nothing extraordinary in the lines mentioned above. And yet, in their integrity, not a single word or phrase is out of place. This is perfection of the whole, a completeness where nothing stands out and everything is just and right. An art extremely difficult to accomplish, a lesser hand might have been tempted to throw in decorative verse or lapse into extreme detail. Passages like this make up the whole poem.

...At once
The muskets clamoured out, the bullets sped,
Deadly though few; again and yet again,
And some of the impetuous faltered back
And some in wrath pressed on; and while they swayed
Poised between flight and onset, blast on blast
The volleyed death invisible hailed in
Upon uncertain ranks. The leaders fell,
The forward by the bullets chosen out,
Prone or supine or leaning like sick men
O'er trees and rocks, distressed the whole advance
With prohibition by the silent slain.

This poem should have been one of the national poems of India, ranked as an equal to Bankim Chandra's 'Vande

Mataram' or Tagore's 'Jana Gana Mana' or Iqbal's 'Sare Jahan se Acchha.' Though not as lyrical as the other three, 'Baji Prabhou' is unique as a minor epic, in theme if not in rhythm. Ranking as an equal in importance if not in popularity, an ascetic and masculine rhythm captures well the soul of a nation at war with its colonizers for its existence and freedom.

> ...Then wrath
> Rose in the Prabhou and he raised himself
> In soul to make an end; but even then
> A stillness fell upon his mood and all
> That godlike impulse faded from his heart,
> And passing out of him a mighty form
> Stood visible. Titanic, scarlet-clad,
> Dark as a thunder-cloud, with streaming hair
> Obscuring heaven, and in her sovran grasp
> The sword, the flower, the boon, the bleeding head—
> Bhavani.

Enjambments, caesuras and alliterations create the right mood to sense a presence that towers above the limited individual. A greater vision is presented even while a character's end is related. As the number of Maratha fighters thins, the count is divulged without losing the flow in description. Until the hero offers himself joyfully as sacrifice for the liberation of his motherland.

In our own times, Robinson Jeffers has written the rugged poetry of hills and rocks and eagles, but even he finds it hard to live up to the stoicism he tries to depict, unable to sustain the intemperate and the intrepid. Every time I read 'Baji Prabhou' I learn something about the art of poetry, how to write and describe, how to tell a tale in verse, and to widen one's vision and elevate one's consciousness in doing so. It is wider in scope and detail than the other national anthems or songs, profounder, though less lyrical, and as powerful and Indian in theme and essence.

15.

Urvasie

Blank verse is the commonest and most abused verse form in English. Every Tom, Dick and Mungeri tries his hand at it. But in the hands of modern poets, the meter is lax, uninspiring, blank and unexceptional. According to a survey I found on the internet, according to someone named JP on *American Poetry* in Blendspace, 75 percent of poetry in English is written in blank verse. Thus, 75 percent of the stuff written these days can be safely discarded.

Perhaps I am not being fair. For blank verse is tough to master. Whoever said it is not. "The art is long, life is short, opportunity fleeting, experimentation perilous and judgment difficult," as Hippocrates noted aphoristically (Vita brevis, ars longa, occasio praeceps, experimentum periculosum, iudicium dificile.) Perilous it may be. But experiment we must.

And blank verse needs constant innovation, even though the dense wall of Milton or the breathtaking gift and scope of Shakespeare might appear to have been an unsurpassable summit. It is not that after them, there were no other great poets who wrote in this meter. Wordsworth, Coleridge, Keats, Shelley and Tennyson tried to break away from the past and, to some extent, succeeded. Yeats, Frost and Stevens continued to bring new sources of inspiration into its extremely challenging cadence in an attempt to infuse it with something new and different.

I have already noted how I admire the stark, rugged blank verse that Sri Aurobindo used to great effect in 'Baji Prabhou.' I feel that in 'Urvasie,' he touched greatness at moments while adhering to a traditional and Elizabethan mode of expression. It is the story of love between king Pururavus and an *apsara*[53], Urvasie. This is perhaps the most breathtaking introduction to his achievement in this minor epic:

> He moved, he came towards her. She, a leaf
> Before a gust among the nearing trees,
> Cowered. But, all a sea of mighty joy
> Rushing and swallowing up the golden sand,
> With a great cry and glad Pururavus
> Seized her and caught her to his bosom thrilled,
> Clinging and shuddering. All her wonderful hair
> Loosened and the wind seized and bore it streaming
> Over the shoulder of Pururavus
> And on his cheek a softness. She, o'erborne,
> Panting, with inarticulate murmurs lay,
> Like a slim tree half seen through driving hail,
> Her naked arms clasping his neck, her cheek
> And golden throat averted, and wide trouble

[53] Heavenly maiden.

In her large eyes bewildered with their bliss.
Amid her wind-blown hair their faces met.
With her sweet limbs all his, feeling her breasts
Tumultuous up against his beating heart,
He kissed the glorious mouth of heaven's desire.
So clung they as two shipwrecked in a surge.
Then strong Pururavus, with godlike eyes
Mastering hers, cried tremulous: "O beloved,
O miser of thy rich and happy voice,
One word, one word to tell me that thou lovest."
And Urvasie, all broken on his bosom,
Her godhead in his passion lost, moaned out
From her imprisoned breasts, "My lord, my love!"

Bringing love and eroticism in art with intensity is perhaps the most difficult *sringara rasa*[54] to depict. A lesser hand would veer either towards excessive physicality or superficial sentimentalism. But it is a rare feat to accomplish a balance between the awakened force of passion with the decorum of honor, style and beauty. I feel one can write a book on its inexhaustible riches of ornamentation, intensity, rhythm and imagery and still not have fully exhausted its treasures.

This passage noted above, to my mind, can compare with the best of Yeats or Eliot in sheer sustained intensity in the

---

[54] A very crude translation of this Sanskrit phrase would be the ornamental or decorativeness in taste.

last century. How is it that this achievement has not been acclaimed in any anthology of English poetry? Then again, my question too is superfluous. Perhaps, as pointless as the anthologies we see today of such shallow times.

16.

The Vigil of Thaliard

This is perhaps the most haunting verse written by Sri Aurobindo. And the sound-effects enhanced by rhyme and rhythm create a mesmeric Coleridge-like atmosphere. Just when I thought I had read all of his poetry and there were no more surprises, I came across these lines:

Where Time a sleeping dervish is
Or printed legend of Romance
Mid lilies and mid gold-roses
Of mediaeval France…

Time as "a sleeping dervish" is indeed a strange metaphor with layers of significance. The fourth line with a length one-syllable less than the rest creates a close that is at once abrupt and decisive. Sri Aurobindo has used this forcefully with several passages in what may be considered as his juvenilia, written at the age of nineteen or twenty.

For if throughout the monstrous night

Unblest by ave or by creed
By witchèd water Christian wight
Do finger bead by bead
His scarlet rosary of sins
And leave his soul ajar,
What hour the sleepy Evening pins
Her bodice with a star,
Until, the pitchy veil withdrawn
That swathes the looming dune,
The crowing trumpeter of dawn
Blows addio to the moon…

The music is addictive and grows on one slowly. These are lines that can be committed to memory very easily with sheer logopoeia. To paraphrase Walter Pater, one might say that this fragment depicts 'the strangeness of reality in poetic form.'

The warden of the starry waste
Who walks with orange-coloured lamp
And weird eyes nursing fire, paced
Night's silver-tented camp.
The rose-lipped golden-footed day,
A flower by maiden culled,
Beneath star-blossomed arras lay

In Evening's bosom lulled.
The water seemed a damson crust
With golden sugar poured,
Or mirror caked with purple dust
In lady's closet stored.

Harold Bloom has called romantic poetry as 'an enchantment of the marvelous' in his book *The Ringers in the Tower: Studies in Romantic Tradition*. A daemonic sense pervades the twenty-six stanzas that make up this fragment.

His eyes were drops of smelted ore
That in a foundry chase:
His lips a cruel promise wore,
A marble pride his face.
As shows thro' gold caparison
Laburnum dusky-stemmed,
Thro' silks in Persian harem spun
His gorgeous body gleamed...

One may perhaps notice a riot of sights and sounds here, of colors and gleams and flashes of brilliance. As his art matured, Sri Aurobindo moved to a more controlled and measured imagery in his later years. But if Eliot is right that only those who will risk going too far can possibly find out how far one can go, then this seems to be an attempt to explore the limits and possibilities of poetry.

> A blue papyrus-leaf designed
> With fretted curls of fire,
> A purple page with coronet lined
> Or labyrinthine spire:
> The fiery-coloured bee of night
> With folded purple wing,
> Or solitary chrysolite
> Shut in an emerald ring:
> The vellum binding of a book,
> A scented volume spiced with Ind,
> A magic purse by Genie shook
> To loose a murmuring wind.

One does not get tired of this rhythm and only wishes that the poet had continued with his inspiration and given us a longer poem. But that was not meant to be. Romantic poetry for its own sake, or aesthetic poetry, was only a detour. It was left to Sri Aurobindo to pursue another line of development in English poetry, which pushed the frontiers of a new kind of poetry: that which approached sound as its own experience and rhythm as its own revelation.

17.

Rose of God

Rose of God, vermilion stain on the sapphires of heaven,
Rose of Bliss, fire-sweet, seven-tinged with the ecstasies seven!
Leap up in our heart of humanhood, O miracle, O flame,
Passion-flower of the Nameless, bud of the mystical Name.
...
Rose of God, like a blush of rapture on Eternity's face,
Rose of Love, ruby depth of all being, fire-passion of Grace!
Arise from the heart of the yearning that sobs in Nature's abyss:
Make earth the home of the Wonderful and life beatitude's kiss.

'Rose of God' is a difficult poem even though on the surface it appears simple. Is the 'Rose of God' a natural and physical rose that is taken as a symbol in the manner of Yeats and Eliot? Or is it a vision that the Mahayogi had, and he is only describing it? Is it a metaphor for the soul, the *anahata*, the psychic being, at its intensest devotion and flowering? Or is it the seeker himself seeing his own whorls and gyres, shades, and mysterious form? Or is it all of these?

Helen Gardner describes in *The Composition of Four Quartets* that for T.S. Eliot there were "actually three roses: the sensuous rose, the socio-political Rose and the spiritual rose and that the three must in some way be identified as one." The rose is also the symbol of Mary, as the Divine Mother of Christ. According to the Rosicrucians, the rose symbolizes the soul on the cross. In a letter to a disciple Sri Aurobindo wrote, "The rose is usually taken by us as the symbol of surrender, love, etc. But here it is not used in that sense, but as the most intense of all flowers it is used as symbolic of the divine intensities—Bliss, Light, Love, etc."

In another letter, he wrote,

> 'Rose of God,' like a previous poem 'In Horis Aeternum,' is written in pure stress metre. As stress and high accentual pitch usually coincide, it is possible to scan accentual metre on the stress principle and stress metre also can be so written that it can be scanned as accentual verse; but pure stress metre depends entirely on stress ictus. In ordinary poetry stress and natural syllabic quantity enter in as elements of the rhythm, but are not, qua stress and quantity, essential elements of the basic metre: in pure stress metre there is a reversal of these values; quantity and accentual inflexion are subordinate and help to build the rhythm, but stress alone determines the metrical basis. In Rose of God each line is composed of six stresses, and the whole poem is built of five stanzas, each containing four such lines; the arrangement of feet varies freely to suit the movement of thought and feeling in each line. Thus,

Róse of| Gód, | damask fórce of| Infínity, | red ícon of| míght,
Róse of| Pówer | with thy díam|ond hálo | piércing | the níght,
* Abláze | in the wíll of | the mórtal, | desígn | the wónder of|*
thy plán,
Ímage of | Ímmor|tálity, | outbréak of | the Gódhead | in
man.[55]

It is also curious that the lines in most of the poem are predominantly trochaic. The first foot is usually stressed throughout, except in lines eleven, fifteen and nineteen. The trochaic metrical units give an impetus to the rhythm. Dactyls and anapests interspersed throughout the poem give it a delicate and subtle lengthening of rhythm sometimes sounding like Latin hexameters.

So much for the technique. The line I love the most is this:

Rose of Light, immaculate core of the ultimate seeing!

This is a most mysterious image. Is the rose glowing with light or is there a mystical glow about it? Or is it Light manifesting as a rose? And this Light itself is the core of the seeing? Some unique kind of fusion between the object and the observer has happened. And the image of a rose of light with its spiraling petals and the vortex of color and form lends itself to endless meditation, to paraphrase Harold Bloom.

The next line which hits me in the solar plexus is this one:

Sun on the head of the Timeless, guest of the marvellous
Hour.

---

[55] CWSA, Vol.2, p.568

Here, the 'Rose of Light' has become the Sun but in a timeless world and only appears in phenomenal time as a guest. The four dactyls in this line makes one think of Sun as the symbol of *Sat-Chit-Ananda*, or Truth-Consciousness-Bliss, in a Vedic image. Rose of God has several such visionary images that confound and enlighten at the same time and to appreciate them, one needs to almost develop a new taste.

And then we come across this line which takes this blinding insight further:

> Rose of Power with thy diamond halo piercing the night!

The line reminds one of the poem 'Shiva' written by Sri Aurobindo and the dawn of his epic 'Savitri.' As if the ray of light is its fiat and the force of Shakti as depicted in Shiva. But, above all, it is a fascinating image of the rose sending out beams of diamond-glow and clarity.

And then, these perplexing lines:

> Rose of God, smitten purple with the incarnate divine Desire,
>
> Rose of Life, crowded with petals, colour's lyre!

Is it the soul that is aspiring for the Divine and has changed in color with its singular intensity? In a synesthesia of color and sound, the rose becomes a musical instrument. It reminds one of Yeats' famous line:

> Far off, most secret, and inviolate Rose…

...Your great leaves enfold

...the helms of ruby and gold

Of the crowned Magi...

Where "the rose is a remote ideal seen in the far distance transcending the world of time ... symbolizing ideal beauty, eternal love, perfection, incorruptibility, and the realm of the mysterious, mythical and magical ..." as elaborated by Rachel V. Billigheimer. In 'The Motif of the Rose in the Poetry of William Butler Yeats,' Zavrsni rad opines that "it is certain that the addressee is a woman ... It could be Maud Gonne, but it could also be Ireland ... perhaps there might in fact be two entities being referred to."

Or Yeats aspiration in his poem 'To the Rose upon the Rood of Time':

Red Rose, proud Rose, sad Rose of all my days!

Come near me while I sing the ancient ways...

And thine own sadness, whereof stars, grown old

In dancing silver-sandalled on the sea...

Eternal beauty wandering on her way...

Or the Yeatsian incantation about 'The Lover Tells of the Rose in His Heart':

All things uncomely and broken, all things worn out and old,

The cry of a child by the roadway, the creak of a lumbering cart,

The heavy steps of the ploughman, splashing the wintry mould,

Are wronging your image that blossoms a rose in the deeps of my heart.

The wrong of unshapely things, is a wrong too great to be told;

I hunger to build them anew, and sit on a green knoll apart,

With the earth and the sky and the water, re-made like a casket of gold

For my dreams of your image that blossoms a rose in the deeps of my heart.

Kristel Marie Pujanes in an essay 'Featured Poem: The Lover Tells of the Rose in His Heart' by W.B. Yeats points out that it is a love poem written for both a "dream lover" and "the dream of a better nation."

We meet the rose in Walter de la Mare's lyric 'All That's Past':

Very old are the woods;

And the buds that break

Out of the brier's boughs,

When March winds wake,

So old with their beauty are—

Oh, no man knows
Through what wild centuries
Roves back the rose.

Something wistful, a deep longing for a reality within seems to come to us in the image of the rose. Something that aspires and wishes to be the completest flowering of itself, and in that blossoming be the transformation that the world needs. Two great poets of mystery, Yeats and Walter de la Mare have used the rose symbol exquisitely and with great effect. Sri Aurobindo moves beyond the realm of profound feeling within to a vision that towers above us. Amal Kiran in *Talks on Poetry* felt that the 'Rose of God' is a work of metaphysics and psychology, in which "the Divine is feelingly visioned and visionarily comprehended and comprehendingly felt." Amal sees 'Rose of God' as primarily an incantatory poem that is meant to evoke the vision it describes with rhythm and suggestiveness.

The Yeatsian rose according to Amal is metaphysically not only "visioned in the deeps of the heart" but could also be "elsewhere in a vaster pervasion" when he sings in 'The Rose of Battle,'

Rose of all Roses, Rose of all the world…
But gather all for whom no love hath made
A woven silence, or but came to cast
A song into the air, and singing passed…
Beauty grown sad with its eternity

Made you of us, and of the dim grey sea.

They have gone down under the same white stars…

Perhaps in the same vein we could also say that the Aurobindonian rose is not only of the world but also above the world, not only immanent but also cosmic and transcendental. That is the only way the symbol makes sense to me.

18.

Sri Aurobindo and Milton

Milton, the poet who attempted to subsume all great poets of the past, Homer, Virgil, even the Bible, ended up subsuming future poets for the next few centuries. The mighty wall of Milton, while noble and powerful, had no hidden harmonies or flexibility and stifled anyone who attempted new things in blank verse. Keats, Shelley and Tennyson tried, but the former two died young and Tennyson could only produce a meter far weaker and ineffective, perhaps more due to the thinness of his themes and temperament.

But it seems to me that the mighty wall of Milton has been breached. At least the way to do so has been shown and new possibilities opened and lines of development created. Sri Aurobindo, in his early blank verse poems, 'Love and Death' and 'Urvasie,' made some innovations but largely stayed confined within the safe firewalls of the past.

His early innovations are thus more an inspiration and an easy felicity than a breakthrough in meter, as in 'Urvasie,' here, depicting the moment King Pururavus picks the fainted *apsara* back into his chariot, having saved her from the demon, Cayshie:

Nor King Pururavus pursued but checked
His rushing chariot on the quiet snow
And sprang towards her and knelt down and trembled.
Perfect she lay amid her tresses wide,
Like a mishandled lily luminous,
As she had fallen. From the lucid robe
One shoulder gleamed and golden breast left bare,
Divinely lifting, one gold arm was flung…
And soon she moved. Those wonderful wide orbs
Dawned into his, quietly, as if in muse…
Slowly; last, sudden, they brighten and grow wide
With recognition of an altered world,
Delighted: so woke Urvasie to love.

The rhythm is managed in a masterly manner, with feminine and masculine endings, with caesura and weighting of syllables, assonances and modulations. The line, "Those wonderful wide orbs dawned into his" is the high-point of this section with its quiet gentleness, romance of feeling and slow movement.

Later, we come to a passage even more extreme and intense, quoted earlier, and even Whitman, Eliot or Yeats would be hard-pressed to match its sustained power, rapidly moving images and magnificence:

He moved, he came towards her. She, a leaf

Before a gust among the nearing trees,
Cowered. But, all a sea of mighty joy
Rushing and swallowing up the golden sand...
...
And Urvasie, all broken on his bosom,
Her godhead in his passion lost, moaned out
From her imprisoned breasts, "My lord, my love!"

What a tour de force! Let us look at 'Love and Death,' written when he was 27 years old, another poem with some powerful breakthroughs of energy and eloquence:

Replied to Ruru, "Mortal, I am he;
I am that Madan who inform the stars
With lustre and on life's wide canvas fill
Pictures of light and shade, of joy and tears,
Make ordinary moments wonderful
And common speech a charm: knit life to life
With interfusions of opposing souls
And sudden meetings and slow sorceries:
...
O mortal, all deep-souled desires and all
Yearnings immense are mine, so much I can."

And then he rises to an even higher pitch with another passage of enchantment, vigor and enduring passion:

In a thin soft eve
Ganges spread far her multitudinous waves,
A glimmering restlessness with voices large,
And from the forests of that half-seen bank
A boat came heaving over it, white-winged,
With a sole silent helmsman marble-pale
...
Love shall draw half thy pain into my limbs;
Then we shall triumph glad of agony.

But this too is only a temporizing solution. Milton still lurks, unexpiated, in the background, with his marble balustrades and high ramparts, preventing any flights, unless some lasting solution is found. The efforts made by later poets failed to match the Samson-like potency of these lines from Book 1 of 'Paradise Lost':

Him the Almighty Power
Hurld headlong flaming from th' Ethereal Skie
With hideous ruine and combustion down
To bottomless perdition, there to dwell
In Adamantine Chains and penal Fire,
Who durst defie th' Omnipotent to Arms.

Or these lines of singular pain and sense of injury again from Book 1:

But his doom
Reserv'd him to more wrath; for now the thought
Both of lost happiness and lasting pain
Torments him; round he throws his baleful eyes
That witness'd huge affliction and dismay
Mixt with obdurate pride and stedfast hate:
...
In utter darkness, and their portion set
As far remov'd from God and light of Heav'n
As from the Center thrice to th' utmost Pole.

Compare this with Tennyson in 'Ulysses' and the difference in tone and cadence is immediately palpable:

It little profits that an idle king,
By this still hearth, among these barren crags,
Match'd with an aged wife, I mete and dole
Unequal laws unto a savage race,
That hoard, and sleep, and feed, and know not me.
I cannot rest from travel: I will drink
Life to the lees: All times I have enjoy'd

Greatly, have suffer'd greatly, both with those
That loved me, and alone, on shore, and when
Thro' scudding drifts the rainy Hyades
Vext the dim sea: I am become a name;
...
Gleams that untravell'd world whose margin fades
For ever and forever when I move.

The two "falls" that Milton depicts in his epic are felt and seen by the reader sensually. Take an example from Tennyson's 'Morte d'Arthur,' and difference between the Miltonic vital energy and the Tennysonian false simplicity and faux sentimentality is obvious:

So all day long the noise of battle roll'd
Among the mountains by the winter sea;
Until King Arthur's table, man by man,
Had fallen in Lyonnesse about their Lord,
...
Delight our souls with talk of knightly deeds,
Walking about the gardens and the halls
Of Camelot, as in the days that were.

Keats did much better in his fragment 'Hyperion' and it is a pity he died so early. Otherwise, perhaps, he could have cracked the code of this "most difficult of all English metres," as Sri Aurobindo once noted in a letter to a disciple. That may be because Keats was far more authentic as a voice even though he had just begun to find it:

> He enter'd, but he enter'd full of wrath;
>
> His flaming robes stream'd out beyond his heels,
>
> And gave a roar, as if of earthly fire,
>
> . . .
>
> The blaze, the splendour, and the symmetry,
>
> I cannot see—but darkness, death and darkness.

Yet, the problem remains. How do we create another possibility in blank verse that lets one escape the shackles of the past, allows the poet 'to master and possess' the achievements of the past, as Bloom has pointed, and tear down the iron enclosure that has enclosed us more than four centuries? I believe it was Sri Aurobindo who first accomplished this with his little recognized and still under-appreciated epic, 'Baji Prabhou.' Here is the beginning (quoted earlier) from the sparse, bare, rocky, direct poem that hits one in the solar plexus, not as intensely as Milton perhaps, but in a different manner, stark and parched as its landscape:

> A noon of Deccan with its tyrant glare
>
> Oppressed the earth; the hills stood deep in haze,
>
> And sweltering athirst the fields glared up
>
> Longing for water in the courses parched

Of streams long dead.
...
Therefore they stayed not for the choking dust,
The slaying heat, the thirst of wounds and fight,
The stumbling stark fatigue, but onward pressed
With glowing eyes.

This may be the tiny door through which modernist poetry can escape the oppressive art of Milton without resorting to the artificial and clever craftsmanship of a Tennyson. D.H. Lawrence had advocated poetry that was instantaneous, simple in language and unaffected in style. Perhaps a solution incorporating his directness and the starkness of modernist unsentimental non-sententious verse can open up new prospects. Here is another section that is raised to high pitch by the fierce patriotism of the protagonist, his love of land and fearless willingness to sacrifice his life:

Then Baji first broke silence, "Lo, the surge!
That was but spray of death we first repelled.
Chosen of Shivaji, Bhavani's swords,
For you the gods prepare. We die indeed,
But let us die with the high-voiced assent
Of Heaven to our country's claim enforced
To freedom." As he spoke, the Mogul lines
Entered the menacing wide-throated gorge,

Carefully walking, but not long that care
Endured, for where they entered, there they fell.
Others behind in silence stern advanced.
They came, they died; still on the previous dead
New dead fell thickening. Yet by paces slow
The lines advanced with labour infinite
And merciless expense of valiant men.
For even as the slopes were filled and held,
Still the velocity and lethal range
Increased of the Mahratta bullets; dead
Rather than living held the conquered slope,–
The living who, half-broken, paused.

"They came, they died; still on the previous dead/New dead fell thickening." Eliot might have been thrilled at this stripping away of adjectives and Victorian affectations, since he could be quite a votary of starkness when evaluating other poets. I end with this section of the minor epic since it seems to me to be its greatest height ascended, a revelation of the hidden godhead of the nation to the dying hero, the culmination of his life's work and, finally, his success in protecting his motherland from the invaders:

Small was the space for fight,
And meeting strength with skill and force with soul
The strong and agile keepers of the hills

Prevailed against the city-dwelling hosts,
With covert and the swiftly stabbing blades
O'erpowering all the feints of Agra's schools.
...
And Baji knew the goddess formidable
Who watches over India till the end.
Even then a sword found out his shoulder, sharp
A Mogul lance ran griding through his arm.

This might be one approach. A sublime theme with charged feelings, a patriotic and noble protagonist, a battle that decides the fate of the nation and its supreme leader, the conscious sacrifice of a chosen band in an elevated spiritual light and the Divine presence depicted at a critical moment pictorially to bring the epic to its denouement. In a rhythm that is bare as the rocky landscape, stark as the situation, direct as the stakes. In my opinion, it opens possibilities and breaks from the shackles of the past.

T.S. Eliot complained of the "dissociated sensibility" of Milton, where the auditory imagination took precedence over the visual or the tactile. He believed this caused a deterioration of the language which crimped even great poets such as Keats. But Milton succeeded because he happily chose the epic situation that suited his genius, the unseeable or unseen characters who are not human but archetypes, in the nebulous beginnings of the world. And he succeeded as a great poet because he brought something new to the language, a power that was not necessarily inherent in the regular use of the language but one of its possibilities, and despite his flaws, he was so successful in his execution at a particular stage of the language's development that he left a permanent imprint on the poetic diction of English. That achievement should no longer be seen as a disability but as an opportunity. Milton's fierce dedication to his life's purpose is something to be emulated, his faith in his destiny as a bard, his invention and higher mental plane of conceptualizing and execution. His singular focus on improving the lot of his people, no matter how great his failures, is admirable. And his persistence and faith in his poetic destiny despite the risk of termination by the rulers of the day, should be inspiring to all of us poets whom he makes look minor just by his devotion to the art of poetry.

We will need to be more, or at least as inventive as him, with fiercer selves than him, and keep trying to learn from poets who attempted something new, no matter their recognition. Marlowe with his mighty lines such as:

> See, see, where Christ's blood streams in the firmament

Or

> Was this the face that launched a thousand ships
> And burnt the topless towers of Ilium?

This could give us an opening, as Sri Aurobindo pointed out. Or Keats' attempts in 'Hyperion' could serve as a template to attempt something afresh.

Let us look at another possibility. I quote the opening scene of 'Paradise Lost,' one of the greatest accomplishments in English poetry ever in its long and illustrious history, again:

> ...Of Man's First Disobedience, and the Fruit
> Of that Forbidden Tree, whose mortal taste
> Brought Death into the World, and all our woe,
> With loss of Eden, till one greater Man
> Restore us, and regain the blissful Seat,
> Sing Heav'nly Muse, that on the secret top
> Of Oreb, or of Sinai, didst inspire
> That Shepherd, who first taught the chosen Seed,
> In the Beginning how the Heav'ns and Earth
> Rose out of Chaos: Or if Sion Hill
> Delight thee more, and Siloa's Brook that flow'd
> Fast by the Oracle of God; I thence
> Invoke thy aid to my adventrous Song,
> That with no middle flight intends to soar
> Above th' Aonian Mount, while it pursues
> Things unattempted yet in Prose or Rhime...

Remember this rhythm, its breathlessness, piling up of hammered beats, its intensity packed up in the pentameter, which almost seems cloistered and agoraphobic with tense suspirations, and now try this new rhythm in The Symbol Dawn from 'Savitri':

It was the hour before the Gods awake.
Across the path of the divine Event
The huge foreboding mind of Night, alone
In her unlit temple of eternity,
Lay stretched immobile upon Silence' marge.
Almost one felt, opaque, impenetrable,
In the sombre symbol of her eyeless muse
The abysm of the unbodied Infinite;
A fathomless zero occupied the world.
A power of fallen boundless self awake
Between the first and the last Nothingness,
Recalling the tenebrous womb from which it came,
Turned from the insoluble mystery of birth
And the tardy process of mortality
And longed to reach its end in vacant Nought.
As in a dark beginning of all things,
A mute featureless semblance of the Unknown
Repeating for ever the unconscious act,
Prolonging for ever the unseeing will,
Cradled the cosmic drowse of ignorant Force
Whose moved creative slumber kindles the suns
And carries our lives in its somnambulist whirl.

Athwart the vain enormous trance of Space,
Its formless stupor without mind or life,
A shadow spinning through a soulless Void,
Thrown back once more into unthinking dreams,
Earth wheeled abandoned in the hollow gulfs
Forgetful of her spirit and her fate.
The impassive skies were neutral, empty, still.

The first line itself is a stretching of the length of the pentameter, as it were. There is a deliberate slowing of the meter, as if there is an eternity to contemplate, and time is only a means to move into some stillness. There is a sound in the background, as if the Indian *veena* with its undertones, and the poet has forced this temporizing on the reader.

There is no rush as of "Siloa's brook that flowed fast by the Oracle of God" but "the abysm of the unbodied infinite" where "a fathomless zero occupied the world." A new meter had been discovered and formalized, a new sound as of the Vedas and Upanishads caught, reflecting the theme and the imagery, and it was only a matter of time when "a power of fallen boundless self awake … turned from the insoluble mystery of birth and the tardy process of mortality" in verse.

Let us compare the best passages again, both poets dealing with the "fallen state of mankind" with their own mythology and theological constructs, both attempting to study if not "justify the ways of God to men." Keats seemed to admire the lines below from Book I of 'Paradise Lost' in a letter to his brother for their "light and shade … their black brightness—the bon diamonding … the sorrow, the pain, the sad-sweet melody … the thousand Melancholies and Magnificences of this Page,"

> but he his wonted pride
> Soon recollecting, with high words, that bore
> Semblance of worth, not substance, gently rais'd
> Thir fainting courage, and dispel'd thir fears.
> Then strait commands that at the warlike sound
> Of Trumpets loud and Clarions be upreard
> His mighty Standard; that proud honour claim'd
> Azazel as his right, a Cherube tall:
> …
> Awaiting what command thir mighty Chief
> Had to impose:

Compare this with the quiet and intense pain described in Canto Two of 'Savitri', held by her secretly while she faces the impending death of her husband, Satyavan:

> Awhile, withdrawn in secret fields of thought,
> Her mind moved in a many-imaged past
> That lived again and saw its end approach:
> Dying, it lived imperishably in her;
> Transient and vanishing from transient eyes,
> Invisible, a fateful ghost of self,

It bore the future on its phantom breast.

...

The strength, the silence of the gods were hers.

In her he found a vastness like his own,

His high warm subtle ether he refound

And moved in her as in his natural home.

In her he met his own eternity.

Again, the same radical shift in rhythm, and an imagery and theme appropriate to the protagonist, but an entirely different treatment and approach. It is my belief that there are great possibilities in absorbing rhythms from other languages like Sanskrit, Japanese, Persian or Arabic to help create new resonances in English. English has constantly renewed itself from an infusion of new sounds whether from Italian and French early on, or from Spanish and Arabic from the British conquests of imperial lands, or from Sanskrit and other Indian languages as we see here with 'Savitri.'

Sri Aurobindo seems to have shown us the way. One criticism of 'Savitri' made by modernist critics is that it is extremely focused on sound, sometimes to the detriment of imagery. But that is precisely the point. To match the mighty wall of Milton, we needed the quiet and insistent bulldozer of a new harmony and new solutions.

As Eliot noted in his famous essay on Milton, "... the development of blank verse may be likened to the analysis of that astonishing industrial product coal-tar. Marlowe's verse is one of the earlier derivatives, but it possesses properties which are not repeated in any of the analytic or synthetic blank verses discovered somewhat later." We need to open ourselves up to disruption and invention just like Milton did, and if they are successful like Sri Aurobindo, despite the length of the epic and despite its enormity and extravagance, we need to use its vibrancy to "break the new wood (since) now is the time for carving," as Ezra Pound noted about Walt Whitman.

Keats again, in another letter to his brother, with his appreciation of Milton from Book I, "a sense of independence, of power, from the fancy's creating a world of its own by the sense of probabilities … we imagine after them—but not their realities if we had them nor our fancies in their strength can go further than this Pandemonium":

> Anon out of the earth a Fabrick huge
> Rose like an Exhalation, with the sound
> Of Dulcet Symphonies and voices sweet,
> Built like a Temple, where Pilasters round
> Were set, and Doric pillars overlaid
> With Golden Architrave; nor did there want
> …
> With Naphtha and Asphaltus yeilded light
> As from a sky.

And again, place this against my favorite passage from all of 'Savitri' from Book III, Canto 2 (The Adoration of the Divine Mother):

A stillness absolute, incommunicable,
Meets the sheer self-discovery of the soul;
A wall of stillness shuts it from the world,
A gulf of stillness swallows up the sense
And makes unreal all that mind has known,
All that the labouring senses still would weave
Prolonging an imaged unreality.
Self's vast spiritual silence occupies Space;
. . .
A black veil has been lifted; we have seen
The mighty shadow of the omniscient Lord;
But who has lifted up the veil of light
And who has seen the body of the King?

Can anyone still question if a new rhythm can be created? Nor are there any poets I know of who can sustain this level of elevated speech for 24,000 lines. Milton himself started losing his vision, in more ways than one, in the later books of Paradise Lost. It is only his indomitable will and his force of rhythm along with the story that allowed him to continue in this vein for nearly 11,000 lines.

To quote T.S. Eliot again, as he spoke of Yeats in a lecture delivered for Yeats Society, "Now, blank verse has been a dead metre for a long time. It would be outside of my frame to go into all the reasons for that now: but it is obvious that a form which was handled so supremely well by Shakespeare has its disadvantages. If you are writing a play of the same type as Shakespeare's, the reminiscence is oppressive; if you are writing a play of a different type, it is distracting." Replace Shakespeare with Milton, and you will get the insight why attempting in a dead meter, after an illustrious history of great poets who made the meter a bit 'used,' can be challenging and needs great awareness on the part of the poet seeking to change the terms on his own.

And I will give the last selection from 'Savitri' here, as another potential line of development where the rhythm while intenser, yet is far more spread out, almost like a hexameter built into the pentameter with the stretching of its time and its 'metrical phrase':

> A giant dance of Shiva tore the past;
> There was a thunder as of worlds that fall;
> Earth was o'errun with fire and the roar of Death
> Clamouring to slay a world his hunger had made;
> There was a clangour of Destruction's wings:
> The Titan's battle-cry was in my ears,
> Alarm and rumour shook the armoured Night.
> …
> Their tread one day shall change the suffering earth
> And justify the light on Nature's face.

It will not do to pick up stray passages from 'Savitri,' as some critics are wont to do, and show their lack of power. In such a long epic there are bound to be sections where the afflatus is less powerful. The poet let the rhythm flow in the natural stream of its meter. But these sections are few and far in between. Sri Aurobindo was a master of building his paragraphs and passages in an architectural manner fitting the whole edifice as in an old Indian temple built of one rock, where the sculptor-architect works on one body.

Again, T.S. Eliot, in his essay on Milton is relevant here: "It is the period, the sentence and still more the paragraph, that is the unit of Milton's verse; and emphasis on the line structure is the minimum necessary to provide a counter-pattern to the period structure. It is only in the period that the wavelength of Milton's verse is to be found: it is his ability to give a perfect and unique pattern to every paragraph, such that the full beauty of the line is found in its context, and his ability to work in larger musical units than any other poet—that is to me the most conclusive evidence of Milton's supreme mastery." Sri Aurobindo accomplishes the same with his end-stopped lines, building the epic line by line, passage by passage, canto by canto.

We must understand as did Eliot in his critical review of Milton that "a different meter is a different mode of thought; it is a different kind of punctuation, for the emphases and the breath pauses do not come in the same place," and for a new kind of meter to happen, we have to ascend to a different manner and mode of thought as did Sri Aurobindo.

Thus, to recover blank verse, the most difficult meter in English, to my mind, these will be the requirements of the future:

> Stick to being simple, use modern English, try not the inversions and Latin words that would seem artificial in

most hands, avoid high power words unless they are precise and not pedantic.

Themes have to be carefully selected: Eliot was right that 'Paradise Lost' suited the genius of Milton and was a happy selection; but for sublime themes, one may need to move to great leadership, patriotic themes, spiritual realizations, etc.

To not focus primarily on auditory imagination but all senses fully represented; the focus only on hearing can prove to be a poet's undoing.

Blank verse has to be appropriately handled with stresses, quantity, accents, modulations, caesura, assonances, internal rhymes, feminine endings, a kind of sculptor-architect is needed as Sri Aurobindo suggested, who will build the edifice, line by line, passage by passage without letting boredom set in.

No falsetto, or superficial approaches, or cleverness or sententiousness or sentimentality, unlike Tennyson; the modernist discipline to describe things as they are is a good training.

Training in the more comprehensive or deeper cosmology; while the poet does not have to be a philosopher, the use of mythology and theology can be fraught with danger especially if there is an inherent contradiction in the vision; failure of vision will limit the poet, as it did for Milton, and perhaps Blake, as T.S. Eliot pointed out.

Developing a consciousness of this Miltonic block that makes one write like him; mastering new rhythms, meters, sound harmonies, perhaps from other languages or exploring a new sound; a good poet has awareness of the 'other' and of the self. And has the immense fortune and

> ability to stand as his unconditioned self to look at the 'other' and as the detached 'other' to look at the self; the anxiety of influence has to be overcome, by making it overtly conscious and not buried, by sensitively picking up the Miltonic high note and eliminating it when it shows up inadvertently.

The challenge of Milton to the future poet is immense; yet it is also an opportunity to learn from him, and to try new things in blank verse. This, I believe, was the single greatest contribution of Sri Aurobindo to the growing and immense body of English verse.

19.

Sri Aurobindo and Shakespeare

Sri Aurobindo and Shakespeare are two oceanic personalities in English literature. Only Milton comes anywhere close to them in reach, in originality, in creativity, in mastery and deployment of language, in character development and in heights of intensity. Shakespeare, of course, is foremost among the top poets and dramatists of all time, matched only by Homer, Vyasa, Valmiki at his level of output and ability to create a Universe like a demiurge, according to Sri Aurobindo.

If we compare the two geniuses, Sri Aurobindo and Shakespeare, we will find some overlap, but we will also find that each occupies a unique space all his own. The anxiety of influence that Harold Bloom discovered among several great poets and writers is not visible in Sri Aurobindo because he worked in genres where Shakespeare did not. And also because Sri Aurobindo had a wider set of influences from classical Greek, Latin, French, Italian, Sanskrit and Bengali literature, among other languages that he had mastered.

Sri Aurobindo is unique in his own space as a *darshanik*, critic, translator, linguist, sociologist, futurist and a letter-writer of the highest order. In this, he bears no competition from Shakespeare. If we take Sri Aurobindo's dramas, they are his early works before his full maturity as a writer. Although these plays are fine, especially *The Viziers of Bassora* and the translation from Kalidasa, *The Hero and the Nymph*, they are no match to the power, breadth, inspiration and heights of splendor that Shakespeare achieves in at least twenty-five of his thirty-eight plays.

What Sri Aurobindo achieved as a *darshanik* with *The Life Divine*, *The Supramental Manifestation*, *The Mother* and *The Synthesis of Yoga* is beyond the pale of most philosophers and writers of prose, as I have attempted to show by comparing him with the greatest western philosophers. His commentary on the Gita is the greatest in modern times in any language. As a work of literary criticism, *The Future Poetry* ranks with the finest works of Samuel Johnson or Emerson. His translations of the Vedas and the Upanishads transformed our understanding of the roots of Indic culture and ancient Vedic symbolism. His research into the shared etymologies of Sanskrit, Tamil, Greek, Latin and English are groundbreaking and need to be carried forward and the possibilities shown by him need much more exploration. *The Human Cycle*, *The Ideal of Human Unity* and *War and Self-Determination* are far-reaching works of global importance and present a new approach to human development and evolution. The thirty volumes of his collected works are stupendous not just in sheer output but also quality and impact on the nation and the world.

Of his prose, Gabriela Mistral said, "Sri Aurobindo, the master, the highest of mystics, happily presents the rare phenomenon, an exposition clear as a beautiful diamond, without the danger of confounding the layman. This is possible because Sri Aurobindo is a unique synthesis of a scholar, theologian and one who is enlightened..." And Romain Rolland, had nothing but the highest praise for his writings, "[Sri] Aurobindo Ghose, the foremost of Indian thinkers, has realised the most complete synthesis achieved up to the present between the genius of the West and the East. ... The last of the great *rishis* holds in his outstretched hands the bow of creative impulse." And the *Times Literary Supplement* (London) had this to say of him, "Sri Aurobindo is no visionary. He has always acted his dreams... So from individual self-discipline he has gone to the life of humanity. The Psychology of Social Development, Ideals and Progress and The Ideal of Human Unity should be carefully considered by all those who are busy preparing blueprints for the future."

When we come to poetry, Sri Aurobindo's unique contributions to English poetry as an innovator are quite radical since they challenge the fundamental bases of English prosody. Sri Aurobindo realized that while accent is an important basis in measuring the feet and length of a line, there are other elements too such as stress and quantity. With the right principles of scansion and listening carefully with the ear, a new basis for meter can be attempted. This was a departure from established theory. His success in creating half a dozen samples that illustrated these concepts are a singular contribution to the music of English verse. 'An Image,' 'Descent,' 'Shiva—The Inconscient Creator,' 'Ocean Oneness' and passages from 'Jivanmukta,' 'Musa Spiritus' and 'The Life Heavens' prove that new meters are possible in English that are natural, spontaneous and robust.

His blank verse, as I have attempted to show, especially with 'Baji Prabhou' and 'Savitri' is an advancement past the boundaries imposed by Milton. And his devotional and religious poetry take off after a space of almost three centuries from where Donne, Herbert and Vaughan had left. Sri Aurobindo too experimented with sonnets but perhaps here Shakespeare steals a march over him; but the 'Nirvana' sonnet is second to none in the language and may be listed among the best five sonnets of all time in any language.

'Savitri' is a work that has not received full attention from the reading public since post-independence Indian critics have been antagonistic to it, caught in an exclusivist enthusiasm for realism and unstructured poetry. It may be time to state without fearing the clique of professional critics and literary societies that the peaks of 'Savitri' are equal to the best of Shakespeare, in rhythm, intensity, revelation, creativity and inspiration.

Wittgenstein said that Shakespeare is a creator of language. He said, "Shakespeare's similes are, in the ordinary sense, bad," and suggested in the very next sentence: "So if they are nevertheless good – and I don't know whether they are or not – they must be a law to themselves" (Wittgenstein [1998: 56]). But he never illustrated his observations with examples. Wolfgang Heumer in the Routledge Companion to Shakespeare and Philosophy believes that several of these remarks seem to suggest that he regarded Shakespeare as a lonesome genius who played in a league of his own and who could not, in consequence, be captured in the framework of our established categories.

Wittgenstein adds, "I do not think that Shakespeare can be set alongside any other poet. Was he perhaps a creator of language rather than a poet? ... Shakespeare's work needs to be judged according to a law of its own."

I agree that Shakespeare created a unique world full of vital energy, human passions and turbulence. In Wittgenstein's idiom this is a new language. Shakespeare had the advantage in having Chaucer create a new basis for English prosody, based on accent. The influence of Petrarch and Boccaccio on Sir Henry Wyatt and Henry Howard also helped transplant blank verse and the sonnet form into English. And the genius that he was, Shakespeare took it to new heights of expression. He vitalized the language and made it capable of great creations in his capable hands and helped make English a remarkably supple and robust language and a fit instrument in the hands of traders, artists, shopkeepers, businessmen and poets to come.

Whether his immense success as a dramatist made it difficult for future playwrights to succeed is another matter. Like a Ghalib or Tagore, he gave birth – if not to the language itself – to the immense possibilities of diction, eloquence, elusiveness, nuance and metaphor in English and gave it the ability to sustain the artist's creativity. After Marlowe had prepared the medium of drama for him, he took it to heights as great as any Greek play by Sophocles, Aeschylus or Euripedes. His ability to create multiple personalities is unsurpassed and as puissant as if a "work of nature" in themselves as Ben Johnson noted in the introduction to Shakespeare's First Folio.

Sri Aurobindo too is a creator of a new language, if one may borrow Wittgenstein's phrase in the same context. A new world of spiritual, mystical and neo-romantic reality, with new significances, a new ecosystem of meanings and cross-meanings, texts and subtexts, inter-defined, inter-related, linked and referenced as by a demiurge or *anahad nada*[56] itself. Or as Makarand Paranjape describes it in 'Sarojini Naidu: Selected Poetry and Prose', "an ideological and spiritual project" on a superhuman scale.

For Sri Aurobindo's begins his challenge to the reader and listener where Wittgenstein ends his *Tractatus*: "That whereof we cannot speak, thereof we must remain silent." But Sri Aurobindo describes that unspeakable in terms of language, whether through resonant sounds or symbolism or mythic legend or commentary or phonology or *darshana*. He expresses the Silence not just in words or word-meaning, but also sound-music, imagery, orchestral overtones and undertones and meaning as with the ancient Indian mantra where the sound is the experience. Word thus not a symbol as in our modern languages but itself the deeper meaning.

That discovery was critical if we were to attempt to reach the silence not via meaning but through feeling directly. That is a science in itself and a new language, or shall we call it a super-language. Shakespeare had Chaucer, Marlowe, Walter Raleigh to help build his language, not with meanings but with vital rhythms, situations, intensity. The stage was set for him to walk in and perform if I might be allowed a pun.

Sri Aurobindo had no stage and had to rely on ancient Indian vedic principles and create anew a world of expression that takes language beyond itself into meaning or rather experience. This is his greatest contribution to English even greater than the new classical forms and meters he created. In

---

[56] *Anahad nada* is the name given in yogic philosophy to the cosmic sound or the so-called "white noise" that is present everywhere, without being actively made in a way that can be perceived. From Sanskrit, *anahata* or *anahad* means "un-struck" or "unbeaten," and *nada* means "to flow." (Taken from Yogapedia)

this, he ranks supreme, as the Shakespeare of *The Future Poetry*.

20.

Sri Aurobindo and Herbert

There are very few exceptional devotional poets in English. One thinks mainly of John Donne, George Herbert and Henry Vaughan from the Elizabethan age, and Gerald Manley Hopkins and Christina Rossetti from the Victorian. Harold Bloom calls George Herbert to be the devotional poet proper in English, by any standard. It should be noted that devotional poetry is not necessarily religious poetry or metaphysical poetry. Nor is it the same as spiritual poetry of which there have been extremely few practitioners in English. Sri Aurobindo is the most prominent poet to write spiritual poetry in English in the last century; T.S. Eliot in the Four Quartets touches it at moments and William Wordsworth in his theophanic moments of experiencing nature is another powerful example.

Luke Hankins in 'The Poem as Devotional Practice' published in the *Contemporary Poetry Review* describes four categories of devotional poetry: confession, petition, praise and meditation. Perhaps to this, another category of spiritual devotion may be added which is the way Sri Aurobindo wrote: connection and realization.

Anthony Low in his book, *Love's Architecture: Devotional Poets in Seventeenth-Century English Poetry*, indicates four types of devotional practice: vocal, meditative, affective and contemplative. These affect the nature and expression of the devotional verse. Perhaps other types of devotional practice may be reported: that of disappearance and the other of intimacy or unity. These last two are more esoteric and may be ecstatic and mystical. In esoteric mysticism, the seeker or poet either loses his identity or begins to feel the Divine possessing his identity in intense togetherness.

"George Herbert is either our most major minor poet in English literature or he is the most modestly exquisite of our major poets," says John Tobin. Either way, his authenticity was praised by T.S. Eliot as the most fundamental and vital element in his verse. And Eliot says, "When I claim a place for Herbert among those poets whose work every lover of English poetry should read and every student of English poetry should study, irrespective of religious belief or unbelief, I am not thinking primarily of the exquisite craftmanship, the extraordinary metrical virtuosity, or the verbal felicities, but of the content of the poems which make up 'The Temple.' These poems form a record of spiritual struggle which should touch the feeling, and enlarge the understanding of those readers also who hold no religious belief and find themselves unmoved by religious emotion."

The question then is, "Can religious or devotional art be appreciated by the secular?" If we study technique, then Herbert, and in equal measure Donne, is a master of metaphysical poetry, with "elaborately extended metaphors or conceits, paradox, linguistic inventiveness and ingenuity or wit." Or similarly, can Hopkins be appreciated for his sprung rhythm and compound words even by the non-religious?

The answer seems to be yes, for devotional verse uses the same techniques to enhance itself, sometimes more intensely so, to deliberately evoke in the reader a sense of the Divine, the Beloved. It may use "affective exuberance of sound," as Emma Mason notes in *The Oxford Handbook of British Poetry 1660-1800*, or it might take to the visual and the visionary as with the Romantics. Prosody is critical since sound helps open the gateways to feeling and experience. Thus, great devotional poets necessarily must be masters of the art and craft of poetry.

We must remember that these "travels in realms of gold," as Keats described the dominion of poetry might be equally used for the world of religious experience. Which is why it is no surprise that the greatest scriptures of the world use poetry as a means to enhance their message. George Herbert and Sri Aurobindo attempted the same, George with prayer, Sri Aurobindo with experience.

Here is Herbert in 'Love (III),' with the highly dramatized accounts of Love and Guilt,

> Love bade me welcome. Yet my soul drew back
>
> Guilty of dust and sin.
>
> But quick-eyed Love, observing me grow slack
>
> From my first entrance in,
>
> Drew nearer to me, sweetly questioning,
>
> If I lacked any thing.
>
> ...
>
> You must sit down, says Love, and taste my meat:

So I did sit and eat.

Sri Aurobindo, on the other hand, describes the most intimate experience of the Divine in the sonnet, 'Because Thou Art,'

Because Thou art All-beauty and All-bliss,
My soul blind and enamoured yearns for Thee ;
It bears Thy mystic touch in all that is
And thrills with the burden of that ecstasy.
...
Time voyages with Thee upon its prow
And all the future's passionate hope is Thou.

In one of his most famous poems, 'The Collar,' Herbert puns his way on "collar and choler," to show the priest's dissatisfaction and denial of the religious life, until he hears the voice of the Lord at the end, and he immediately responds,

I struck the board, and cried, "No more;
I will abroad!
What? shall I ever sigh and pine?
My lines and life are free, free as the road,
Loose as the wind, as large as store.
Shall I be still in suit?

...

Methought I heard one calling, Child!

And I replied My Lord.

This is beautiful but even more fulfilling to the seeker is 'The Golden Light,' which describes the descent of the godhead in clear and precise terms.

Thy golden Light came down into my brain

And the grey rooms of mind sun-touched became

A bright reply to Wisdom's occult plane,

A calm illumination and a flame.

...

Thy golden Light came down into my feet,

My earth is now Thy playfield and Thy seat.

Mario A diCesare in *George Herbert and the Seventeenth-Century Religious Poets* notes that meditation is a close cousin of poetry. A.G. Nutall in *The Shocking Image* refers to 17th-century handbooks offering instruction in devotional practice, "The handbooks taught that a man should train his imagination as an athlete trains his body. It is natural that such a system should produce certain champions, gymnasts of the imagination, whose powers should spill over into their poetry." Luke Hankins avers that the composition of a poem may itself be a devotional practice. This ties in extremely well with Sri Aurobindo's insistence that literature is not to be written just for literature's sake but for a higher purpose and that the *saadhak*[57] should use writing poetry as a means to augment his *sadhana*.

We do not know if Herbert used "the unfolding of poetry," to borrow a phrase from Robert Frost, as a prayer or practice. But we know how he "artfully rejected artfulness and craftily denied the craft" and attempted to be simple and direct in his worship to Christ his Master in 'Jordan I',

Who says that fictions only and false hair
Become a verse? Is there in truth no beauty?
Is all good structure in a winding stair?
May no lines pass, except they do their duty
Not to a true, but painted chair?
...
Shepherds are honest people; let them sing;
Riddle who list, for me, and pull for prime;
I envy no man's nightingale or spring;
Nor let them punish me with loss of rhyme,
Who plainly say, my God, my King.

Sri Aurobindo describes 'The Word of the Silence' in his sonnet, simply and directly too,

A bare impersonal hush is now my mind,

[57] Spiritual practitioner and seeker

A world of sight clear and inimitable,

A volume of silence by a Godhead signed,

A greatness pure, virgin of will.

. . .

All turns from a wideness and unbroken peace

To a tumult of joy in a sea of wide release.

As Emma Mason has noted in 'Christina Rossetti: Poetry, Ecology, Faith', logopoeia is immensely helpful in creating the sense of a vast impersonal Silence that widens the reader's awareness. Sri Aurobindo left us a body of work that takes devotional verse in English to a new level. Where the sound becomes the experience. The sense becomes the realization.

Samuel Johnson, and later John Dryden, passed strictures against devotional verse. "That the good and evil of eternity are too ponderous for the wings of wit." Wit perhaps might not be sufficient in itself to bear the Universe. But Sri Aurobindo gave us a different approach, that of the sound bearing the Universe and eternity. And, accomplishing this, he added a new mansion to the estate of English verse.

21.

Sri Aurobindo and Yeats

One of the most famous literary personalities of the 20th century, William Butler Yeats in many ways gives us an idea of the contributions made by Sri Aurobindo to his own nation and culture. Their lives ran parallel in several instances. Both were born in countries that were under the rule of the British. Both were intense nationalists and great artists, writers, and poets. Both were cultural ambassadors and advocates for their people and nations in their writings, philosophy, politics, and interests. The poet of Ireland and the poet of India were not just idealistic and visionary patriots. Each was also unique in his immense contribution to English literature.

Yeats became famous as a poet of the Celtic twilights and mysticism. He was able to capture the subtle worlds of Irish ethos and mythology in his earlier poems as he became one of the leaders of the Irish Literary Revival. And he had the power to make the reader experience the worlds created by him of the dreamworlds that were a constant reality to the Celtic fabulist, poet, or ethnologist. Far more than any other writer, except for James Joyce perhaps, he advanced the Irish culture and Gaelic sensibility. And it is because of him that today we can experience Irish spirituality and re-live its magical universe.

According to *WB Yeats: A New Biography by* A. Norman Jeffares, Yeats promoted the Irish Dramatic Society (later to become Abbey Theater) and contributed to its defiance of English censorship by writing a series of avant garde plays. He wrote their manifesto which declared, "We hope to find in Ireland an uncorrupted and imaginative audience trained to listen by its passion for oratory... and that freedom to experiment which is not found in the theaters of England, and without which no new movement in art or literature can succeed." He remained associated with the theater until his death in 1939. Along with leading the movement to revive theater, he also helped establish the Dun Emer Press. He sought to "find work for Irish hands in the making of beautiful things." He experimented with Japanese Noh plays and adapted their methods to support a resurgence of Irish literature and cultural traditions.

Sri Aurobindo in a similar vein rediscovered the ancient writings of the Vedas for a global readership, explained them in modern language and through his writings awakened India to its own heritage and *dharma*. His translations and interpretations of the Upanishads and the Gita were remarkable in their vivacity, authenticity and creative power and brought the original afflatus back to the reader and made them easily available to a modern mind. His poems on Indian legends such as Urvashi or Ruru and Priyumvada or Savitri and Satyavan advanced an appreciation of Indian mythology not only to the western reader but also to the Indian. For the natives seldom realized their own legacy so conditioned were they by the bastardized education system of Thomas Babington Macaulay being perpetrated across Indian educational institutions. He captured the spirit of Indian *dharma* and its unique psyche in his copious letters to his disciples, his aphorisms, essays, criticism, sociology and commentaries. More than anyone else, he brought India back to the front, without apology and with confidence, raising its profile among a global audience and ready to take back its place of prominence and leadership as in the distant past. Sri Aurobindo's spirituality went far deeper than Yeats who was, nonetheless, himself influenced by Indians such as the theosophist Mohini Chatterjee or Tagore or Sri Purohit Swami, a Hindu teacher.

Amal Kiran in his book *Sri Aurobindo, the Poet* has reported that Sri Aurobindo was "the sole Indian poet whom, as Francis Watson reported in a radio talk from England in 1951, Yeats had singled out as writing creatively in English." And Yeats was one who had not much respect for Indians writing in their babu-English.

Sri Aurobindo called Yeats "a very great poet" in his talks with Nirodbaran. In a letter to a disciple he noted,

> Yeats' contact [...] is not so much with the sheer spiritual Truth as with the hidden intermediate regions, from the faery worlds to certain worlds of larger mind and life. What he has seen there, he is able to clothe rather than embody in strangely beautiful and suggestive forms, dreams and symbols. I have read some of his poems which touch these behind-worlds with as much actuality as an ordinary poet would achieve in dealing with physical life – this is not surprising in a Celtic poet, for the race has the key to the occult worlds or some of them at least – but this strange force of suggestive mystic life is not accompanied by a mental precision which would enable us to say, it is this or that his figures symbolises. If we could say it, it might take away something of that glowing air in which

> the symbol stand out with such a strange unphysical reality. The perception, feeling, sight of Yeats in this kind of poetry are remarkable, but his mental conception often veils itself in a shimmering light — it has then shining vistas but no strong contours.

He also wrote in another letter,

> The perfection here of Yeats' poetic expression of things occult is due to this that at no point has the mere intellectual or thinking mind interfered—it is a piece of pure vision, a direct sense, almost sensation of the occult, a light not of earth flowing through without anything to stop it or to change it into a product of the terrestrial mind. When one writes from pure occult vision there is this perfection and direct sense though it may be of different kinds, for the occult world of one is not that of another.... Yeats does that too, very often, but he does it by bathing his thought also in the faery light; in the lines quoted however, he does not do that, but leaves the images of the other world shimmering in their own native hue of mystery.

In *The Future Poetry*, Sri Aurobindo discussing the newer trends in English verse exulted thus:

> Yeats, a supreme artist in rhythm, this spiritual intonation is the very secret of all his subtlest melodies and harmonies and reveals itself whether in the use of old and common metres which cease to be either old or common in his hands or in delicate new turns of verse ... very near to the ear of the sense, that inaudible music floating the vocal music, the song unheard, or heard only behind and in the inner silence, to catch some echo of which is the privilege

of music but also the highest intention of poetical rhythm.

How is Sri Aurobindo different from Yeats? Sri Aurobindo was also classical as Yeats and pre-dated the modernism ushered in by Eliot and Pound. Sri Aurobindo too was able to sustain passages of inspired rhythm and passionate intensity in his early works such as 'Love and Death' and 'Urvasie.' It is my opinion that Sri Aurobindo broke through into a new line of development in blank verse with 'Baji Prabhou,' the minor epic, with a gaunt, ascetic rhythm and milieu.

But Sri Aurobindo goes deeper through the subtle worlds that Yeats inhabited in his poems and moves into the causal or intuitive illumined states from where his poetry takes on a different hue. His poetry is no longer limited to human emotion or the twilight world of dream, myth, and imagination sung by Yeats. But Sri Aurobindo reaches the vision and clarity of perception that we see sustained in a similar manner by the Vedic or Upanishadic *rishis* and poets such as Ved Vyasa.

Let us look at some famous lines 'The Lake Isle of Innisfree,' from the early Yeats that illustrate his half-lit subliminal shades, the world that lurks behind the physical bathed in strangeness and glow:

> And I shall have some peace there, for peace comes dropping slow,
>
> Dropping from the veils of the morning to where the cricket sings;
>
> There midnight's all a glimmer, and noon a purple glow,
>
> And evening full of the linnet's wings.

Sri Aurobindo creates a similar mystical atmosphere in 'The Sea at Night' too in one of his very early poems:

> The grey sea creeps half-visible, half-hushed,
> And grasps with its innumerable hands
> These silent walls. I see beyond a rough
> Glimmering infinity, I feel the wash
> And hear the sibilation of the waves
> That whisper to each other as they push
> To shoreward side by side…

Or if we select the luminous high-romanticism of Yeats in 'He Wishes for the Cloths of Heaven':

> Had I the heavens' embroidered cloths,
> Enwrought with golden and silver light,
> The blue and the dim and the dark cloths
> Of night and light and the half light,
> I would spread the cloths under your feet:
> But I, being poor, have only my dreams;
> I have spread my dreams under your feet…

And place it next to 'Night by the Sea' written by Sri Aurobindo before he immersed himself into the spiritual mysteries of India:

Love, a moment drop thy hands;
Night within my soul expands.
Veil thy beauties milk-rose-fair
In that dark and showering hair…
We shall lose, ah me! too soon
Lose the clear and silent moon,
The serenities of night
And the deeper evening light.

It seems to me that Yeats' artistry here is more complete even though Sri Aurobindo's technical mastery is not inferior in any way. I have always surmised that this is so since Yeats had found his home in the Gaelic occult and had no impetus to go any further. But Sri Aurobindo would not settle in the *sookshma jagat*[58] for it was only a passageway for him. And he ploughed through the lunar-scapes and starlit glimmer where glow-worms dazzle and swans wing, the native terrain of Yeats, to emerge into the golden splendor of the *karana sharira*[59]. Or, if we may use the symbolism of *Isha Upanishad*, we might say that Sri Aurobindo removed the golden lid above the head that separates the normal human consciousness from the resplendence of Truth and rose above. Thus, Sri Aurobindo discovered the more intimate and sheer vision of the *kavi*, one who can not only behold the truth but also reveal it to others. When he wrote in 'Savitri' about the

---

[58] Subtle world.

[59] Causal body.

radical shift in awareness experienced by the protagonist, he gave us something that Yeats could have never been intimate with:

> Across a void retreating sky he glimpsed
>
> Through a last glimmer and drift of vanishing stars
>
> The superconscient realms of motionless peace
>
> Where judgment ceases and the word is mute
>
> And the Unconceived lies pathless and alone.

Or when he bursts into a powerful dactylic beat at the end of 'Musa Spiritus,' he gives us a new meter in English along with an ecstatic invocation of the Divine Word:

> Weave from my life His poem of days,
>
> His calm pure dawns and His noons of force.
>
> My acts for the grooves of His chariot-race,
>
> My thoughts for the tramp of His great steeds' course!

At his heights, Sri Aurobindo stands on par with the best of Shakespeare, Milton, Wordsworth, or Yeats, but his special gift to us is the Upanishadic sound brought into English with an alive almost physical force.

When we look at them as translators, we find to our delight that Yeats translated the Upanishads with the help of Purohit Swamy. Let us look at Verse 5 of *Mandukya Upanishad* as translated by him,

> In deep sleep man feels no desire, creates no dream. This undreaming sleep is the third condition, the intellectual condition. Because of his union with the Self and his unbroken knowledge of it, he is filled with joy, he knows his joy; his mind is illuminated.

And place it next to Sri Aurobindo's translation of the same verse:

> When one sleepeth and yearneth not with any desire, nor seeth any dream, that is the perfect slumber. He whose place is the perfect slumber, who is become Oneness, who is wisdom gathered into itself, who is made of mere delight, who enjoyeth delight unrelated, to whom conscious mind is the door, Prajna, the Lord of Wisdom, He is the third.

And here is Verse 7 of the *Mandukya Upanishad* as translated by Yeats and Purohit Swamy,

> He is not knowable by perception, turned inward or outward, nor by both combined. He is neither that which is known, nor that which is not known, nor is He the sum of all that might be known. He cannot be seen, grasped, bargained with. He is undefinable, unthinkable, indescribable.
>
> The only proof of His existence is union with Him. The world disappears in Him. He is the peaceful, the good, the one without a second. This is the fourth condition of the Self—the most worthy of all.

And again, compare it with the translation done by Sri Aurobindo:

> He who is neither inward-wise, nor outward-wise, nor both inward- and outward-wise, nor wisdom self-

> gathered, nor possessed of wisdom, nor unpossessed of wisdom, He Who is unseen and incommunicable, unseizable, featureless, unthinkable, and unnameable, Whose essentiality is awareness of the Self in its single existence, in Whom all phenomena dissolve, Who is Calm, Who is Good, Who is the One than Whom there is no other, Him they deem the fourth; He is the Self, He is the object of Knowledge.

To me, Sri Aurobindo is far more poetic, incantatory, and closer to the vision than Yeats whose translation is flatter and more mental. This might have been so because Yeats was not a master of Sanskrit and unlike Sri Aurobindo was not able to capture the spirit of the original in a facile manner.

And yet, as a poet Yeats was quite the master of incantation when he wrote such iambic-anapaestic lines in 'Aedh Tells of the Rose in his Heart':

> All things uncomely and broken, all things worn out and old,
>
> The cry of a child by the roadway, the creak of a lumbering cart,
>
> The heavy steps of the ploughman, splashing the wintry mould,
>
> Are wronging your image that blossoms a rose in the deeps of my heart.

Compare this with 'Rose of God' by Sri Aurobindo in a trochaic-dactylic beat that uses the same symbol of rose with mantric reverberations:

> Rose of God, vermilion stain on the sapphires of heaven,
>
> Rose of Bliss, fire-sweet, seven-tinged with the ecstasies seven!...
>
> Rose of God, smitten purple with the incarnate divine Desire,
>
> Rose of Life, crowded with petals, colour's lyre!

Something more intense, vermilion-stained, explodes through Sri Aurobindo's lines, something stripped of all veils and blinds. Sri Aurobindo did not think too highly of Yeats as a critic. I agree with this assessment. Apropos to this one might repeat what Auden said in his elegy of Yeats, "You were silly like all of us. Your gift survived it all." Sri Aurobindo was a far more comprehensive, balanced, and harmonious critic than Yeats and his corpus of philosophical works, literary critique, commentaries and essays on human evolution and linguistics may be ranked as among the best in world literature.

In his later years, Yeats re-invented himself and moved away from the occult worlds of the Irish collective subconscious. He became more bitter, sparse, direct, and almost became another poet. T.S. Eliot, in his memorial lectures on Yeats, admired his ability to create a new avatar of himself. But, to my mind, the early Yeats is far more beautiful, alluring, and subtle than the later Yeats. Sri Aurobindo too became a different poet as he withdrew from an active political life to an intenser spiritual adventure of consciousness and joy. But Sri Aurobindo became an even greater poet in his later mystical work.

Both were great poets. Yeats was also a great dramatist, mythologist, and apocalyptic visionary. Sri Aurobindo, a greater critic, philosopher, translator and nationalist, made some splendid contributions to English prosody, blank verse, and new meters in English which are beginning to getting appreciated now. Both lived through the end of 19th century, the tumult of World War I and had the satisfaction to see the liberation of their nations.

Yeats lives on yet, with narrower influence limited mostly to his verse, his criticism mostly relegated to historical interest. On the other hand, Sri Aurobindo, visionary, poet of the future, philosopher, and harbinger of the zeitgeist, keeps growing in stature across the globe becoming more and more relevant each day.

22.

Sri Aurobindo and Tagore

The only artist from India of Sri Aurobindo's stature in the last century is Rabindranath Tagore. And it is of interest to note that they both had the highest regard for each other. Sri Aurobindo, called him "a wayfarer towards the same goals as ours in his own way," in a letter to D.K. Roy. While Tagore honored him after his arrest by the British in August 1907 for sedition as editor of the *Bande Mataram*:

> Rabindranath, O Aurobindo, bows to thee!
>
> O friend, my country's friend, O voice incarnate, free,
>
> Of India's soul! No soft renown doth crown thy lot,
>
> Nor pelf or careless comfort is for thee...
>
> The fiery messenger that with the lamp of God
>
> Hath come - where is the king who can with chain or rod
>
> Chastise him? Chains that were to bind salute his feet,
>
> And prisons greet him as their guest with welcome sweet...
>
> And then to Him I bow Who in His sport cloth make
>
> New worlds in fiery dissolution's awful wake,

From death awakes new life; in danger's bosom rears
Prosperity; and sends his devotee in tears...

Tagore, a poet, novelist, playwright, story-writer, essayist, travel writer, composer, painter and educationist, single-handedly energized the Bengal Renaissance in literature and music. While reviled for his compositions and paintings by many modernist critics, he remains the high watermark of creativity, wisdom, lyricism and idealism in modern India, the standard against whom all poets to follow were appraised, and even in criticism and deprecation acknowledged as a dominant influence and a giant. It almost became an emblem of honor for a critic to have attacked Tagore. But Tagore is like the Himalayas. Which peak shall one attack as lowly or not attained enough? Which snowcap pales in lustre to the others in its company?

His word music is enchanting even to those who do not fully understand Bengali. His paintings depict a different way of seeing, despite the fact that he had had no formal training in draftsmanship. A natural artist, flowing like the mighty Ganges, taking vast tracts of terrain in its wide embrace, all we can do with this wonder of creative flowering is behold quietly as one gazes at a wonder of the natural world.

Girish Karnad criticized the lack of movement in his plays which might have some validity. Pritish Nandy might take issue with Rabindra Sangeet. But it seems to me that even trying to defend Tagore is an impertinence to him. It is as if one attempted to defend the culture and art of a nation, such was his deep identification with the genius of the people he loved.

Sri Aurobindo appraised him as one of the forbears of *The Future Poetry* and his lyricism and spirituality with a fine sensitivity and an artist's spontaneous ease of expression are mentioned with respect and critical praise. And Sri Aurobindo says in *The Future Poetry*,

> The poetry of Tagore owes its sudden and universal success to this advantage that he gives us more of this discovery and fusion for which the mind of our age is in quest than any other creative writer of the time. His work is a constant music of the overpassing of the borders, a chant-filled realm in which the subtle sounds and lights of the truth of the spirit give new meanings to the finer subtleties of life.

And Tagore saw the great seer and *rishi* in Sri Aurobindo when he came to Pondicherry. And he described his visit on May 29, 1928 in his journals thus,

> …the French steamer on which I was travelling touched Pondicherry and I came to meet Aurobindo. At the very first sight I could realise that he had been seeking for the soul and had gained it, and through this long process of realisation has accumulated within him a silent power of inspiration. His face was radiant with an inner light and his serene presence made it evident to me that his soul was not crippled and cramped to the measure of some tyrannical doctrine … I felt that the utterance of the ancient Hindu Rishi spoke from him of that equanimity which gives the human soul its freedom of entrance into the All. I said to him, "You have the Word and we are waiting to accept it from you. India will speak through your voice to the world, 'Hearken to me.'

> Years ago I saw Aurobindo in the atmosphere of his earlier heroic youth and I sang to him, "Aurobindo, accept the salutation from Rabindranath." Today I saw him in a deeper atmosphere of a reticent richness of wisdom and again sang to him in silence, "Aurobindo, accept the salutation from Rabindranath."

How does one compare the two, both renaissance men, both vast beings in their fields and genres, both representative men of the Indian nation in its gathering potential, both great mystics, nationalists and revolutionaries in their own realms? It is sufficient to realize our great fortune that we are so close to their presence spatially and temporally, with barely a few degrees of separation. It is sufficient to know that we represent them in our journey forward as their chosen people.

If Tagore invented the genre of the Bengali short story or created the Bengali that we hear today, Sri Aurobindo rediscovered the secret of the Vedas and gave us the greatest *bhashya* of the Gita in modern times. If Tagore established Bengali renaissance after Bankim and Michael Madhusudan Dutt, Sri Aurobindo initiated the national renaissance at about the same time as Gurudev Rabindranath. If Tagore gave us international recognition with his universalism, idealism and pacifism, Sri Aurobindo announced the new age of earth's evolution in *The Life Divine* and *The Supramental Manifestation*.

And yet, each is incomparable. Attempts to contrast their contributions are both odious and otiose. Each is a unique synthesis of the great fountainheads of Indic civilization. Each uniquely honoring each other as two ancient *rishis* born in modern times, seeing each other's life blossoming in public and in deepest inner seclusion. They are each a lesson to us, as beacons and guideposts, as a reminder of our own possibilities and the greatness they encompassed in their lives as infinitely as humanly possible.

Tagore never got the translations of his poetry that he deserved, not even when he did them himself. A normal translation often observes Heisenberg's Principle of Uncertainty. When it catches the rhythm, it loses the meaning; when it brings out the meaning, the music of the original becomes flat. But there have been no translations of Tagore that I know of yet that have been able to capture his celestial resonance, his Indian harmonies or his reverberating assonances. This is why after a period of fame, his poetry has mostly been forgotten by the western world. Yeats, Ezra Pound, Pablo Neruda, among others, thought highly of him but a larger audience and influence outside Bengal still awaits Tagore. Perhaps a new generation of translators that will be sensitive to his spirit and catch it in other languages will do justice to him. Interestingly, instead of Hindi, I have found better translations of Tagore in Rajasthani which perhaps need to be popularized much more.

Sri Aurobindo has a wider global reach since he wrote in English with a natural flow and could experiment in meters and music in the language. And I believe his experiments in rhythm and meter, as masterly as Tagore, are being discovered more and more and will have a profound impact on English prosody as they grow in influence.

I have often wondered why Tagore or Sri Aurobindo are not studied or, more importantly, recited in our schools. I feel our education system would impart more culture and creativity to our youth if they learnt to appreciate our greatest and best artists. Nothing more is needed if one begins to appreciate and get inspired by these two greatest of littérateurs. This is the true tragedy of our system that is churning out clones of Macaulay. And yet, it is not too late. The Sun and the Moon of our literary horizons will now spark another efflorescence of our nation's creative spirit. This is my firm conviction.

23.

The Viziers of Bassora

Sri Aurobindo wrote several plays in his revolutionary days. From the information available in his archives, it seems that the last attempts to rewrite or recreate his plays were in 1915. After the Arya, he turned to matters of other interest and other genres.

The Viziers of Bassora is perhaps his earliest play which has an interesting history. It was confiscated by the British during the Alipore Case and given up as lost forever. However, in a unique turn of events, it was saved by a conscientious civil servant and discovered in 1951. To me, it is a fascinating look into the creative evolution of Sri Aurobindo.

The Viziers of Bassora is a light-hearted comedy, called a "Dramatic Romance" by its author. The story derived from the *Arabian Nights* is the tale of two viziers in the kingdom of Bassora, which came under the suzerainty of Caliph Haroun Ul-Rashid. Each has a young son, who is wanton, lustful and dissipative of his energy in the superficial pleasures of women and wine. But Nureddene, son of Alfazzal Ibn Sawy, the kind and wise vizier, has a romantic side to his hedonistic pursuits. Fareed, son of Almuene Bin Khakan, the evil vizier, is ugly in desire, unlovely and vile in his seekings.

Both sons seek the same slave-girl, Anice-Aljalice who falls in love with Nureddene. Anice is bought for the Caliph by Ibn Sawy. However, Nureddene manages to win her favors and is able to win her from her father, who is yet conscientious and scandalized. Ibn Sawy leaves on a mission for the Caliph and leaves half his wealth to Nureddene, who promptly squanders it all. Almuene plots the end of Nureddene but Nureddene escapes with Anice to Baghdad where he meets Haroun Al Rasheed and manages to impress him with the genuineness of his love for Anice.

Haroun appoints Nureddene as the King of Bassora but in another sinister plot, Almuene gets Nureddene almost executed by Alzayni, the present King of Bassora. Anice convinces Haroun to save Nureddene and remove Alzayni and order the execution of Almuene. Nureddene becomes King and ascends with Anice, having grown wiser and chastened, and is destined to be a kind and good sovereign to his subjects.

The Viziers of Bassora has been called a morality play by some critics. Archana Singh and Shailendra Singh have reviewed the characteristics of Morality in a study published in *Pune Research*, an international journal in English. They point out that "The main objective of the morality plays provides the audience with moral guidance and encourages men to live a righteous life. Sri Aurobindo's *The Viziers of Bassora* fulfills the moral purpose of this play. The character of Nureddene signifies that despite the entire worse situation one has to keep full faith in God." In the words of S.S. Jaiswal, "Sri Aurobindo here suggests that cheers and tears are the warp and woof of man's life. To be able to overcome the difficulties and sorrows punctuating his life, man must plead for God's fatherly love and kindness, for these, rather than justice, can bring him peace and harmony."

Another characteristic of the morality play is that the supporting characters are personifications of good and evil. *The Viziers of Bassora* absolutely follows this characteristic of the morality play. Mr. Seetaraman observes, "The sets of opposite characters in the play are radically opposite temperaments with basically different orientations of the energies of life."

S.S. Jaiswal writes, "If one character stands for the type made in God's image and growing more and more in that image of Love, Light and Grace, the other is its exact opposite, as written in the play; 'a brutish amalgam of gorilla and Barbery ape'."

Prof. K.R.S. Iyengar is of the view, "The story of the two viziers, Ibn Sawy and Almuene, and of their sons, Nureddene and Fareed, can almost be read as a morality play; but no! the poetry of the play and the comic spirit that presides over it will permit no such critical excrescence." But as this play has been written by Sri Aurobindo, a yogi, a philosopher and a spiritualist, despite its comic spirit, one can not deny the deep purpose of this play. As in the words of A. Nicoll; "If a poet has high soul like Sophocles, his influence will always be moral, let him do what he will."

Archana and Shalilendra Singh conclude that "… it can be said that the conflict between good and evil and ultimately the triumph of good over evil makes the play *The Viziers of Bassora* to stand in the category of the morality play." Personally, I tend to agree with K.R.S. Iyengar. This play of youth, insouciant and 'playful,' seems more a farce to me. A farce can be more incisive and lethal than a morality play in the tradition of Jonathan Swift or Oscar Wilde.

Sri Aurobindo depicts life and culture in the times of Haroun Ul-Rashid , the most illustrious and upright of the Abbasid Caliphs of Baghdad, and a picture of Arab civilization as a whole as shown in the *Arabian Nights*. A subtle humor runs throughout the drama but at times one wonders if it is a caricature of the life of the privileged in those times. The hypocrisy of a people who deem themselves highly religious is scathingly observed without giving offense and in a spirit so light-hearted that in a first reading one might almost miss it. And yet, the sharp edge of the *khanjar*[60] is barely covered in a velvet of pretentiousness and *tehzeeb*[61].

It is impressive how deep a knowledge Sri Aurobindo had of the religious creed of the people, with careful but succinct observations on the place of usury or human equality or God's will in Islam. It shows his eclecticism and range of awareness beyond his own times and culture which makes the play effective and satirical.

When one reads Ibn Sawy reflecting on his mission to buy the "the fairest of all slave-girls" for the Caliph, one cannot but feel the tip of a rapier go through the veneer of joviality:

> …Ten thousand golden pieces hardly buy
>
> Such wonders,— so much wealth to go so idly!
>
> But princes must have sweet and pleasant things
>
> To ease their labours more than common men.

---

[60] *Khanjar* means knife

[61] *Tehzeeb* means etiquette

Their labour is not common who are here
The Almighty's burdened high vicegerents charged
With difficult justice and calm-visaged rule.

At another place, Sri Aurobindo is equally caustic towards other cultures, though in the same gentle and honeyed languor, when Ibn Sawy speaks to Almuene:

...Never, Vizier,
Was such a scandal until now allowed
In any Moslem town. Why, it is just
Such barbarous outrage as in Christian cities
May walk unquestioned, not in Bassora
Or any seat of culture. It should be mended.

Or this exchange:

Almuene
Let him be anything, he is a Vizier's son.
The Turk forgot that.
Ibn Sawy
These are maxims, brother,
Unsuited to our Moslem polity.
They savour of barbarous Europe. But in Islam
All men are equal underneath the King.

Almuene

Well, brother Turk, you are excused.

Hidden underneath the genteel religiousness is the same crude and racist rhetoric as we see even today, creed or no creed. Mankind remains unevolved in the garb of religion. Sometimes it seems to me that Oscar Wilde and plays such as these were precursors of the absurdist drama that came to the fore especially after World War II.

Elsewhere, there are delightful lines that surprise us and remind us of the essential poet who pens the play.

Khatoon

You have indulged the boy till he has lost

The likeness even of manhood. God's great stamp

And heavenly image on his mint's defaced,

Rubbed out, and only the brute metal left

Which never shall find currency again

Among his angels.

Sri Aurobindo did not indulge much in metaphysical poetry and has always seemed to me in the romantic mold, bringing "a strangeness to beauty" in his art, to borrow a phrase from Walter Pater in his brilliant essay, *The Classic and the Romantic in Literature*. But this conceit about "the coin of youth" above appears to be a reference to Donne, an effective and apt allusion. Elsewhere, Almuene vaunts the "lusty pattern" of his son, Fareed:

…Give way,
Give way to the inspired blood of youth
And you shall have a man, no scrupulous fool,
No ethical malingerer in the fray;
A man to lord it over other men,
Soldier of Vizier or adventurous merchant,
The breed of Samson. Man with such youth your armies.
Of such is an imperial people made
Who send their colonists and conquerors
Across the world, till the wide earth contains
One language only and a single rule.
Yes, Nature is your grand imperialist,
No moral sermonizer. Rude, hardy stocks
Transplant themselves, expand, outlast the storms
And heat and cold, not slips too gently nurtured
Or lapped in hothouse warmth. Who conquered earth
For Islam? Arabs trained in robbery,
Heroes, robust in body and desire.
I'll get this slave-girl for Fareed to help
His education on. Be lusty, son,
And breed me grandsons like you for my stock.

Lines such as these might cause riots today, were the offended cultured enough to read such literature. That is perhaps our last sanctuary today, the refuge of non-commercial art. And yet, the slave-trade, the treatment of women as chattel, the desire to conquer pagans and idolaters with brute force, is all shown, without the veneer of a false aesthetic.

Flashes of poetic brilliance appear intermittently, without being overbearing on the easy flow of the play. There are writers such Manoj K. Mishra who believe that *The Viziers of Bassora* anticipates *The Life Divine.* I do not see how. It is critical to allow Sri Aurobindo's literature to be a fox rather than always being a hedgehog, to borrow from Isaiah Berlin's classification of writers and their creative output in his famous book on Leo Tolstoy, *The Hedgehog and the Fox.*

Sri Aurobindo is not a Shakespeare as a playwright, nor does he attempt to be in his blank verse. This gives him space to avoid falsetto and the weight of Elizabethan verse that has hung on our dramatists since Marlowe, Ben Johnson and Shakespeare showed us its possibilities. T.S. Eliot laments the death of the verse drama but his own plays ended up showing us more clearly how we continue to fail.

No sermonizing is needed with depictions of action, dialogue and narrative on stage. Nor is a play an overt critique unless its structure and gestalt is itself a critique. Sri Aurobindo accomplishes this extremely well in what was to be a dalliance in his canon prior to far more serious works. Yet, *The Viziers of Bassora* succeeds in being minor even as it lacerates to the bone. As all great and unpretentious art should.

24.

Perseus the Deliverer

T.S. Eliot, a greater poet than literary critic, and a far greater literary critic than social-cultural critic, was uncharacteristically sapient in his essay, *The Possibility of a Poetic Drama.* He compared the structure of the Athenian or Elizabethan drama to the comedy of 'ideas' made popular by Shaw and Galsworthy and showed that the drama is not a platform for overt philosophy. The undigested 'idea' or idea-emotion is not separate from the action or plot, or rather, the intellect is in the action. Or shall we paraphrase Marshall McLuhan and say that the movement is the message. That does not mean that one may not discuss the ideas but that the ideas are not divorced from the staging of life that a drama is.

Perseus the Deliverer, an early work by Sri Aurobindo, is a mythological play with nationalist symbolism. Andromeda is India, Perseus the spirit of the freedom fighter, Polydaon the priest as the Viceroy and the unregenerate and rapacious Poseidon as the British. The play is not preachy or sanctimonious but presents action on stage as its own import and meaning. The message is subtle but pervades the whole play. It can be easily picked up by the laity and is a popularization that is yet classy.

The only limitation, to my mind, is that it uses a European mythos to invoke the spirit of Indian nationalism. Sri Aurobindo, educated from a very young age of five in classical Greek and Latin in England, was still under the influence of their ancient legends and attempted to transplant them in the Indian soil. I am not certain if most Indians could relate to its significances and nuances except the most educated ones, and those too of the literary kind. It seems that Sri Aurobindo soon realized the foreignness of his symbols in the play. And he moved to a more ethnic mythology and native figures in his poetry and plays. By 1914, he had fully Indianized his heart, mind and consciousness by steeping himself deep in Indian culture, arts, literature, languages and *darshana*.

So profound was his assimilation of Indian mythology and symbols in his awareness, that his creative expressions began using them naturally and organically. His understanding of the Indic way of being was more extensive than most Macaulized Indians. He brought the rigor and the systematic and methodical approach of a mind trained in the west to the arcana and esotericism of the east. In this, he energized Indic literatures and influenced writers and poets across the land to adopt our own folklore and stories to new creations.

The play moves from an initial confrontation between Pallas Athene, the goddess of wisdom and warfare, and Poseidon, the sea god. Athene is the symbol of democracy, freedom and quiet strength of purity. And Poseidon the Olympian predator of storms, earthquakes and horses. They each choose a champion to represent them. Athene picks

Perseus, son of Danae and Zeus. Poseidon is represented by his sea-monster.

Perseus finds Andromeda, daughter of Cepheus and Cassiopea, chained to a rock, to be devoured by the sea-monster as sacrifice and atonement for her mother's impiety. He slays the monster, rescues Andromeda and weds her. Sri Aurobindo creates a play in the Elizabethan model or a romantic story, depicting the human vital with its energies and movements. And he executes it well, except that he has not yet found his own voice, his own symbology and vision. The play is derivative and more a matter of historical interest and as a study in the evolution of Sri Aurobindo the artist and unique writer.

Marlowe's drama tends to end with an evocation of the greatness of human spirit; Shakespeare on the other hand, especially in his tragedies, depicts the unfolding of human weakness and folly, in his best-known plays such as *King Lear*, *Othello*, *Macbeth* and *Hamlet*. Sri Aurobindo is even more celebratory of man's spiritual potential than Marlowe as *Perseus the Deliverer* is a triumph of its protagonist over barbaric and violent life-forces. And it depicts a stage in human evolution as it advances in civility, harmony, gentleness and the first seekings of spirituality.

Perseus the Deliverer is a play that one may enjoy if one is able to see a revolutionary in the making. Though not one who indulges in violent insurrections of an external world. Rather, a mutineer who with stillness and love overthrows falsehood, savagery and evil and brings about a true metamorphosis of earthly life. These are the inchoate beginnings of transformation in a prolific and creative mind. And we can see the exploration of themes, interests and tropes that he was to develop further in his maturer works with far greater power and expansiveness.

25.

Savitri as Play

I have often wondered if 'Savitri' could have been written as a play. And I am aware immediately that most of the action happens in this epic in the inner worlds, which are not obvious and may not be interesting to the audience. And yet, this may be one of the frontiers that the future drama may wish to explore.

As we evolve globally and our lives and arts turn subjective and inward, there must be a way for this most outward-looking form to make visible the inscape and make audible, as Wallace Stevens poetizes in *Notes Toward a Supreme Fiction,* "... the hum of thoughts evaded in the mind." Our spiralliform turning away from the classic to the romantic, from Milton to Wordsworth, or Chaucer to Carl Jung, can perhaps be depicted in gesture and external activity, in spoken word and stage direction.

The Absurdist Theater has advanced thespian art to a new way of looking and feeling, where the stage is literally stripped of all adornments, where narrative and plot become secondary and time and space too are constructs. Ionesco and Beckett made the drama stark and existential, meaningless and closer to the reality buried constantly under the surface. Would a different, more subjective and psychological action, be stageable?

Sri Aurobindo discussed this in response to *Chaitanya*, a play written by his disciple D.K. Roy, in a letter written on January 21, 1950 and wrote,

> Advocates of the old style drama might object to the great length of the discussions as detrimental to compactness and vividness of dramatic interest and dramatic action and they might object too that the action (though this does not apply to the Jagai-Madhai episode) is more subjective and psychological than the external objective succession of happenings or interchanges represented on a stage would seem to demand; this was the objection to Shaw's most characteristic and important plays. But where the dramatic interest is itself of a subjective and psychological character involving more elaboration of thought and speech than of rapid or intensive happening and activities, this kind of objection is obviously invalid; what matters is how the subjective interest, the play or development of ideas, or if high ideas are involved that call to the soul how their appeal is presented and made effective. Here it is great spiritual ideals and their action on the mind and lives of human beings that are put before us and all that matters is how they are presented and made living in their appeal. Here there is, I think, full success and that entirely justifies the method of the drama.

Perhaps, a three-act dramatization of 'Savitri' is possible. I have heard that several stagings of the longest-poem in English language have been done and a dance drama had been planned in the past by some illustrious actors in Bollywood. But any attempt to convert it into a play would require tremendous creativity, sensitivity and an appreciation of its inner spirit. There is enough external action in the story that can be preserved. Yet, a way can be found to depict the inner movements of consciousness, experiences and feeling.

The traditional way in which the psychological realms have been depicted in India have been not only via the written or spoken word but also via music and dance. A theater should be possible that uses *mudra* or pose of hands, *bhangima* or gesture and *raga* and mantra to invoke the occult and the spiritual. Whether we can make such an attempt with 'Savitri' or other works is a challenge that the future drama holds for us. If that happens successfully, a new possibility in arts might become available to us, reflecting what is already happening in life, perhaps nudging it along just a little bit more.

26.

What is the Mantra?

The mantra is a unique achievement of Indian poetry. It encompasses in itself, in theory and practice, articulation and understanding, the Indic civilization. It is our *darshana*, yoga, aesthetics and psychology, all brought to the summit of realization. It is tantra and Vedanta, *sankhya* and *bhakti*, the meaning of the Vedas and Upanishads. The mantra is the highest possibility of poetry.

"Poetry," says Harold Bloom in his essay *The Art of Reading Poetry*, "is figurative language, concentrated so that its form is both expressive and evocative." The mantra takes to wing with inspired rhythms and harmony and a seeing that pierces the veils of human mind and appearance and ascends higher and farther. And with its oceanic harmonies captured in the immediacy of the instant, it can transform the consciousness of the hearer.

And Bloom reaches the summit of his understanding as he ends the essay with these words, "I think that poetry at its greatest – in Dante, Shakespeare, Donne, Milton, Blake – has one broad and essential difficulty: it is the true mode for expanding our consciousness ... Consciousness is the central term here."

Owen Barfield expands this further in *Poetic Diction*, "Consciousness is to poetry what marble is to sculpture: the material that is being worked. Words are figurations of consciousness: metaphorical of consciousness ... A felt change of consciousness occurs when ordinary consciousness is shed like an old garment and one sees in a new and strange light."

But there is a whole art to the mantra. How to approach it, with stillness and self-gathering, how to receive it and perform its *uccharan*[62]! And this we must perfect this art once again, I feel, to reach our own highest possibilities.

D.H. Lawrence famously said in his essay on Walt Whitman that great literature changes your blood-consciousness. He was right. The mantra is transformative to the mind, the heart, the vital and the DNA. Truly, it is a journey towards self-awareness and a total experience. Not just feelings artistically explored. Nor thoughts strung in meter. Nor even visions articulated with creativity and imagination.

It is the sound of the syllables and the words, the rhythm and the harmonies, and the music in the background, the sound behind the sound. One needs to listen to it with utmost attention and silence, not with the physical ear, but in a deeper listening, *srotrasya srotram*[63]. Let it vibrate through the marrow, be heard with the diaphragm, resonate layer by layer to the psychic, down the spine to the toes and into the ground, and reverberate into space, endlessly. As if it is eternal, which, in reality, it is.

---

[62] Pronunciation

[63] *Kena Upaniṣad* -1.2 - श्रोत्रस्य श्रोत्रं मनसो मनो यद्, वाचो ह वाचं स उ प्राणस्य प्राणः।

It is said that our *ragas* came from the mantra. With even a couple of words, a few *beeja*[64] sounds, it can shatter our edifice of mind. It can liberate prior to the meaning coming through, almost like a mathematical formula or a sublimely orchestrated *raga*. The highest fusion of sound and vision and meaning, of form and content, it is a *dhyana*[65] and a *sadhana*[66].

That is why when we read a shloka from the Upanishads or the Gita, we should realize that each line is the sound-body of the *kavi*, the one who can see and reveal, and who can hear the *sruti*. It is the *tatva*[67] of the *rishi* still present to us, as the nectar they have left us. So we may return to it again and again, and accelerate our growth.

When we read the Gita it is as if Sri Krishna came and touched us. It is up to us now, whether to ignore him or embrace him in return with fullest gratitude and adoration.

The mantra is not fast food. We need to slow down and imbibe it drop by drop, note by note. For each drop is the sea, each note is *Nada Brahman*[68].

Sri Aurobindo expresses this far more radiantly in his letter to a disciple,

> The word is a sound expressive of the idea. In the supra-physical plane when an idea has to be realised, one can by repeating the word-expression of it, produce vibrations which prepare the mind for the realisation of the idea.

---

[64] Seed

[65] *Dhyana* means meditation

[66] *Sadhana* is the systematic approach and process of self-evolution or yoga

[67] *Tatva* means literally thatness or the essence

[68] Transcedental sound

That is the principle of the Mantra and of *japa*[69]. One repeats the name of the Divine and the vibrations created in the consciousness prepare the realisation of the Divine. It is the same idea that is expressed in the Bible, "God said, Let there be Light, and there was Light." It is creation by the Word.

And he adds,

> … the mantra in poetry, that rhythmic speech which, as the Veda puts it, rises at once from the heart of the seer and from the distant home of the Truth, — the discovery of the word, the divine movement, the form of thought proper to the reality which, as Mr. Cousins excellently says, "lies in the apprehension of a something stable behind the instability of word and deed, something that is a reflection of the fundamental passion of humanity for something beyond itself, something that is a dim shadowing of the divine urge which is prompting all creation to unfold itself and to rise out of its limitations towards its Godlike possibilities." Poetry in the past has done that in moments of supreme elevation; …

No better description of the mantra has been given, itself sounding like a mantra. It was his hope and fervent aspiration that the poetry of the future once again reach its inevitability, the fullest perfection that is the mantra.

---

[69] Chanting, repetition of mantra

III.

Sri Aurobindo, the Aphorist

1.

Sri Aurobindo's Aphorisms[70]

Of all the literary avatars of Sri Aurobindo, I love this persona of him the most. I say love, but I must also add that I am intrigued, puzzled, surprised, startled, enlightened and liberated in its presence. For, it seems to me, that he is most himself as an aphorist. Free to not create systems of thought or constructs or write long narrative poems, but to laugh at everyone and himself. To be contrarian for effect, to commit heresy, to dance and to sing, and then to suddenly disappear: to let us figure out what he said, to complete with the emptiness that we are. *On Thoughts and Aphorisms* is a uniquely Aurobindonian collection of his pithy and sagacious maxims.

The aphorism that I enjoy the most from this collection is this: "What is the use of admiring Nature or worshipping her as a Power, a Presence and a goddess? What is the use, either, of appreciating her aesthetically or artistically? The secret is to enjoy her with the soul as one enjoys a woman with the body."

---

[70] All the aphorisms from Sri Aurobindo quoted in this essay are taken from *On Thoughts and Aphorisms*

This is Sri Aurobindo at his most insouciant and irrepressible, unsettling us with an image perhaps a blasphemer like Nietzsche would have used. And yet, what a great spiritual truth expressed with concision and vividness! One may realize the truth of it as one grows in spiritual practice and ascesis.

A corollary to this apothegm following immediately after is, "To commit adultery with God is the perfect experience for which the world was created." How many writers can speak like this with confidence and fearlessness? Perhaps only a God-knower and one who has realized God intimately. So intimately, that he can play with the Divine as one plays with a friend or beloved.

Bold as he is, he pushes the envelope even further, when he challenges us to see God no longer with fear and as someone apart but as a playmate. "If you cannot make God love you, make Him fight you. If He will not give you the embrace of the lover, compel Him to give you the embrace of the wrestler." What religion has missed in abject deification of God, true spirituality discloses to us. "When one has the vision in the heart, everything, Nature and Thought and Action, ideas and occupations and tastes and objects become the Beloved and are a source of ecstasy."

"Discipleship to God the Teacher, sonship to God the Father, tenderness of God the Mother, clasp of the hand of the divine Friend, laughter and sport with our Comrade and boy Playfellow, blissful servitude to God the Master, rapturous love of our divine Paramour, these are the seven beatitudes of life in the human body. Canst thou unite all these in a single supreme and rainbow-hued relation? Then hast thou no need of any heaven and thou exceedest the emancipation of the Advaitin." A profound identification with the Divine in all its aspects and manifestations, this is the highest yoga and wisdom. And one may see these *Mahavakyas*[71] as windows into the heart and mind of this great poet-seer, who had another facet to his personality, that of a humorist and a rhapsodist.

And here, another perennial favorite of mine, "The seeker after divine knowledge finds in the description of Krishna stealing the robes of the *Gopis* one of the deepest parables of God's ways with the soul, the devotee a perfect rendering in divine act of his heart's mystic experiences, the prurient and the Puritan (two faces of one temperament) only a lustful story. Men bring what they have in themselves and see it reflected in the Scripture." Sri Aurobindo with his epigrams gives us an openness of space where we may not only meditate over his words and interpret them, we may also begin to absorb his incandescence of discovery and delight.

And here is another, a Universe in itself, dense and alchemic, "My lover took away my robe of sin and I let it fall, rejoicing; then he plucked at my robe of virtue, but I was ashamed and alarmed and prevented him. It was not till he wrested it from me by force that I saw how my soul had been hidden from me." One is reminded of Pascal's *Pensees* in their enlightening anti-Cartesian surrender to the heart than to the mind and their breakthroughs of non-discursive argument.

"Canst thou see God as the bodiless Infinite and yet love Him as a man loves his mistress? Then has the highest truth of the Infinite been revealed to thee. Canst thou also clothe the Infinite in one secret embraceable body and see Him

---

[71] A *mahavakya* is a grand, profound saying that has great importance to a spiritual yogic practice. (Taken from Yogapedia)

seated in each and all of these bodies that are visible & sensible? Then has its widest and profoundest truth come also into thy possession." One of the fundamental characteristics of an aphorism is its concision or pithiness. These *sutras*[72] can say what elaborate systems may not. And, to me, it seems that these oracular and enigmatic 'threads' are a great companion to his more discursive prose and even poetry.

Another favorite of mine from these maxims is, "Divine Love has simultaneously a double play, an universal movement, deep, calm and bottomless like the nether Ocean, which broods upon the whole world and each thing that is in it as upon a level bed with an equal pressure, and a personal movement, forceful, intense and ecstatic like the dancing surface of the same Ocean, which varies the height and force of its billows and chooses the objects it shall fall upon with the kiss of its foam & spray and the clasp of its engulfing waters." Aldous Huxley at the end of *Eyeless in Gaza* describes the shift in consciousness of the protagonist when he feels a descent into the substratum of identity and he experiences unity and subaqueous peace even beneath the divisions. How simply and eloquently, Sri Aurobindo expresses a tremendous mystical reality and truth! He almost gives us the realization of oneness, even as he invites us to share it with him.

Andrew Hui in his book *A Theory of Aphorism—From Confucius to Twitter* discusses the "effectiveness of the incomplete" that Nietzsche employed with devastating effect. Sri Aurobindo does not disrupt and destroy so much as make us feel whole. And yet, he is also capable of rousing us as God's servants to be his fighters and protectors, "There are two works that are perfectly pleasing to God in his servant; to sweep in silent adoration His temple-floors and to fight in the world's battlefield for His divine consummation in humanity." He surprises us with new adages for the age, "Pity is sometimes a good substitute for love; but it is always no more than a substitute," or, "Self-pity is always born of self-love; but pity for others is not always born of love for its object. It is sometimes a self-regarding shrinking from the sight of pain; sometimes the rich man's contemptuous dole to the pauper. Develop rather God's divine compassion than human pity," or, "Not pity that bites the heart and weakens the inner members, but a divine masterful and untroubled compassion and helpfulness is the virtue that we should encourage."

Adam Gopnik in his essay, *The Art of Aphorism*, opines that the empirical test of the aphorism is laughter, then longevity. If so, Sri Aurobindo touches a peak with these two gnomic apothegms, "Sometimes one is led to think that only those things really matter which have never happened; for beside them most historic achievements seem almost pale and ineffective."

And, he follows with this most satiric and memorable gist of human ignorance and pride, "There are four very great events in history, the siege of Troy, the life and crucifixion of Christ, the exile of Krishna in *Brindavan* and the colloquy with Arjuna on the field of Kurukshetra. The siege of Troy created Hellas, the exile in Brindavan created devotional religion, (for before there was only meditation and worship,) Christ from his cross humanized Europe, the colloquy at Kurukshetra will yet liberate humanity. Yet it is said that none of these four events ever happened."

The unique aspect about these aphorisms is that Sri Aurobindo wrote them during the early years of his yogic development, during 1913 to 1914. He never came back to this genre again. It is also surprising to me that even critics sympathetic to his vision have not commented on them as far as I know.

But aphorisms themselves are at the periphery of what we call canonical literature although aphoristic prose by great writers such as Wilde, Pascal, Nietzsche and Shaw has been acclaimed through the years. They have not been studied or analyzed as a genre the way drama, story and poetry are. Wittgenstein's *Tractatus* has an axiomatic style and G.B. Shaw attempts to establish brocards of evolution in *The Revolutionist's Handbook and Pocket Companion*. Yet, the style of aphorisms that makes them memorable, relatable and a unique art like a haiku is not a subject that is frequently written on or researched.

When Sri Aurobindo says in one of his aphorisms, "Only those thoughts are true the opposite of which is also true in its own time and application; indisputable dogmas are the most dangerous kind of falsehoods," he is not only pronouncing a great truth that is of relevance in today's world, he is also sharing an essence that normally he would use dozens of pages to nail in, say a chapter of *The Life Divine.*

It does not appear that he intended to publish this adagio of adage, that is special since in these pregnant expressions, he indicates his vision and ideas that he would later build into more detailed exposition. They are perhaps his most personal and intimate prose before it evolved into an impersonal style even by the time he began writing for *Arya*, his journal, from 1914 onwards.

Growing in self-mastery, also called yoga, he often states what seems contrarian to our normal instincts, "When I read a wearisome book through and with pleasure, yet perceived all the perfection of its wearisomeness, then I knew that my mind was conquered." Mental mastery is achieved once one is free of duality and the illusion of good and evil, "I knew my mind to be conquered when it admired the beauty of the hideous, yet felt perfectly why other men shrank back or hated."

Same happens to our conception of God, "Because God is invincibly great, He can afford to be weak; because He is immutably pure, He can indulge with impunity in sin; He knows eternally all delight, therefore He tastes also the delight of pain; He is inalienably wise, therefore He has not debarred Himself from folly." Herman Hesse has written about the god-devil, the True Divinity that unifies even this duality and Sri Aurobindo seems to pre-date him, centered in a spiritual unity, "There is no mortality. It is only the Immortal who can die; the mortal could neither be born nor perish. There is nothing finite. It is only the Infinite who can make for Himself limits; the finite can have no beginning nor end, for the very act of conceiving its beginning and end declares its infinity."

And then there are prophetic and Delphic atomisms that make one want to read his later works for more elaboration, "Europe prides herself on her practical and scientific organisation and efficiency. I am waiting till her organisation is perfect; then a child shall destroy her." Who is this child? Is it a new awareness? We can perhaps surmise his hints and make educated guesses for, as Andrew Hui says, "Aphorisms love to hide." Or his grand statement on the spiritual übermensch, not the vitalized Superman of Nietzsche or the mental Overman of Shaw, "Evolution is not finished; reason is not the last word nor the reasoning animal the supreme figure of Nature. As man emerged out of the animal, so out of man the superman emerges."

"Almost all books of aphorisms, which have ever acquired a reputation, have retained it," John Stuart Mill wrote in 1837 and added, "How wofully the reverse is the case with systems of philosophy." In Sri Aurobindo's case, the opposite seems to be true. In my opinion, though, this aspect of his literary avatar too shall be known and widely received once we realize its importance in his formative years as the future philosopher, essayist, thinker who always saw farther than his fellow humans and on a far vaster scale. These aphorisms are perhaps the first articulations of his literary projects in prose or poetry.

The tradition of the *sutra*[72] or the *Mahavakya* is an ancient Upanishadic one. The four great sayings that encompass the wisdom of Vedanta are formulas that the disciple would intensely meditate on to help open up the knots in their own consciousness. The spiritual tradition of the Master's statements becoming the seed for one's personal growth is also seen with the *Analects* of Confucious, or the *Tao Te Ching*, or with Heraclitus or the *sutras* of the Buddha. Sri Aurobindo is part of the same lineage as he imparts his 'micro-models of empirical inquiry,' as John Stuart Mill described them. He added that to be unsystematic is of the essence of all truths which rest on specific experiment.

Aphorisms are esoteric but we can test them against our common experience. They derive their folksy approach from the proverb, adroitness or provocative delight from the

---

[72] Refers to an aphorism or a collection of aphorisms in the form of a manual or, more broadly, a condensed manual or text. (Taken from Wikipedia)

epigram and ambivalence from the parable. And yet, the difference may be in their bold evocation of truth that may be mystical or disruptive, funny or silly, revelatory or explosive.

Max Beerbohm once suggested in a moment of aphoristic insight, in this spirit, that Sappho's work does not survive in fragments but was written in fragments. As Adam Gopnik suggests, Pascal's non finito manner, with little brought to a conclusion, is a deliberate defiance of the Cartesian system-building. The illogic of one cryptic fragment colliding with the next cryptic fragment vindicates soul over system. Our universe and the God within it are too big to be systematized; we see Him or Her most clearly in glimpses. Nietzsche perhaps gave us the best definition of the luminous and fragmentary nature of these expressions in *Thus Spake Zarathustra*, "In the mountains the shortest way is from peak to peak: but for that one must have long legs. Aphorisms should be peaks, and those spoken to should be big and tall."

Thoughts and Aphorisms are the peaks of Sri Aurobindo's vast personality. Not the highest perhaps but early indications of the Everests and Kanchenjungas that were to come later in our journey into the Himavant[73] of his body of writings even as they are atomic, *anvic*[74], and granular.

---

[73] The personification of the Himalayan mountains, which are also known as the *Himavant* Mountains.

[74] *Anvic* is Sanskrit for atomic

IV.

Sri Aurobindo, the First Post-Modernist Translator Before Modernism

1.

Essays on the Gita: A Bhashya as Primary Text

In the tradition of commentary in ancient and medieval India, a *bhashya* is an exposition of any primary or secondary text. It can mean interpretation, individual viewpoint or explanation of the commentator and may adopt certain guidelines such as elaborating the meaning of words in the *sutras*, citations, quotes, references, verifications, reasons, and finally, conclusion of the *bhashyakara* or author of the *bhashya*.

And the bhashya may take various stances, such as *alochana* (criticism), *vivechana* (discussion), *vishleshan* (descriptions), *tippani* (commentary), *teeka* (exegesis), *sameeksha* (analysis), *vyakhya* (elaboration) to the final inference and proof, *pramana*. And there are times when the *bhashya* elaborates with such authority equal to the original text, with an epiphany as bright and brilliant, equal in inspiration, wisdom and reach, in metaphysics and impact, that it becomes its own authoritative text. Examples of such are the *Brahma Sutra Bhashya* by Madhvacharya or the *Gita Bhashya* by Adi Sankara.

Essays on the Gita is such a *bhashya*, an exposition of the Gita by Sri Aurobindo, that not only simplifies, but makes lucid its complex harmony, as a faithful reproduction of its synthesis, and is perhaps the best interpretation of the ancient scripture in modern times. Sri Aurobindo rises in afflatus to poetic heights, resonating with the themes and the central import of the Gita, largely because he is as great a philosopher, metaphysician and integrator as the original singer of *The Song Celestial,* Sri Krishna. The Mother of Pondicherry said that with Sri Aurobindo's commentary, the action of the Gita "became decisive." Swami Prabhupada, no admirer of dialectics and the *sankhya* interpretation of the Gita, called the essays "masterly." Swami Paramhansa Yogananda deemed *Essays on the Gita* as the best translation of the scripture in English.

Essays on the Gita may be considered now as a companion volume, equal in significance and value, since it makes the Gita accessible in our times without compromising on its message. Various commentators have given their own slant to the Gita over the past millennia, due to their own personal inclinations but for a true appreciation of the work, one must learn to share the same synoptic and integrative vision.

Two of the greatest *darshaniks* and exponents of Indian spirituality, Sri Krishna and Sri Aurobindo, although perhaps 3,000 to 4,000 years apart, come together in reviving their ages and giving them a new vision and a more integral worldview. Sri Krishna admonishes Arjuna, his friend, disciple and chosen instrument, and awakens him to his *dharma*, his duty, calling, responsibility and ideal standard of action, and bids him fight the forces of darkness and of evil. Sri Aurobindo in the early 20th century invokes the Indian spirit and initiates the Indian renaissance with growing self-confidence in asserting the nation's right to be independent, realizing its true *dharma* and nature, fulfilling its destiny as a leader among nations.

Both with their call for decisive action, no matter how terrible, *ghor* or sanguinary, synthetized the seemingly diverse or even opposing *panths* or creeds of spirituality prevalent in their times in the society, revitalized their country and the entire civilization. Neither was a proponent for a quietistic escapist withdrawal from life and action. And each laid down in essence and form, the foundation of a subtler freedom from the world and its three *gunas*[75], with emphasis on an inner grounding in *samata*[76] and a total surrender to the Divine alone.

Both made Indian spirituality and metaphysics more complete, although it always was so in essence, but due to some perversion in understanding and acceptance had become narrow and exclusive. Both took all the prevalent paths of metaphysics in their times and unified them into a coherent whole such that the truth of none was denied, yet the comprehensive vision was not limited or skewed in any way, was truly universal and eternal and timeless in scope and application.

Sri Krishna essentially gave us a manual for *dharma*, in eighteen chapters, the progressive enlargement of understanding with each chapter, nay each *shloka*, without deviating in any way from the immense need for action and the pragmatic side of spirituality. He addresses Arjuna's ethical, practical and vital difficulties, his desire to escape the

---

[75] Quality, peculiarity, attribute, property

[76] Equanimity

consequences of his particular station in the epic crisis of nations, and his incomprehension and sudden bankruptcy of morality when faced with 'the holiday of fight.' The Gita is a to-do guide-book, a work of meta-ethics as it were, pointing out not only what thou shalt do but also how thou shalt do. For it is not only a profound work of metaphysics, but also of psychology since Indian tradition always took human psychology as the determinant of our culture, sociology, philosophy, arts and sciences. And by discovering the secrets of the human psyche and consciousness, the secrets of metaphysics, spirituality and *darshana* can be organically revealed.

The Gita proceeds not with a Socratic rationalism or method of questioning but by an intuitive and experiential approach that immediately impacts, what we may call in modern educational terminology, our behavioral and emotional competencies. Sri Aurobindo, profoundly indebted to the Gita in his own development as a yogi and a bearer of its message, a fact he acknowledged readily several times in his life, brings out the spirit of the Gita that he intimately lived and deeply realized in his own being.

And this reflects in the 'magisterial' work that he created, a master-work of philosophy and metaphysics, psychology and ethics, that just like the original the *Essays on the Gita* became the pivot and the axis for an age. In his later development, Sri Aurobindo continued down the lines of the same integrative and unifying approach of the Gita in *The Life Divine* and *The Supramental Manifestation*.

2.

Sri Aurobindo: An Approach to 'the Impossibility of Translation'

A translation may mean many things to many people. On the one hand, there are transliterators that faithfully stick to the meaning of the original; on the other hand, there are transcreators, who take the original as a kind of jumping board and create something entirely different. Omar Khayyam translated into the 'Rubaiyat' is an entirely different work of art; Edward Fitzgerald stuck to the main themes, even to the imagery, but he mixed lines freely from one *rubai* to another, creating his own significances, nuances, hidden layers of meaning. He largely adhered to the philosophy of hedonism and materialism of the original but missed the symbolism of the wine, the tavern, the *saqi*, that is part of the mystical traditions of Islamic poetry. Then there are poets such as Ezra Pound who blend in their own creative articulations. Pound maintained in his theory of translation that "no translation has to reproduce all aspects of the original and each translation should be a new poem in its own right."

To the general mind, an ideal translation captures the original meaning without changing it as far as that is possible. It gives to the new work a body of rhythm and sound that attempts to capture the harmonies and meter of the original to the extent it is manageable in an alien language; at the very least, it should give a form, even if it is in prose that expresses the content as an aesthetic whole. The translation delivers the imagery, metaphors, motifs, idioms of the primary as close and as faithful as possible. This is a tall order and a complex wish-list, almost impossible to manage. But, at the end, despite all these demands, a translation has to create a living work, one that is independent and autonomous.

In reality, a translation is seldom that. As T.S. Eliot hinted while introducing Ezra Pound's *Selected Poems* that, even at its best, his translations were "a translucency" and an invention. Lawrence Venuti denotes the failure to acknowledge the impossibility of translation in *The Translator's Invisibility: A History of Translation* as a cultural, political and economic scandal, not acknowledging the possibility of "remainder" or "the possibility for variation in any linguistic conjunction." Dryden maintained that a translation can be a "metaphrase," word for word equated to the original, or "paraphrase," that keeps the sense of original, or an "imitation," a new work that builds off the original idea or theme. Borges felt that dropping the images in translation by using poetic equivalents makes us lose the flavor and impact of the original.

Being a physician, I see a translation as a transplant – it is as if the surgeon placed the heart of the donor in the recipient's body – the post-operative period critically watched to see if the patient survives. Any kind of ventilatory support can only be transient and eventually the patient has to live on of his own. A new corpus, yet beating with someone else's heart, that yet stays unseen—this is the trope I often use to focus on the final outcome. After all the theories are considered and put aside, is the patient vital, functional, robust? Something essential has been placed in an alien body. Do they mount an allergic and immunologic reaction against each other or are able to tolerate each other's antigens so that the 'self' and 'non-self' co-exist, and eventually thrive?

Venuti in his seminal work on the theory of translating cultures examined

> ...the enormous power translation exercises in the formation of cultural identities and the construction or representation of foreign cultures. Translation has both reinforced existing institutions and served as a form of resistance to these same institutions and their respective societies, as is readily apparent in parts of Asia, Africa, the Caribbean, and South America.

He shows how the colonizers' ruthless effort to force English literacy upon its conquered population actually has worked against the colonizer, and has produced a form of literary and political insurgency. Venuti also claims that

> ... scholars knowingly have neglected translation studies, even though a large amount of their research and classes are based on translated texts. Likewise, the study of philosophy in the first world is based, almost exclusively, on translated texts. Yet scholars have claimed that philosophy is a scientific language, based on exact logical formulations, and thus the translation of this material is accurate precisely because of its scientific nature. This attitude, leaves no room for cultural assumptions made by the original author, inherent in any work of literature. If anything, scholars have been known to blame the inability

> to translate this "scientific language" on the inability of the translator, rather than focus on the cultural discrepancies between past and present societies.

We need to appreciate as Venuti points out that basically a translation is

> ...not an ethics of sameness, but one of difference. The focus on the marginality of translation is strategic. It assumes that a study of the periphery in any culture can illuminate and ultimately revise the center. In this Venuti directly refers to the relationship between hegemonic or dominant cultures over subordinate or developing cultures.

With this background, how do we approach translations that are not attempting to do creative 'remakes,' to make a new form similar in effect to that of the original, as Michael Alexander points out, but bring the meanings, nuances, symbolism, and cultural significances of the original with as much fidelity as possible to the reader? This is the challenge Sri Aurobindo faced when he attempted to translate the Upanishads. And to stay close to the original, he adopted a two-pronged approach: to give a translation that is a 'metaphrase' with close signification of each historical, literary, psychological or cultural device used alongside an elaborate commentary on the philosophy, cosmology, psychology and metaphysics of the original.

He translated the *Isha* and *Kena Upanishads* adhering to the unique import and implication of each word of the primary text, annotating any variation in translation by other authors or poets, referencing his intention and reason for a particular slant in meaning and then followed it up with a *sameeksha* or critique and even detailing the schema and thought process of the original. In this, he was perhaps far ahead of his times, desiring to preserve the sense of the original to the utmost for the natives whom he wished to awaken to their own heritage and legacy.

T.S. Eliot stated that "each generation must translate for itself" as a critique of Pound's translation, or rather, adaptations. But Sri Aurobindo has created the translation for an age, plugging all possible leakage, trying to preserve "whatever was unique to the language and what part of poetry should not be lost by translation," to paraphrase Pound. His language is simple, direct, yet poetic, without all the encumbrance of alien cultural and spiritual concepts, so that any modern reader can read them without the need of a dictionary or encyclopedia.

The *Isha*, one of the oldest extant *Upanishad*, which challenged "even the greatest mind that ever walked on earth," Adi Sankaracharya, such that he abandoned his attempt to translate it, is brought out in all its relief in equal lucidity and measure for the uninitiated and the scholar. The *Isha* is critically important as a *sruti* or revealed scripture since it is one of the earliest available statements of monotheism on earth with a life-affirming message that encompasses a Universe in eighteen *shlokas*. It also profoundly influenced the Gita with insights and worldview.

This is how I believe Sri Aurobindo addressed the challenge of translating old Sanskrit with its Vedic symbolism and devices of *shlesha*[77] into modern English:

---

[77] Pun

He steeped himself in the original, lived its ideals and philosophy, such that he mastered the concepts of the source text not in theory but in practical living.

He studied, Sanskrit, the original language, in detail, with such mastery that he was able to unlock the ancient mystery of why the Vedas seem so puerile and barbaric while their *darshana* enunciated in the Upanishads is universal and extremely sophisticated.

To translate the Upanishads faithfully, he brought out the symbology, with detailed review, the literary devices of metaphor, puns based on etymology and seed sounds, and rhythm thus became secondary in this venture. However, being a master of English and a poet himself, his translations are rhythmic and often catch the symphonic and orchestral harmonies of the original. With the use of alliteration, assonance, imperfect and internal rhymes, even his prose rises in pitch to a poetic intensity reminiscent of the original.

His commentaries on *Isha* and *Kena*, with detailed exposition of the Logos of the original and consideration of its entire ontology, and what would perhaps be called today an early 'deconstructionistic' and the 'structuralist' approach to linguistics and psychology of the original seers and poets.

He translated other Upanishads too, the *Katha*, *Mundaka*, *Taittreya* and *Aittreya*, but did not leave us the detailed expositions of these latter, to my utmost regret. But he left a methodology for future translators to perhaps follow. And he enlarged on all these concepts in his masterly work, *The Life Divine* and brought them to a coherent whole in an integral manner.

It is curious to see that Sri Aurobindo merged commentary and translation in *Essays on the Gita*, although the essence and *darshana* are utterly faithful to the original. The inspired aesthetic and cognitive whole of these series of essays with references did not focus on translation per se but in imparting the spirit of the original.

The approach taken in the translation of the *Isha* and *Kena Upanishads*, and those of the Vedas, is a contribution to the art of translation with a unique approach, that might serve as a benchmark for future scholarly work and guiding us in how to translate a very important text so that no 'remainders' are neglected or rejected.

3.

Sri Aurobindo: The Scandal of the Vedas

Of all the translators, Sri Aurobindo is the one who perhaps has the most unique approach. As he himself pointed out, he saw his translations of the Vedas more as a rendering than a word-by-word transcription. In his own talks with his disciples, he noted that the spiritual experiences described in the Vedas and their import, that had been forgotten by Indian commentators themselves, were independently experienced by him. And when he read the *shlokas* he could identify what the ancient *rishis* had described in a symbolism couched with literary devices like the *shlesha* or pun.

Or after reading a verse, he would intimately experience the realization described in Sanskrit. In fact, he did not attempt to translate at all but let the spirit and the inspiration guide the 'rendition' into English. This is not a usual translator's approach who is willing to catch some nuance or aspect of the original, something interesting that the reader might like, and practice what Pound call "excernment," leaving that which cannot be translated. However, for an extremely significant compilation like the Vedas, which defines a whole culture, civilization and was the origin of its vast philosophy, literature, art, sciences and *dharma*, a transactional, fly-by-night adaptation would never do.

To use modern terminology, Sri Aurobindo wrote from the same gestalt or *nous* as the *rishis* and wrote, not by 'metaphrasing,' or doing literal remakes, but from their insight and intuition. It was only after the rendering that he would look at the linguistic and scholastic interpretation made of the ancient Sanskrit by other scholars such as Sayana or Max Mueller. Many a time he would disagree with them, with Sayana for his literalness that was external and superficial, and with Max Mueller, for his fanciful leaps inspired by his own biases. Sri Aurobindo then chose the interpretation that was closest to his spiritual experience.

His translation was based on the psychology of the sounds based on their yogic significance and his vast research into the *beeja dhvani* or seed sounds is extremely instructive in how he connected the ancient language of Sanskrit with Latin and Greek and used this knowledge to render the original sense of the primary text. He did this not from a western point of view but from the center of his own culture and native understanding—in this perhaps, he anticipates the criticism of Venuti and latter's insistence on the impossibility of translating.

Sri Aurobindo followed his rendering with a detailed commentary, at least on the first mandala of the *Rig Veda* (he had wanted to translate the entire *Rig Veda* in this manner), with detailed consideration of various meanings and nuances to bolster his interpretation. Sri Aurobindo's rendering is akin to a master pianist playing a concerto of Beethoven. He is faithful to the chords and notes, but the feeling, style and interpretation are entirely his own. Thus, multiple interpretation of the concerto are possible, as many as there are virtuoso pianists in the world.

However, Sri Aurobindo, realizing the immense value of Vedas to the Indian renaissance, continued to interpret the Vedas his whole life in the light of his intuition and yogic development. He brought these insights later into his magnum opus, *The Life Divine*, and each chapter of the massive work of philosophy, metaphysics and dialectics begins with a *shloka* of the Vedas or Upanishads or the Gita and is an integral aspect of its thematic exposition.

Initially, Sri Aurobindo's interpretation was not accepted by scholars and critics but today it is an axiomatic understanding of Indology and Indic sciences. The revolutionary insights turned out to be accurate and valid and this was helped significantly by the knowledge of linguistics, phonology and etymology that he brought to the vast and complex subject.

He followed up on the renderings of the *Rig Veda* and his detailed commentary on *The Secret of the Vedas* with the significance of each sound and phrase in the original, the primal roots and esoteric mindset of the *rishis*—and this made his approach authentic and genuine to his people.

Such was the respect for him as a spiritual authority and literary figure that he single-handedly gave a new impetus to the awakening of India. And the *Vedas* that had been neglected, forgotten, rejected for millennia as 'the mere babblings of an infantile humanity', suddenly were seen with a fresh eye, as the profound utterance of a highly evolved people far ahead of their times who inspired the Upanishads and the later development of the entire subcontinent.

Each shloka to him was a revelation, especially from the *Rig Veda*—hidden in a language that could transmit the epiphany to the listener or reader if he would be open to it and transform his mind and heart with its sound that was itself the bearer of the rich and visionary experience. And this transmission was not merely auditory but visual and tactile, a mutation as it were, known to the Vedic seers as the mantra. Listening to the mantra is akin to holding the weight of each syllable on the tips of one's fingers, to paraphrase Virginia Woolf. If I might add it would be akin to hearing with the body and seeing with the skin.

Sri Aurobindo clarified the significance of the symbols used in the verses. For example, the *yajna*[78] which had come to be seen as a ritual in which ghee, or purified butter, is poured in the sacrificial flame, as the chants invoked the Sun-God to pull its horses, dripping with the ghee, or the Moon to grant *soma-rasa* or wine to the barbaric priest. But each symbol had an inner significance, an experiential and conscious equivalent, covered by the literary devices of puns and allegory. Thus, the Sun was a symbol of the highest awareness of man, the *Sat-Chit-Ananda*, Truth-Consciousness-Bliss, seen in physical or holographic imagery. The ghee was the purified aspiration and energy poured into the pure psychic center and fire of one's being. The *soma-rasa* became enlightenment or the opening and lightness one feels while enjoying wine. And the horses were the heightened energy of ascesis or *tapasya* that helped one transcend the mere physical to a more evolved state of living.

Hinduism had unfortunately lost itself in *karma kanda* or empty ritualism that forgot the inner significance of each act or the symbolism behind the repetitive movements of self-

[78] Sacrificial fire in which ancient Indians poured sacrifices and libations to invoke the gods but the whole ritual is a symbol of one's inner development and purification and offering to the divine within.

purification. It is surprising that even after the Adi Sankara had established the victory of Vedanta and Advaita over mere Vedic ritualism, they were carried on in the society as an established fact of *dharma*, along with the same continuance for idolatory. The psychological reality of the Vedic gods was forgotten in polytheistic or henotheistic practices. Sri Aurobindo once again firmly established the bases of Sanatana [79] Dharma, by taking us to a profounder understanding of subtle and inner worlds and helped recover the *Uttara Mimansa*[80] that Sankara had already proclaimed as the foundation of Indian *darshana*.

Ezra Pound announced that every translation is a critique of the original. Sri Aurobindo seems to have taken this literally and offered a critique with every translation. And supplied us the key with which to unlock the mysteries of the original and all other Vedas and Upanishads ourselves. No translation may fully capture all the aspects of the primary text but the Veda require "not less than everything" for their transformative action. Sri Aurobindo by giving us a comprehensive, multi-faceted and multi-dimensional treatment of the original, tries to bring us the *rasa*[81] of the Vedas in all its flavors.

As we have pointed out, his later works continue the process of translation or rendering that he had done in his early years of yoga, and with works such as *The Supramental Manifestation* or the final versions of 'Savitri,' he continued

---

[79] Eternal

[80] *Uttara* means later or subsequent. *Mimamsa* means critical inquiry or exegesis. *Uttar Mimamsa* is one of the most significant of all Indian philosophies.

[81] Essence, nectar, taste.

his paraphrasing of the *srutis* in the light of his dynamic and personal transformation as a seer, philosopher and prophet.

It is curious that Sri Aurobindo saw the linguistic connections among Greek, Latin and Sanskrit when he began to study Tamil and translate the 'Tirukkural.' He discovered that all these languages were essentially one family and found missing links in their connections with a deeper research and study of Sanskrit.

Owen Barfield, who studied the history of English words, made a singularly important contribution to the understanding of comparative philology. He showed with extensive research in *Poetic Diction: A Study* in *Meaning* how each word is a multi-dimensional entity, almost like an organism or a person—with its own history, birth, evolution, its cognate siblings or off-springs, and its readings and missed meanings. He also showed how the discovery of Sanskrit by European scholars in the 18th century turned philology into an exact science showing the resemblances among Indo-European or Aryan languages. And how the advent of phonology laid the foundations of modern scholarship that could begin to 'date' words and affix their ancient meanings, thus transforming ethnology, anthropology, sociology and history in one fell swoop.

No translation, as we have pointed out, can exhaust the original. But in Sri Aurobindo's world, the Vedas is no longer a book external and preserved from a period of time, but the eternal knowledge in the heart of each human being, that could be explored, lived and established with a consciousness which had an "evolutionary appetite," to use a phrase coined by G.B. Shaw.

Sri Aurobindo restored the original to its own people—to whom it had always been available, though not accessible or comprehensible. To use the paradigm of Venuti, a translation is an attempt to colonize the alien people. Here, it was scholars like Max Mueller, who with their imaginative and prejudiced minds had practiced a kind of literary imperialism. And it was Sri Aurobindo who freed the minds of his people from the neo-colonialism of such scholars and by his interpretation liberated the concept of translation from its inherent contradiction.

Nor was this unique rendering based on an intimate experiencing of the original an unconscious process. Sri Aurobindo opened it up to scientific study and scholarship without losing the living poetry of the original. He shared his literary processes with his students and disciples, inspiring them to attempt translations on their own, critiquing them by comparing the primary and secondary texts with each other, not just literally but as aesthetic and cognitive equivalents. Finally, he compared the spirit of the original and the translation, their inspirations, their intuitive understanding and capacity to make the phrasing inevitable.

Eventually, the proof is in the rendering. Does the value of the rendition as living literature equal the original as 'cognate' work of art, delivering an experience to the reader or listener, with a "blood-seeing" as Rilke aspired for eventually? In this, and by using these criteria only, Sri Aurobindo triggered a metamorphosis of Indic literatures and languages, the effects of which will be felt for ages, in my opinion.

Thus, a threefold approach to translation was taken by Sri Aurobindo with the three most important works of Indian literature or *srutis* which include the Vedas, the Upanishads and the Gita, anticipating the more modern criticisms of the validity and authenticity of a translation. For the Vedas, a rendering based on his own spiritual discoveries, a linguistic, phonologic and psychologic assessment of Sanskrit and other Aryan languages to uncover the secret of the Vedas, a critique with a review of the erroneous approaches of the past especially by Sayana, Adi Sankara and Max Mueller, and a lifelong application and investigation of their explorations and intuitions in his own life and yoga. Such seem to be his methods by which he restored to the Indian people the sense and meaning of the Vedas which had formed the bedrock of Indian civilization.

To translate the Upanishads, he took a more direct approach by interpreting their more intellectual and less intuitive articulations and writing a commentary on the *Isha* and *Kena Upanishads*. For the Gita, his *bhashya*, at once a commentary on the Gita and its translation, in highly fused and inspired essays creates a parallel work equal in significance and action.

Sri Aurobindo also translated Kalidasa and Bhartrihari. Unfortunately, one of his translations of Kalidasa has been lost, likely forever, though a few fragments remain that tell us of their beauty and refinement. These translations are more traditional, more literary and conservative in approach than those of the Vedas, Upanishads and the Gita, although his translation of Kalidasa's prose into poetry was another bold departure from the conventional treatment of the great dramatist and poet.

He also translated *Prières et Méditations* written by the Mother from Pondicherry (originally written in French) into simple and lucid English *Prayers and Meditations*. Six hundred pages of translation besides those of the *srutis*, from Sanskrit, Bengali, Tamil, Latin and Greek verse are a significant body of work in his poetic avatar as *anuvaadak*[82].

Innovations created by him to translate Latin and Greek poems into a quantitative verse in English need more research. Perhaps modern prosody will someday catch up with his experimentations to replicate the rhythms from these ancient languages into Anglo-Saxon harmonies which improve upon those of Clough, Longfellow and Bridges. His essay on quantitative meter gives a more 'sound' basis to measure and structure metrical feet or units to the accentual considerations of the past.

Sri Aurobindo may be considered as the Leonardo Da Vinci of translation. With his voluminous output of original writings in prose and poetry and critical diversions by other causes, global or nationalist, constraining his time, he was unable to complete many of these translations that he had begun from various poets in half a dozen languages. Yet, he created radically new possibilities and departures that can and must be explored in the future, suggestions that might make attempts by others less strenuous and more fruitful. In that, he may be considered to have initiated an Indian renaissance in translation just as he did in literary criticism and philosophy.

---

[82] Translator

4.

Vikramorvasie or the Hero and the Nymph

(Translated from the Sanskrit Play of Kalidasa)

Vikramorvasie is the only play of Kalidasa translated to completion by Sri Aurobindo, the other being *Meghduta* that was unfortunately lost. *Vikramorvasie* is unique since it is a translation of Kalidasa's poetry in blank verse, while *Meghduta* was in terza rima.

To capture Kalidasa's spirit is the challenge that Sri Aurobindo seems to have set himself as he wrote in an essay 'On Translating Kalidasa' and by this he meant, not just the most outward form or imagery but also the feel and the feeling, the thought and the theme, the sounds and the spirit.

In the aforementioned essay, in a beautiful metaphor comparing the body of the poem with the body of man, he describes the various layers of a poem that merit translation:

> The mere quantities are but the most mechanical and outward part of meter. A fanciful mind might draw a parallel between the elements of man and the elements of meter. Just as in man there is the outward food-plasm and within it the vital or sensational man conditioned by and

> conditioning the food-plasm and within the vital man the emotional or impressional man similarly related and again within that the intellectual man governing the others and again within that the delight of the spirit in its reasoning existence and within that delight like the moon within its halo the Spirit who is Lord of all these, the sitter in the chariot and the master of its driving, so in meter there is the quantitative or accentual arrangement which is its body, and within that body conditioning and conditioned by it the arrangement of pauses and sounds, such as assonance, alliteration, composition of related and varying letters, and again within it conditioning and conditioned by this sensational element and through it the mechanical element is the pure emotional movement of the verse and again within these understanding and guiding all three, bringing the element of restraint, management, subordination to a superior law of harmony, is the intellectual element, the driver of the chariot of sound; …[83]

Sri Aurobindo maintains that Kalidasa's plays are very unlike Greek drama from whom they are alleged to have off-sprung. The Hindu expression of the time was less intellectual, more aesthetic and temperate, "noble, forbearing and gentle." It is possible that there might have been some influences of Athenian art, but the Hindu *Natya Shastra*[84] is an art form that seems to be more Indic than Greek in origin.

He also shows the differences between the Elizabethan and Hindu drama, the latter less vital, critical, excessive and cultured. Indic drama was also "a necessary result of the

---

[83] CWSA, Vol. 1, p. 241

[84] Sanskrit treatise on the performing arts.

principle that aesthetic and intellectual pleasure is the first object of all poetic art." Sanskrit, a language of wider harmonies, resonances and symphonic notes, has always a mantric sonority in the background, even in its most emotional or physical forms of art. And thus, the Hindu drama, according to him, was "written by men of accomplished culture for an educated audience."

Sri Aurobindo has captured the spirit of Kalidasa in his only complete translation available, the imagery, lightness of flow, the humor, the traditional setting and narrative. The blank verse seems well-adapted to the theme and is simple and unaffected. An easy lyricism of feeling and thought is able to bring out the richness of life of those times. The passions among characters, though intense and measured, are not uncontrolled or crude such as we often find in Shakespeare.

It is interesting to note that Sri Aurobindo also wrote a minor epic 'Urvasie' based on the same story, which has passages of far greater intensity and is a study in how a play's structure and story can be used to develop a parallel creation and recital in verse. Kalidasa seems to be forgotten today, as compared to Shakespeare, perhaps due to translations that do not capture his spirit or, more likely, due to the lack of critical appraisal of his oeuvre. But he remains one of the three greatest figures in Sanskrit poetry after Valmiki and Vyasa and it might be time for a renewed effort to research and study his art and poetics. For he is as important as the greatest Greek or Elizabethan dramatists. But he needs to be approached and appreciated on his own terms and not those with the blinkers of an unoriginal education.

V.

Sri Aurobindo, the First Literary Critic of Modern India

1.

The Future Poetry

Modern India has begun to catch up with the profuse and prolific creativity of its ancient and medieval periods in prose and poetry, though not so much in drama or criticism. Amartya Sen, in *The Argumentative Indian* showed that Indian society since ancient times has reveled in public debate and discourse and literary and philosophical criticism was considered as an essential aspect of our tradition and robust culture. Though, I must add, that these debates were not primarily intellectual as he deems them to be but came from a consideration of subtler and deeper realities that were a part of our holistic *weltanschauung*.

Be that as it may, Gordon Bottomley's term of sneer for Indo-English poets, cited by K.R.S. Iyengar in *The Indian Contribution to English Literature*, as "Matthew Arnolds in a saree" may be extended to modern Indian critics too. So derivative and secondary has been their ability to analyze, compare, research, interpret or evaluate other works of literature that there has been no significant contribution made by any Indian to the compendium of modern literary criticism. The only work that may usher in a new way of looking at the historical development of English literature and its evolving trends is *The Future Poetry* by Sri Aurobindo.

The Future Poetry is perhaps the first book of original literary criticism from India in the last 200 years. It reviews the last 600 years of English poetry, its development from the poetry of Chaucer to Shakespeare to Milton and the Romantic poets to the Victorian age of Pope and Dryden ending in the emerging trends with Celtic poetry and Tagore. A detailed section on metaphysical and modernist poetry, though planned, was never completed. However, its broad scale and treatment of the lines of development in English poetry is a radical departure from approaches in the past and its ability to deduce the future a refreshing take from the usual and the discursive.

Modern criticism may need a meta-critical approach to itself as in modern literature. Perhaps a Wittgenstein is needed now to look at the games played by thought with itself in this genre. It seems to me that the last great critic in English was Harold Bloom who recently passed away in 2019 but even his major contributions to our reflective and interpretative literary faculties are more than a few decades ago. We have seen no Isaiah Berlins or even an Allen Tate to shed new light or de-construct the sure and settled past of our understanding in the last few decades.

It may be worthwhile to revisit *The Future Poetry* since it seemed way ahead of its times when it was published in the early 20th century. To my mind, the most significant contribution by Sri Aurobindo to the *Tao of Literature*, to paraphrase a comparative analysis of quantum physics and eastern philosophy by Frijof Capra, is to first begin a historical consideration of the long and successful development of English poetry.

Such an approach, as far as I know has never been taken before. It needs a much more encyclopedic research as far as I am concerned, but Sri Aurobindo gave us a summary of the considerations and the possible conclusions before us in his physically thin but sweeping insightful review. Much more may be revealed as the lines of evolution of literatures in other languages are studied. But a basis for comparative analysis for the *sahitya* of the world canon has been created. Sri Aurobindo's definition of the mantra, its place in Indian critical thought and its possible inchoate appearance in other literatures, especially English, is a remarkable advance in the conceptual figuration and comprehension of language and human semantic evolution.

Sri Aurobindo's thesis is two-fold. The first question he asks is—"What is the nature of poetry and its highest power?" "What is the supreme music that can be extracted from its instrument" and how can it reach an inevitability of expression? And he attempts to give some guiding intuitions, some helpful descriptions, though not with barren and narrow definitions, to enlighten our search.

Poetry is an ancient and high art, as Harold Bloom has pointed out in *The Best Poems of the English Language*. Sri Aurobindo calls poetry the highest form of speech available to man for the expression of his self-vision or world-vision. In his words, "The most inevitable poetry becomes possible when three highest intensities of speech meet and become indissolubly one: and these are the highest intensity of rhythmic movement, verbal form and thought-substance or content and vision of truth. And he calls this fusion of the utmost possibilities of poetry as the mantra."

Rhythm may be the most important aspect of this supreme expression of imagination, creativity, illumination and inspiration but it is not just the rhythm on the surface but the fuller and subtler harmonies that touch our deeper psychology. For these overtones and undertones may be the pinions on which inspiration can wing beyond the horizons into new space. When each syllable has a significance multi-dimensional and alchemic; when economy of sound becomes its power and possibility. And it is heard not by the physical ear, but in stillness by a hearing, that may be described in the language of the Upanishads as the "ear of the ear, that which listens behind the instabilities of word and speech."

The second aspect of the mantra is the style, the thought, the substance. A superficial treatment or temperament falsifies by its poetic inadequacy the truth of our supreme utterance. It is the Word that creates and carries with it all the elements of expression, rather than being dependent on them.

And finally, great poetry not only brings us a vision of Truth universal and eternal, it also makes us see it. Modern poetry lays a predominant value on thought and sensation; while these are important, the poet-seer is able to penetrate the screens of gross appearances and temporal fluctuations to see something that is endlessly joyous and beautiful. This sight is no longer subjective or objective, realistic or ideal, but is spiritual, unified and revelatory. The mind of man might then begin to see more intimately the forces behind life and the powers concealed by our own subjective existence.

Also, in a line reminiscent of what T.S. Eliot was going to declare much later to great fanfare in his essay 'Tradition and the Individual Talent,' the work of the poet depends not only on himself and his age but also on the mentality of the nation to which he belongs and the spiritual, intellectual, aesthetic tradition and environment which it creates for him. Thus, a poet reaches mastery when the nation recognizes its innate character or dharma and articulates it clearly and explicitly. This is what made Greek or ancient Indian poetry the voice of not only its individual poets but also of the collective, the innumerable people who are inseparably connected to one another, giving it a timeless perfection. For voice is not only a personal quality, it is also the unity that is characteristic of any evolved society.

Setting thus the Everest of poetry in our sights, he then proceeds to review the trends of English poetry as described by James Cousins in his book, *New Ways in English Literature*. But Sri Aurobindo casts his sight farther back to the very inception of English poetry and traces it to the developments in early 20th century. He starts with Chaucer and his poetry of external life, and his contribution towards finding a basis for the English meter in accents, alliteration and assonances. No other great poetical literature has had quite such a beginning completely dedicated "to reflecting the external figure and surface of things as near as possible."

This was followed by perhaps the most opulent stage of English poetry in abundance and power, yet not satisfying in its performance fully. From 1587 ACE for the next eighty years, poets of a high order like Spenser and Marlowe towered the scene. But it was Shakespeare, an exception, a genius and one of the greatest poets of all time, who hid the general inadequacy of forms and self-awareness by eclipsing all the rest with his super-creative daemon. The interpretative vision and the mastery of expression was still missing from the rest.

With Milton English poetry began to get a training in poetic and artistic intelligence. But Milton too fell in sustained intensity after the first few books of 'Paradise Lost.' And this, according to Sri Aurobindo, was "due to failure of poetic vision and inability to show us God after he had shown us the Devil." Or perhaps it was the inherent contradiction of the theology that Milton was secretly rebelling against, as A.D. Nuttall in *The Alternative Trinity: Gnostic Heresy in Marlowe, Milton and Blake* has pointed out. William Empson too felt that "Milton had barely managed to keep his temper with the poem's God" in his remarkable study *Milton's God.*

After a comparative lull in power and inspiration in the age of Thomas Gray and William Collins, there came the Romantic revolution in early 19th century. But great as the achievements of Wordsworth, Coleridge, Blake, Keats and Shelly were they were unsustained and restricted in time. Wordsworth petered out early after a decade of immense creativity and became a versifier than a visionary poet. Coleridge belied his immense talent and genius except in the daemonic triad of *Kubla Khan*, *The Rime of the Ancient Mariner* and *Christabel.* Blake, more than anyone else, was able to capture a middle world of vision in his poems; yet, as T.S. Eliot has pointed out, cosmological and theological paradigms were not able to keep up with him and, despite his genius, he could not create a work like Dante, on a wider and profounder scale. Shelley and Keats died early while their art was still maturing.

And then, the age of Pope and Dryden with its dry intellectualism and loss of vision, a perfection of form without greater substance or inspiration, and a superficial approach to life and oneself. To be followed by Tennyson and Browning with their technical perfections and lack of transformative rhythms or style.

And thus, English poetry with all its richness and power of expression still searched for the revelatory Word that had manifested solely in the genius of Shakespeare, more as an exception than a rule. With the advent of a modernistic age, however, and the appearance of Yeats, AE (George William Russell), Tagore and Carpenter, the sight of the poet turned inward, with an opening to the spiritual and the subjective, to the subtler movements behind the gross and material worlds.

In Sri Aurobindo's opinion, the emergence of Celtic and Indian poets with their rediscovery of their nations' genius and *dharma*, brought a new possibility to English poetry. He hoped that as time passed, more and more Indian poets would express the spirituality of their nation in English and bring the element of mantra in our discourse, idealization and comprehension collectively.

Sri Aurobindo's only work of criticism is a masterly and sensitive consideration of the trends in English poetry seen so far and where it could possibly lead to in the future. And, it seems, that despite the brief interlude of modernist poets in the mold of Eliot and Pound, form and romanticism are coming back into the mainstream, as it were. And that Indian poets will have a role to play in the development of English poetry in the next few decades.

Sri Aurobindo was way ahead of his time. He has not been appreciated for his historical analysis of English verse and projection of trends and lines of development. And yet, there will be a time that readers and critiques will see his major contribution to literary criticism or *alochana* as humanity ascends from its inchoate beginnings to a more enlightened understanding. Until then, we will need to learn and evolve together as best as we can and possess our souls with silence.

As one of the most widely-spoken languages in the world with one of the oldest and richest literatures in any language, any impact on the caliber of English literature would immediately impact other literatures, writers, poets, readers, listeners, thinkers and the general mind of humanity. A lot of vital crudeness in our discourse and drives could possibly be refined and our sensual pleasures lend themselves to "more difficult pleasures," as Shelley discovered. Poetry as one of "the enlargements of life," in the eyes of Wallace Stevens, could then be an instrument of a shift in awareness and sensitivity of humankind.

The approach of the Vedas is quite the opposite of modern psychologists like Freud. Vedic thought investigated our superconscious and considered an opening to its vast realms as the first step in our evolution to its heights. It explored the higher levels of awareness, hitherto unknown and unavailable to us, described them in detail in an attempt to make the superconscious a natural and organic parts of our dreams and aspirations. Modern psychology especially in Freud proceeded by studying our nether ranges as the subconscious, without any understanding of the ascent possible to us, and hoped to resolve its ills by means analytical and powerless to effect a change. A systematic, methodical and consistent attempt to bring an inspirational element to our aesthetic and cognitive lives could be the metamorphosis the world needs today.

As the lingua franca of the globe, the language of sciences and the one most studied for artificial intelligence and natural language processing and generation, it is my estimate that as English evolves to different possibilities, it will change our psychology, our philosophies and our humanities and sciences.

Sri Aurobindo brought a historical dimension to criticism in English that no longer focused on individual poets and their lives but on the growth of expression in their verse and the progression in subtlety, range, power and orientation in English poetry over 600 years. Critics who take a narrower view are at risk for making serious errors in judgment. Even T.S. Eliot in his exuberance made proclamations which he later retracted and was often sometimes juvenile in his assessment swayed by the immediate success of a particular style "with visions and revisions which a moment would reverse." A critic capable of looking at the entire Himalaya of English poetry would perhaps be able to measure each peak's individual height and compare it with the others more accurately and with more sympathy and restraint. Sri Aurobindo gives us that perspective in his small but insightful *vyakhya* or elucidation.

2.

Letters on Poetry, Literature and Art

Letter-writing is a lost art. As our analog selves grow digitized, our natural language generated by silicon semiconductors and our native intelligence turned artificial, the gestalt of picking a pen and constructing patiently, lovingly, cursively on blank white sheets maybe remembered like one's first love. The memories often intertwined with the act of writing them.

Great letter writers like Keats and D.H. Lawrence took them as an opportunity to explore, articulate, share, confirm and develop their thoughts and theories. The concept of "negative capability" was first enunciated by Keats in an epistle to his brothers at the age of 22, a precociousness of self-detachment rare at this age. And D.H. Lawrence expounded in correspondence of thousands of letters, his apocalyptic insights of death and "descent into darkness and unknowing," the freeing from the malady of "sex in the head." Arnold and Huxley and Freud use their letters as a medium of self-expression, self-formulation and self-realization while sharing the sacred and intimate space of their dispatches.

Sri Aurobindo brought yoga, philosophy, poetics, anthology, sociology, linguistics, history and a multitude of themes into the missives he scribbled almost till dawn for his disciples. They show a mind supple and lucid, with vast erudition yet not hampered by his knowledge, and incisive insights that are still relevant and fresh. In this essay I shall restrict myself to his letters on poetry and literature, collected from his archives into sections that show us his "delicacy of touch, fineness and depth of observation, and just sympathy and discrimination," qualities he noted are necessary for literary critique.

To me, his aesthetic temper and outlook and a distinctive temperament that always saw things on a wide scale, in a broad expanse of time, with precision and subtlety are a perennial delight and an occasion of dealing with one of the finest minds of last century. Archivists have collated these letters into broad sections on the process, form and substance of poetry, or poetic rhythm and technique, or modern poetry or translations, or Indo-English poetry, etc. But any random page opened discussing the finer points of art from his small room with students who might as well be continents away, is an experience equivalent to the listening to Beethoven or gazing at Michelangelo. A classicism of personality, gentle in outlook, sensitive in approach, modern in expression, a remote greatness that could yet touch intimately and personally with lines penned at wee hours of morning.

There were at least four to five disciples he personally groomed into poets writing in English, and they were no underlings either. Under his guidance, mathematicians, doctors, and revolutionaries turned into bards of the spirit, creating a school of Aurobindonian poetry. The characteristics of this school may be summarized as:

> Turning art into yogic activity, as *bhakti*, like the ancient Vedic ideal of turning art into one's highest calling used to be.

> A focus on more elevated and sublime thought, content and subjects, that could be simple or complex, realistic or idealistic, occult or spiritual, with utmost perfection of form, rhythm and symbolism.

> The goal of the poet was not just to write great poetry but grow individually, to attempt, as Rilke acclaimed, "to be one's own greatest work of art."

> To create poetry that aspired to reach the heights and depths that would transform the consciousness of the reader or listener, the veritable mantra.

The growth of the disciples not just as yogis but as poets, critics, writers, thinkers, to "logicize" them, as he said, to refine their crude and formative vitals, to introduce them to world literature, at least in six to seven languages, to create the future of a resurgent Indian literature and art, this was his attempt which may yet influence aspiring poets who read him today.

His considered or immediate responses, full of humor and profound off-the-cuff remarks, are a lesson in sensitivity, gentle mentorship, concision and humility. And this personal engagement, I believe, did more to improve the disciples' aesthetic and cognitive faculties, their awareness and passion for learning, than all his mighty erudition or repertoire.

More than an *ashram* or literary school, he created what in modern parlance we would call, a Learning Organization or Knowledge-Based Organization. And this passion for culture and self-edification is another aspect of his enormous legacy for us, borne by these thousands of letters that scholars are still trying to pore over and organize.

3.

Indian Literature

Sri Aurobindo elaborated on the history of Indian Literature, its development, salient features, accomplishments and direction in *The Foundations of Indian Culture* in response to a western critic William Archer, who assailed the entire life and culture of India as "a repulsive mass of unspeakable barbarism" in his book *India and the Future.*

In Sri Aurobindo's opinion, literature is "not indeed the complete, but the most varied and ample record of the culture of a people." For literature gives us the most flexible and many-sided self-expression of the spirit, the aesthesis and their creative mind. And "the greatness of a literature, in his words, lies first in the greatness and worth of its substance, the value of its thought and the beauty of its forms, but also in the degree to which it avails to bring out and raise the soul and life or the living and the ideal mind of a people, an age, a culture…"

One of the most salient features of Indian literature is its profound impact on the civilization's mind, the influence that, say, the Vedas and Upanishads had on Indian philosophy, art, culture, ethics, economy and politics. And we see with the Ramayana and the Mahabharata an even closer identification of the common man with the characters and the personages of these epics, the adoption of their stories in the literary and social life of the Indic nations down to the lay person, even in the most remote and rural areas. The impact of Jayadeva's 'Gita Govinda' on the entire medieval nation with his beautiful love story of Radha and Krishna, their human-divine romance and devotion to each other, continued to affect other art-forms, such as music, painting, drama, sculpture and dance. Tulsidasa's 'Rama Charita Manas' became a companion to a whole generation of students teaching them ethics, philosophy and character. And the patriotic songs of Saint Ramadas inspired a whole nation to stand up against the tyranny of the Moguls.

The Sanskrit language itself, one of the most standardized and stable according to modern computer sciences, rhythmic and harmonious, precise, linguistically evolved, sweet and flexible, strong and clearly-formed, full, vibrant and subtle, is evidence of the character and quality of the people whose mind it expressed and reflected.

Sanskrit literature stands in the front ranks of the world's great literature, equaling the productions of ancient, medieval and modern Europe. Add to this, the literatures of Pali, and the dozen Sanskritic and Dravidian tongues, and one can discern a continental body of creation brought forth by some of the most developed and creative peoples on the planet. The Vedas, Upanishads, Ramayana, Mahabharata, Puranas, the drama of Kalidasa and the aphorisms of Bhartrihari and the lyrics of Jayadeva are our great legacies. And these followed by the Buddhistic literature, the Dhammapada and the Jatakas, and later, the Panchatantra, Tulsidas, Vidyaprasad and Chandidas, and Ramprasad, Ramdas and Tukaram are only a first look at the oceanic mass of Indic *sahitya.* And then, the massive works in Dravidian languages, from Tiruvalluvar to

Kamban, the Shaiva saints and the Alwars, down to Subramanium Bharti and Gokak, add an Atlantic to the already described Pacific of the inexhaustible vitality of this civilization. Not to mention the songs of Nanak, Kabir, Mirabai and Tulsi which yet link back to the Gangotri of the Vedas and the Upanishads in spirit and spirituality and the uniqueness of India's genius still existing, surviving and thriving, after 6000 years of robust activity, despite minor periods of inertia, becomes obvious.

Sri Aurobindo showed us with examples how the Vedas are the output of an early intuitive and symbolical mentality, describing an imaged psychological and religious experience. The Upanishads, breaking through and beyond Vedic forms, symbols and images, without entirely abandoning them, reveal the ultimate and unsurpassable truths of self, God, man and world. The epics, Ramayana and Mahabharata, represented the *dharma* of the nation as practiced by men of ideals and high conviction, of realization and dedication, and in their life reflected the heroism and youth of the race.

Thus, the Indic literature saw philosophy, religion and poetry as one and made it thus; the secular was not demarcated from the spiritual. The philosophy not being an abstract or intellectual speculation about truth, was seen, lived, felt and held by the mind of the nation whether in *kathas*[85], songs, stories, exegeses, debate, discourse or drama. Nor was it only mental but instead a vision and a revelation to the whole people by their best and most representative.

The great speculations of modern metaphysics and thought can always find an indication or seed of the same concerns, reflections and speculations in the *darshanas* of the

[85] Narrations

nation in some form or the other. The works of Kalidasa, Puranas and Tantra, continued the momentum of the classical age of ancient Sanskrit literature, but slowly began to move to a less revealed and more conscious and willed body of creation. The derived languages, the daughters of the dialects, assumed the mantle as the new literary instruments accepting the general lines of tradition and developed them further.

Sri Aurobindo thus critiques the historical development of Indian literature just as he did with English literature in *The Future Poetry*, though here the scale is larger and his treatment more limited, but the approach is the same; looking at trends and considering possibilities for the future. He felt that one cycle of its opulent and prolific creation was coming to a close but another cycle was beginning to gather, which would extend itself to spirituality, religion and secular living in equal measure and influence them all just as it had done splendidly in the past history and evolution of the nation.

VI.

The Poetry of Sri Aurobindo

1.

On Quantitative Meter

Sri Aurobindo made an extremely important contribution to English prosody, equal in value to *The Future Poetry*. And this was his innovation in the approach to be taken in adopting classical meters in Greek and Latin into English, especially quantitative hexameter, sapphics, alcaics, hendecasyllables, elegiacs, etc. Its potential value to English verse might be potentially as important as the breakthroughs of Walt Whitman or Gerard Manley Hopkins in rhythm and meter or Wordsworth's Preface to the second edition of *Lyrical Manifesto* wherein he championed the cause of normal speech in poetry.

What is quantitative meter? For those of us, who are familiar with Hindi or Bengali or even Sanskrit prosody, it is obvious that each vowel has a precise metrical value, which is dependent on the time it takes to pronounce the vowel. The time taken to read a line and its cadence are defined by how many of these vowels are there in the line and how they are arranged internally. Thus, a vowel in Hindi can be *laghu* which is short and counted as one unit or *guru* which is long and counted as two units. Traditionally the *dohas*[86] or

[86] A form of self-contained rhyming couplet in Indian poetry.

chaupais[87] in Hindi had designated lengths of each line, e.g., a *doha* had to have to have specific units in each line, usually split between 13 and 11.

For those who are familiar with Greek or Latin poetry a similar principle is followed. English on the other hand depends on accents which is the lilt or slant or roll in the speech usually accompanied by an increased stress or force with which the syllable is enunciated. This is due to the natural genius of the language. Quantity till now has not been used to measure the length of a line in English. It is accent that hitherto has defined the length of a line and its cadence. A line in pentameter would have five accents while tetrameter would have four. A pentametric line that predominantly consists of iambs would be a line in iambic pentameter. The rhythms of English that we enjoy today were developed by monks, chroniclers, romancers, and troubadours, and by a happy coincidence taken up by Chaucer to establish the accentual principle as the key mode of English poetry.

In an extremely important essay 'On Quantitative Meter,' Sri Aurobindo pointed out the reason for the failure in adopting classical Greek and Latin meters to English. He traced the history of such attempts and showed that even great poets such as Spenser and Sidney failed in making quantity as the basis for scansion early on. Later attempts by Tennyson, Longfellow and Clough were stilted and could not naturalize quantitative meter or other classical meters to English. Only Swinburne was able to create sapphics in English that could stand on their own. But even Swinburne's success was an exception rather than the rule. And if even such a great

[87] A quatrain verse of Indian poetry.

prosodist could accomplish rare feats, what hope was there for the other poets far less endowed in mastery of rhythm and sound compared to him?

It seems to me that Sri Aurobindo clearly identified a few cardinal errors with such attempts in the past. First, that English unlike Greek or Latin had an accentual meter and quantity, if imposed based on mere theory, would make the lines sound artificial and fake. Second, the rules of quantity in Greek or Latin did not automatically apply to English, for example, a vowel followed by two syllables does not automatically become a long foot in English. Third, stress could not be abandoned in any kind of prosody in English since stress is an integral part of its meter.

He then suggested that stress along with the quantitative length of a foot be considered an integral part of any consideration of quantity in English since the hammer-stroke of stress is an integral part of its metrics. It is stress that bears the weight of the lighter feet about it and holds the rhythm together. Once this is accepted the problem of quantitative meter in English becomes easier to solve. For whatever theory is offered, it must adhere to the natural genius of the language and not conform to a foreign tongue. And the theory needs to satisfy the ear of the listener and not some arbitrary rules of grammar concocted by theorists.

Sri Aurobindo gave considerable latitude to other elements such as modulations, allowing some feet with intermediate length or stress to be considered as long depending on their ability to bear the weight of the rhythm. And then, he proceeded to show with the help of examples on how his new approach to scansion might work. And that the march and swing of the hexameter is not alien to the genius of the English language.

In a brilliant essay, 'English Hexameter Verse, with a Specimen' published by David Douglas, Edinburgh in 1897, the author Thomas Stewart Omond showed how the hexametric verse in English – which traditionally consists of five dactyls followed by a spondee where the first four dactyls may be replaced by a spondee – is destined for failure since it has been built after alien models. He also noted like Sri Aurobindo that the attempts in the past by great poets and versifiers such as Spenser, Longfellow, Tennyson, and Swinburne to replicate the Greek and Latin models of prosody could never attain the naturalness in English that would help them soar and ascend in a sovereign manner like all great poetry should. The galloping effects of Greek or the oceanic roar and swing of Latin became labored in English, rigid and artificial.

Omond also with the help of examples clarified how the English foot is different from the Greek one; to this I would add, from the Hindi or Bengali one too. English verse cannot be measured by syllables or feet since accent in English is too variable and uncertain, depending often on the speaker, to be able to supply a rigid system of longs and shorts. Nor do we have accurate spondees in English. We need verse that 'sings itself' and not a pedantic, stifling and strangely expedient verse just for the sake of scanning.

Omond proposed that we study what has been done in English in the past to find examples of quantitative meter and he found forty such examples in the Bible. These examples were similar in rhythm to their Greek models but were much freer, suppler, and natural to the genius of the English language. He also proposed that instead of a rigid system of 6 feet in the English hexameter, we adopt a line of six periods. These periods would be "prevailingly dactylic or trochaic in character." The exact feet would be replaced by intonation or cadence of the line, with rapidity of movement and vivid emphasis of accent as the basis. Thus even 4 to 5 syllables could be crowded in a period if necessary and much more license to use redundant syllables at the beginning of a line would be allowed in English. Also, the partition between anapestic and dactylic cadences would be discarded.

Omond prophesized as he concluded his essay that it would take a great poet to confirm that quantitative meter could be adapted and naturalized in English. What is needed is "the sweep and stress of a great poem, compelling the reader's attention, dominating him with the fervor of its thought or passion, fascinating him by the charm of its style and challenging his submission to the witchery of its music." The nerveless dactyls, cantering rather than galloping, with tepid interest for a shallow plot would be replaced by a plastic power and supreme utterance.

So much for theory. Let us look at the examples given by Sri Aurobindo directly and see what we hear and hear what we see:

> Come lovely and soothing death,
>
> Undulate round the world, serenely arriving, arriving,
>
> In the day, in the night, to all, to each,
>
> Sooner or later delicate death…
>
> Approach strong deliveress,

When it is so, when thou hast taken them I joyously sing the dead,

Lost in the loving floating ocean of thee,

Laved in the flood of thy bliss O death....

And the sights of the open landscape and the high-spread sky are fitting,

And life and the fields, and the huge and thoughtful night.

An intense unified movement ready to sweep the Universe in its sustained inspiration, Whitman in 'When Lilacs Last in the Dooryard Bloom'd' above touched at the core of free verse, that which gives it beauty and music despite its apparently loose structure. A powerful dactylic start in lines 1, 2, 3, 7 and 8 brings the gallop and rush that we seek from classical meters. And if we agree with T.S. Omond's views that a dactylic and anapestic meter have fundamentally the same roll of wave if one is not looking at the phonemes with one's eyes alone, then we can hear the effect of his longer sound-units as compared to lines composed solely of iambs and trochees. The point is that the ear is the judge of the rhythm and not the eye and we have to constantly keep reverting to hearing as the final arbiter.

The second example given by Sri Aurobindo of Whitman's powerful innovations is from 'Song of the Broad-Axe':

Weapon, shapely, naked, wan!

Head from the mother's bowels drawn!

Wooded flesh and metal bone! limb only one, and lip only one!

Gray-blue leaf by red-heat grown! helve produced from a little seed sown!

Resting the grass amid and upon,

To be lean'd, and to lean on.

Again, a predominantly trochaic-dactylic meter with the first five lines opening with stressed feet. T.S. Omond proclaimed in 1897 that we are entering the dactylic era and that during the previous thirty years, dactylic meters had come immensely more into favor especially with Swinburne, Tennyson, Morris, Browning and Rossetti. If that is true, then tastes are changing, our ears and the ability of poets are opening to new possibilities. And the iambic-anapestic lines, beautiful and delightful as they are, have a new counterpart in the trochee-dactyl rhythms.

In reviewing the patterns of speech in the prose of Bible and Shakespeare, Sri Aurobindo again finds a quantitative basis, not fixed by a theorist but by the natural cadences of the language:

Consider the lilies of the field, how they grow;

they toil not, neither do they spin:

yet I say unto you, that even Solomon in all his glory

was not arrayed like one of these.

(*Matthew 6: 28-29*)

Similarly, the opening verses of the Sermon on the Mount give us "a sufficient analogy to warrant us in expecting that some such form of structure might find favor with poets" in the future, to paraphrase T.S. Omond. The five lines quoted below enhances the clear guidance of Jesus with a sound-basis that augments his meaning with rhythm as a parallel subliminal movement:

> Blessed are the poor in spirit, for theirs is the kingdom of heaven.
>
> Blessed are those who mourn, for they will be comforted.
>
> Blessed are the meek, for they will inherit the earth.
>
> Blessed are the merciful, for they will be shown mercy.
>
> Blessed are the pure in heart, for they will see God.
>
> (*Matthew 5: 3-8*)

Or, as Sri Aurobindo excerpts from St Paul:

> Though I speak with the tongues of men and of angels, and have not charity,
>
> I am become as sounding brass, or a tinkling cymbal.
>
> And though I have the gift of prophecy,
>
> and understand all mysteries, and all knowledge;
>
> and though I have all faith, so that I could remove mountains,
>
> and have not charity, I am nothing.
>
> (*1 Corinthians 13: 1-2*)

Again, St Paul is as dactylic as can be. If we remove the redundant 'and' at the beginning of lines 3-6, "outside and beyond the regular beat of the verse, but which our ear in reading accepts … almost without notice," as advised by T. S. Omond, the entire passage has a quantitative intonation. Or a soliloquy from Shakespeare's *Hamlet*:

… this goodly frame, the earth, seems to me a sterile

promontory; this most excellent canopy, the air—

look you, this brave o'erhanging firmament, this

majestical roof fretted with golden fire—why, it appears

no other thing to me than a foul and pestilent congregation of vapors.

What a piece of work is a man! How noble in

reason, how infinite in faculty! In form and

moving how express and admirable! In action how like

an angel, in apprehension how like a god! The beauty of

the world. The paragon of animals. And yet, to me,

what is this quintessence of dust?

Why is all this important? For the poet writes not with a theory in mind but with an impulse or inspiration following the thought or the turn of phrase. But a poet might be helped if he had a framework to help for each poet is a critic too. As

Eliot said that a good poet is always conscious where he ought to be. Also, the influence of bad theory cannot be overemphasized. When Sri Aurobindo rejected the fallacy that English quantitative verse must follow the rules of Greek and Latin blindly in designating which foot is long and which is short, he did the poets and critics a great service. Stress may not be ignored in any quantitative verse; his insistence suddenly makes the quantitative verse easier and more possible in English.

Also, he gives an alternate way of scanning English poetry, particularly free verse. He scanned T.S. Eliot's 'Hollow Men' and showed how the best free verse unconsciously and organically follows the framework of quantity:

We are the hollow men

We are the stuffed men

Leaning together

Headpiece filled with straw. Alas!

Our dried voices, when

We whisper together

Are quiet and meaningless

As wind in dry grass

Or rats' feet over broken glass

In our dry cellar

Shape without form, shade without colour,

Paralysed force, gesture without motion;...

The first six lines begin with either a dactyl, trochee or spondee and set the tone for the first section of the poem. Ezra Pound had said in 'A Retrospect' that the desire for vers libre is due to the sense of quantity reasserting itself after years of starvation. He also noted that progress lies rather in an attempt to approximate classical quantitative meters (NOT to copy them) than in a carelessness regarding such things. Here, for once, Pound was right.

Amal Kiran, in one of his brilliant lectures compiled in 'Talks on Poetry', showed that "to appreciate the full value of a vowel in English, we should have to establish a new principle of meter or rather to develop a principle which is latent in the language and unconsciously operative ... yet not openly recognized. The development has been made by Sri Aurobindo in what he called true English quantity." Amal also pointed out the radical breakthrough in practical scansion of poetry with this principle. In English, there can be, technically, alternative scansions. But he believed that "there is always one scansion which is of true help to the significance and the feeling of a line."

He gave the example of a line from Sri Aurobindo such as,

> Measuring vast pain in his immortal mind...

How is one to scan it? Should each foot be comprised of two syllables each, in which case one syllable hangs loose at the end? Or one could keep two syllables in the first foot and assign three to the second, breaking it into "measur" which would be a trochee and "ing vast pain" as the second foot. Or the third choice, to keep three syllables in the first foot as "measuring" which would be a dactyl and the rest of the feet would each comprise of two syllables each. Amal showed how a foot containing one slack and two stresses is not part of normal English prosody and the adjective "vast" was too important to be slurred over with a minor accent in option two. And that "vast pain" should not be divided arbitrarily. The suggestive power of "measuring" is also "maimed when the word is broken up." He suggested that "dactylising the first foot rendered the participle 'measuring' a strong and deep metrical movement which answered to the psychological act expressed." He showed how this also was apt vis-à-vis the spondaic massiveness of the next foot whose verbal significance – "vast pain" – was intended to be both balanced and combated by the verbal significance of the phoneme "measuring." "The scansion has to be in tune with the inspiration and also with the natural reading of the line" particularly as one attempts to decipher "the inner form … We must see closely to its needs when we scan the outer."

Thus, Sri Aurobindo gives us options to scan a line or stanza quantitatively that is organic to the spirit of the English language. He also brings in new feet like the choriamb and makes the spondee more natural and identifiable in English.

Yet, for me, the proof is in the pudding, or, in this case, the hearing. If I had not seen real-life examples and validations of this quantitative theory of Sri Aurobindo, I would have remained unconvinced. But when I hear and see the colors of 'An Image,' a poem in quantitative hexameter (quoted earlier in the book), I am turned into a believer:

> Rushing from Troy like a cloud on the plains the Trojans thundered,

Just as a storm comes thundering, thick with the dust of kingdoms,
Edged with the devious dance of the lightning, so all Troas
Loud with the roar of the chariots, loud with the vaunt and the war-cry,
Rushed from Troywards gleaming with spears and rolled on enormous.
Joyous as ever Paris led them glancing in armour,
Brilliant with gold like a bridegroom, playing with death and the battle
Even as apart in his chamber he played with his beautiful Helen,
Touching her body rejoiced with a low and lyrical laughter,
So he laughed as he smote his foemen. Round him the arrows,
Round him the spears of the Argives sang like the voices of maidens
Trilling the anthem of bridal bliss, the chant hymeneal;
Round him the warriors fell like flowers strewn at a bridal
Red with the beauty of blood.

These fourteen lines prove the case. *Res ipsa loquitur*, the thing speaks for itself, as they say in Latin. Similarly, the sapphics in 'Descent' capture magnificently in sound, form and meaning, a coming down of spiritual power, awareness, and light:

All my cells thrill swept by a surge of splendour,

Soul and body stir with a mighty rapture,

Light and still more light like an ocean billows

Over me, round me.

Similarly, in the alcaics of 'Jivanmukta,' Sri Aurobindo naturalizes another classical rhythm to English without any false poetic diction or padding:

He who from Time's dull motion escapes and thrills

Rapt thoughtless, wordless into the Eternal's breast,

Unrolls the form and sign of being,

Seated above in the omniscient Silence.

Whether one appreciates the mystical experience he is describing, one can appreciate the new rhythms especially with the hexameter and the sapphics. Or these elegiacs in 'Trance of Waiting':

Filled with a rapturous Presence the crowded spaces of being

Tremble with the Fire that knows, thrill with the might of repose.

Or the hendecasyllables of 'Thought the Paraclete' which bring in Catullus into English as no one could before him:

Over world-bare summits of timeless being
Gleamed; the deep twilights of the world-abyss
Failed below. Sun-realms of supernal seeing,
Crimson-white mooned oceans of pauseless bliss...

Sri Aurobindo, being authentic to his experience, is describing only what he saw and felt. That seems to create a difficulty for the lay reader and critic. But, with time, as a closer sympathy with his widened and heightened consciousness grows among our cognoscenti, his innovations in English verse will be more and more appreciated. This is my conviction.

Has the epic prophesied by Omond been created? It seems to me that the fourteen lines of 'An Image' show us a tremendous possibility. The sapphics of 'Descent' validate once more after Swinburne that English can vitalize harmonies from other languages in its own meter and the alcaics of 'Ocean Oneness' confirm this enormous suppleness and richness of English. It is a unique coincidence that Sri Aurobindo's essay 'On Quantitative Hexameter' touched the same challenges as Omond. His conclusions were not the same though in essence he reflected upon the same failures of the past, the errors in approach by even great technicians of the language, and how a new wing to the opulent mansion of English poetry may be added.

It is our tragedy that we must sometimes read western critics to realize our own genius. But if there were a doubt of the great attempt made by Sri Aurobindo and his significant success, it is cleared by reading this remarkable paper published by Omond at the end of the 19th century. And by reading Sri Aurobindo's poems in the new meters.

VII.

The Prose of Sri Aurobindo

1.

The Prose of Sri Aurobindo

It has always been a mystery to me how and why one of the greatest essayists in any language has been ignored by his own country, the critics, and peers for his Himalayan contribution to world prose. Sri Aurobindo is the master stylist in the classical mode along the tradition of Michel de Montaigne, Samuel Johnson or Ralph Waldo Emerson.

Great prose, unlike poetry, relies on certain aspects of cognitive and linguistic expression: coherence, clarity, comprehensiveness, content and, that most unique but definable aspect of prose, a living style. There is much to learn from him especially the manner in which he constructs the thought and builds it up, presenting a proposition and then considering various aspects of it in a dialectic manner, and then finally, reaching a conclusion in an open manner, almost like a synthesis of the contradictory ideas.

One may divide Sri Aurobindo's prose into certain broad categories:

> Essays: By these I mean his larger pieces that are wide in range, detailed in discussion, particular in consideration, and far-reaching in ramification as philosophy, exegesis, historical and literary critique, comparative linguistics and

spirituality. They demand a lot from the reader, a sustained attention and granular focus on each theme as he develops them, but are ultimately extremely rewarding since almost every paragraph in works such as *The Life Divine* or *Essays on the Gita* is a powerful insight, breathtaking and inspirational. In these essays, Sri Aurobindo rises to a level of intensity rarely seen in English and may be considered to have created a kind of poetic prose, rhythmic and grand in harmonies, in philosophic literature.

Micro-Essays: These are usually 300 word-size passionate and poetic 'shorts,' what we might term as blogs in today's journalistic and attention-deficit induced habituation to reading and writing. An example would be *The Hour of God*, a beautiful and inspiring work of couple hundred words.

Letters: The style in his letters, numbering to thousands sent to his disciples, followers, students, admirers or political associates is simpler, more direct and personal, narrow in scope, yet touching on some of the themes that were close to his heart, such as literature, yoga, the future of India and world, and the evolution of humankind. Archivists, even today, are scanning and trying to compile his voluminous writings, trying to organize them and discovering new aspects of his personality that were hitherto unknown to us.

Thoughts and Aphorisms: Sri Aurobindo's aphoristic style is not hermetic but rather, lively, usually paradoxical or humorous, with profound insights into matters human and divine, and are often radically bold and counterintuitive.

Stories: It is a personal regret that Sri Aurobindo did not

> complete his projected series of tales to be called *Idylls of the Occult*. The only completed story, *The Phantom Hour*, is a brilliant work of suspense that develops a misty surreal atmosphere predating modern fiction by decades. It is a Borgesian tale that precedes Borges by decades, but reminds us of his labyrinthine themes of recurrence.

There are very few writers of this expansive creativity that I know of. The only writers or artists I can compare him with of such creative genius, originality, gift of articulation and widest range of themes and genres, would be Vyasa or Valmiki or Shakespeare. No prose-writer in English has written with such perfection and impersonality unless we consider Shakespeare as a writer of prose though, to my mind, he is the pre-eminent poet of English and western literature. English prose-writers, such as Walter Pater, Oscar Wilde, Shaw, tend to seize us more with their force of personality. Samuel Johnson, Emerson, William Hazlitt and Bertrand Russell might be considered to be of his eminence though not of deliberative range and power.

Nor are there writers who have given us not one but several magnum opuses. Here, I can think only of Plato, Shakespeare and Vyasa at this level of productivity and perfection. Sri Aurobindo has given us several masterpieces of prose through the decades that he wrote in a sustained white flame of inspiration. To my mind, his greatest works in prose are *Essays on the Gita*, *The Synthesis of Yoga*, *The Life Divine*, *The Mother* and his innumerable letters.

One criticism that may be applied to Sri Aurobindo's prose that his sentences are long-winding and involved in the longer essay. To me, it seems though that his form is highly fused with the content, so vast is his expanse, and his thought considering every possible nuance of the thesis that the length of the sentences does not jar or seem out of place. The modern reader, more used to Hemingway or Camus with their short sentences, some as long as one word or syllable, may find it laborious to read through Sri Aurobindo's sweeping reach and ability to turn a Universe of proposition into a phrase. But that seems to me more a case of habit and skill in reading rather than a spot in the Sun of his prose. To me, personally, the long sentences are not distracting and rather help in the buildup of the synthesis of the essays.

In the field of philosophy and metaphysics, intricacy is no crime. Camus limits himself to a very narrow realm although he dwells on it insistently. Hemingway's short stories are a great success; it is in his longer prose, that he often begins to fail since his range is restricted by his personality and perceptivity. There are very few writers in English who are truly profound and yet that depth is organic to them and flows naturally. Emerson who has been called an "encumbrance" by T.S. Eliot can be laborious in his writings. Samuel Johnson can be highly erroneous in his judgments, as he was with his strictures on religious poetry and Milton's 'Lycidas.'

Sri Aurobindo wears profundity with ease. There are no affectations or falsettos in his rhetoric. He approaches the subject with impersonality, focused on nothing but the theme and perfection as his mode, without injecting himself into the discussion consistently unlike Wilde or Shaw. The prose is luminous, with a flame not red, fluctuant or explosive, but white, gathered, still and consistent. He does not pronounce his verdicts like Wittgenstein with his *Tractatus*, nor is he dogmatic, pedantic or pedagogic.

T.S. Eliot has a remarkable description of what good writing should be, in 'Little Gidding.' I quote it here as I feel this is perhaps the best description of what Sri Aurobindo's gem-like delighted and delightful *gadya*[88] is:

> ...And every phrase
> And sentence that is right (where every word is at home,
> Taking its place to support the others,
> The word neither diffident nor ostentatious,
> An easy commerce of the old and the new,
> The common word exact without vulgarity,
> The formal word precise but not pedantic,
> The complete consort dancing together)
> Every phrase and every sentence is an end and a beginning,
> Every poem an epitaph.

It may perhaps be said that Sri Aurobindo is the greatest commentator and metaphysician that India has given to the world since Adi Sankara. He ranks higher than Kant, Descartes and Schopenhauer in his conception, symmetry, beauty, logic, systematic methods and depth of vision. Even seventy years after his passing away, India has not been able to match his vigor, clarity and achievement in prose: perhaps only Bankim Chandra Chatterjee, Tagore and Nehru can match his eminence in the last couple of centuries.

---

[88] Prose

It is my fervent hope that in recognizing his genius as a prose-writer, we will not only improve the calibre of our literary criticism but create an opportunity for our young writers to learn from him in how to write and build and perfect the medium to the maximum.

2.

The Story of an Artist as a Young Man

A story may mean various things to various authors. In the hands of a Somerset Maugham, it is all about a happening, a plot, with a start and a finish. While a Chekhov would share a suggestive cross-section or 'slice of life.' To Kafka it is the depiction of psychological reality, more real than the apparent and superficial world. While Borges turns it into a construct, an abstract that might feed on itself and become limitless in labyrinthine possibility.

In recent times, we have seen movements such as magic realism, meta-fiction and post-modernism. Writers such as R.K. Narayan would just leave the reader with a queer enchanted feeling of a nostalgic time or place. Or a Sartre might smash it in our faces with the immediacy of phenomenologic description of experience. Joyce would have his characters have an epiphany about themselves.

A short story is classically defined as a work of prose that one should be able to finish in one sitting, a limitation insisted upon by Edgar Allan Poe in his essay *The Philosophy of Composition*. It may be described as a "connected series of events told with words and images." With the advent of criticism becoming inherent in the creative process, the author may reflect upon the process of writing itself, as in meta-fiction.

Then where does a story begin and where does it end? Perhaps, one could tentatively call it a literary construct that captures a movement in time and space, with the help of characters, usually a plot, perhaps a beginning and an end, held together with a singular awareness. As I write this interpretation, I realize that every word in it may be legitimately contested. In the case of a story, exceptions might prove the rule. What we might agree on is that the story provides tremendous freedom to the author; there are no longer any limits, restrictions, rules or prescriptions. Thus, a story might be a revelation or an experience or an insight or an awareness. Or none of these.

It is in this light that Sri Aurobindo's story *The Phantom Hour* presents a curious case. Written during his early years in Pondicherry between 1910 and 1914, it anticipates the abstract and metaphysical story that came with Borges by more than half a century in some ways. It is a matter of perpetual ruefulness to me that Sri Aurobindo did not write more stories, *The Phantom Hour* being his only completed work in this genre.

Before Munshi Prem Chand and Saadat Hasan Manto became famous in the Indian peninsula as the great story-writers in Hindi or Hindustani, Sri Aurobindo created for us a masterpiece of characterization, atmosphere, intrigue, buildup, suspense and climax. *The Phantom Hour* leaves us poised on a discovery that fulfills us and leaves us athirst, delights and perplexes us at the same time. If there is a master of the occult, without the macabre of Poe or the eeriness of Kipling, I feel it is Sri Aurobindo. Unfortunately, his planned series of tales to be called *The Idylls of the Occult* was never completed. Two other incomplete short stories remain, leaving us wondering with tantalizing conjecture of what could have been.

If the triple movement of James Joyce's short stories in *Dubliners* may be described as paralysis, corruption and death, the schema of *The Phantom Hour* begins with awareness, that becomes an awakening, to finally culminate in action. In that sense, the story in broad terms hints towards the themes that were to preoccupy Sri Aurobindo in his more mature literary works years later. The layer by layer unveiling of consciousness leads to assimilation or integration of the disparate parts of one's being to finally result in a radical ascent, not just individual but collective and gathered in his later poems, essays and letters.

The Phantom Hour begins with the protagonist Sturge Maynard rising from a book, mystic and medieval in epoch and temperament. He is annoyed by the nebulous mysteries and imaginations suggested by the writer until he begins to relate to its suggestions with his own experiences. And he is moved to see the love of his life despite her injunction to not visit her that day. A series of events, perhaps orchestrated by a daemon, along with inner realizations and remembrances of a past life, transform his original uneasiness into a settled insight. The denouement of the story, at once resolving his original perplexity and his 'hallucinations,' is a happy end and yet another opening. I leave it to the reader to decide if this story is enjoyable or satisfying, but I consider the only story that Sri Aurobindo wrote as a mature work, complete in itself, embodying in miniature his future evolution as a giant of Indian literature.

As an artist, in his early years, Sri Aurobindo attempted various forms to manifest his creative demiurge. He experimented with drama, aphorisms and the story. It seems that he found the essay and poetry to be more suitable for his purpose, to educate and awaken a great civilization to its own true potential and to articulate his realizations in genres more conducive to expression and sharing. He also did not pursue literature for literature's sake, just to be famous as a literary figure. And passed on the easier venues for challenges of a more complex and difficult nature.

VIII.

Sri Aurobindo, the Future of India

1.

The Uttarpara Speech

If there is one speech that every Indian must read, and not once but again and again, it is Sri Aurobindo's speech in Uttarpara on May 30, 1909, after his release from Alipore Jail. It is, in my opinion, greater in significance for the nation than Nehru's 'Tryst with Destiny' or Gandhi's Ahmedabad trial in 1922 where he 'plead guilty' to the Chauri Chaura incident. And it is equal in relevance to some of the greatest speeches that changed the world in modern times, including Churchill's "blood, toil, tears and sweat" and Roosevelt's "a date that shall live in infamy" or Swami Vivekananda's speech in the Chicago Conference of Religions in 1892.

Why is that so? Because a speech is great when it expresses a truth in simple language. When it accomplishes what decades or centuries of strenuous effort could not do. When it awakens men to look up to the sky and dream of their own possibilities and of their nation. When it encompasses in a few words what libraries cannot hold.

Sri Aurobindo, I believe, initiated the Indian renaissance with this eloquent recounting of his revolutionary transformation during one year of solitary confinement in the harshest of conditions. He spoke on invitation to the 'Society for the Protection of Religion.' Inspiration flowed from his words to light up the entire nation, not in a vital conflagration, but in the quiet but intense flame of a yogi of Vedic times. Words that once spoken decide the fate of a people, no matter how long it takes, or how difficult the journey. It is the *tathastu*[89] that our seers uttered and whatever they pronounced was done. *Kala*[90] itself would then be only an unfolding of the divine directive that had been given.

"The best speech is one that may not mark a great event", as Simon Sebag Montefiore points out in *Speeches that Changed the World*, but may itself become the event. The splendor of such a speech is its great clarity, rigor, moral or spiritual strength that captures the essence of a great civilization or humanity itself.

Before the Uttarpara there might have been confusion about what the Indian struggle of Independence meant or what Hinduism was. After its articulation, a direction and meaning had been given to both. A word had been spoken to the nation. And the entire significance of *swarajya*, while immensely valuable in itself, had been enlarged to include all humanity and earth. Religion had been defined as that which is universal and eternal and the only nationalism possible to an Indian was to realize and practice Sanatana Dharma.

And he said, without affectation, as someone who carries a golden ember in his heart, that he shares with all,

> ... as I sat here, there came into my mind a word that I have to speak to you, a word that I have to speak to the whole of the Indian Nation. It was spoken first to myself in jail and I have come out of jail to speak it to my people ... When I went to jail the whole country was alive with

[89] So be it.

[90] Evolving time

> the cry of Bande Mataram, alive with the hope of a nation, the hope of millions of men who had newly risen out of degradation. When I came out of jail I listened for that cry, but there was instead a silence.
>
> A hush had fallen on the country and men seemed bewildered; for instead of God's bright heaven full of the vision of the future that had been before us, there seemed to be overhead a leaden sky from which human thunders and lightning rained. No man seemed to know which way to move, and from all sides came the question, "What shall we do next? What is there that we can do?

A country that had been enslaved for centuries, that had lost its vitality along with its faith in itself, had forgotten itself, robbed of its most precious inheritance of a universal and eternal *darshana*, was ready to awaken to its own *dharma* and truth. And Sri Aurobindo spoke as the prophet of what India means to the world of the future and why it is important not just for itself but for the entire globe.

> … you of Uttarpara who are the first to welcome me, not at a political meeting but at a meeting of a society for the protection of our religion … I knew I would come out. The year of detention was meant only for a year of seclusion and of training. How could anyone hold me in jail longer than was necessary for God's purpose? He had given me a word to speak and a work to do, and until that word was spoken I knew that no human power could hush me, until that work was done no human power could stop God's instrument, however weak that instrument might be or however small. Now that I have come out, even in these few minutes, a word has been suggested to me which

> I had no wish to speak. The thing I had in my mind He has thrown from it and what I speak is under an impulse and a compulsion.

Mark Antony could not have constructed it better in Shakespeare's *Julius Caesar*. For it is a masterpiece of rhetoric, structure and composition. And he laid it out in front of the ten thousand or so people listening to him with pin-drop silence.

> I remembered then that a month or more before my arrest, a call had come to me to put aside all activity, to go in seclusion and to look into myself, so that I might enter into closer communion with Him. I was weak and could not accept the call. My work was very dear to me and in the pride of my heart I thought that unless I was there, it would suffer or even fail and cease; therefore, I would not leave it. It seemed to me that He spoke to me again and said, "The bonds you had not the strength to break, I have broken for you, because it is not my will nor was it ever my intention that that should continue. I have had another thing for you to do and it is for that I have brought you here, to teach you what you could not learn for yourself and to train you for my work."
>
> Then He placed the Gita in my hands. His strength entered into me and I was able to do the *sadhana* of the Gita. I was not only to understand intellectually but to realise what Sri Krishna demanded of Arjuna and what He demands of those who aspire to do His work, to be free from repulsion and desire, to do work for Him without the demand for fruit, to renounce self-will and become a passive and faithful instrument in His hands, to have an

> equal heart for high and low, friend and opponent, success and failure, yet not to do His work negligently.

In a few simple lines, he had compressed the message of the Gita. And he builds on it,

> ...I realised what the Hindu religion meant. We speak often of the Hindu religion, of the Sanatana Dharma, but few of us really know what that religion is. Other religions are preponderatingly religions of faith and profession, but the Sanatana Dharma is life itself; it is a thing that has not so much to be believed as lived ... This is the *dharma* that for the salvation of humanity was cherished in the seclusion of this peninsula from of old. It is to give this religion that India is rising. She does not rise as other countries do, for self or when she is strong, to trample on the weak. She is rising to shed the eternal light entrusted to her over the world. India has always existed for humanity and not for herself and it is for humanity and not for herself that she must be great. Therefore, this was the next thing He pointed out to me. He made me realise the central truth of the Hindu religion.

It may perhaps have been better if I had offered no commentary here but excerpted the entire speech. As a literary device, there could not be a more eloquent discourse, yet every word was heart-felt, lived and true to the speaker.

> I had left it to him (the lawyer) and he took it entirely into his hands, with what result you know. I knew all along what He meant for me, for I heard it again and again, always I listened to the voice within; "I am guiding, therefore fear not. Turn to your own work for which I

> have brought you to jail and when you come out, remember never to fear, never to hesitate. Remember that it is I who am doing this, not you nor any other…
>
> Therefore whatever clouds may come, whatever dangers and sufferings, whatever difficulties, whatever impossibilities, there is nothing impossible, nothing difficult. I am in the nation and its uprising and I am Vasudeva, I am Narayana, and what I will, shall be, not what others will. What I choose to bring about, no human power can stay.

And then the human touch, the simple cry of the soul, the tender moment that makes us realize that he was human too like all of us, who rose to the greatest heights of purity with intense love for his people and his land. And he said,

> Then I found myself among these young men (who were in the jail with him) and in many of them I discovered a mighty courage, a power of self-effacement in comparison with which I was simply nothing. I saw one or two who were not only superior to me in force and character – very many were that, – but in the promise of that intellectual ability on which I prided myself.
>
> He said to me, "This is the young generation, the new and mighty nation that is arising at my command. They are greater than yourself. What have you to fear? If you stood aside or slept, the work would still be done. If you were cast aside tomorrow, here are the young men who will take up your work and do it more mightily than you have ever done. You have only got some strength from me to speak a word to this nation which will help to raise it."

And then, again the personal element,

> I realised in the mind, I realised in the heart, I realised in the body the truths of the Hindu religion … When I first approached Him, it was not entirely in the spirit of the *Jnani* … I hardly had a living faith in Him. The agnostic was in me, the atheist was in me, the sceptic was in me and I was not absolutely sure that there was a God at all … So when I turned to the Yoga and resolved to practise it and find out if my idea was right, I did it in this spirit and with this prayer to Him, "If Thou art, then Thou knowest my heart. Thou knowest that I do not ask for *Mukti*, I do not ask for anything which others ask for. I ask only for strength to uplift this nation, I ask only to be allowed to live and work for this people whom I love and to whom I pray that I may devote my life."

The most intimate secrets were shared not as confession or with pride, but as simple statement of facts and perhaps even lessons in how to approach the Divine in our lives. And he shared with us what he heard in the clear austerity of his heart, the word of Narayana,

> Something has been shown to you in this year of seclusion, something about which you had your doubts and it is the truth of the Hindu religion. It is this religion that I am raising up before the world, it is this that I have perfected and developed through the *rishis*, saints and avatars, and now it is going forth to do my work among the nations. I am raising up this nation to send forth my word. This is the Sanatana Dharma, this is the eternal religion which you did not really know before, but which I have now revealed to you.
>
> When it is said that India shall expand and extend herself, it is the Sanatana Dharma that shall expand and

extend itself over the world. It is for the Dharma and by the Dharma that India exists. To magnify the religion means to magnify the country … the protection of the religion, the protection and upraising before the world of the Hindu religion, that is the work before us. But what is the Hindu religion? What is this religion which we call Sanatana, eternal? It is the Hindu religion only because the Hindu nation has kept it, because in this Peninsula it grew up in the seclusion of the sea and the Himalayas, because in this sacred and ancient land it was given as a charge to the Aryan race to preserve through the ages.

But it is not circumscribed by the confines of a single country, it does not belong peculiarly and for ever to a bounded part of the world. That which we call the Hindu religion is really the eternal religion, because it is the universal religion which embraces all others. If a religion is not universal, it cannot be eternal. A narrow religion, a sectarian religion, an exclusive religion can live only for a limited time and a limited purpose. This is the one religion that can triumph over materialism by including and anticipating the discoveries of science and the speculations of philosophy.

It is the one religion which impresses on mankind the closeness of God to us and embraces in its compass all the possible means by which man can approach God. It is the one religion which insists every moment on the truth which all religions acknowledge that He is in all men and all things and that in Him we move and have our being. It is the one religion which enables us not only to understand and believe this truth but to realise it with every part of our being. It is the one religion which shows the world what the world is, that it is the *Lila* of Vasudeva. It is the one religion which shows us how we can best play our part in that *Lila*, its subtlest laws and its noblest rules.

> It is the one religion which does not separate life in any smallest detail from religion, which knows what immortality is and has utterly removed from us the reality of death.

And there you have it. The *dharma* described by a *brahma-gyani* in lucid crystalline prose, such as would make a Nabokov or Joyce proud.

And he ended with a masterly flourish, such that Cicero, Jefferson or Lincoln would have topped with,

> …this movement is not a political movement and that nationalism is not politics but a religion, a creed, a faith. I say it again today, but I put it in another way. I say no longer that nationalism is a creed, a religion, a faith; I say that it is the Sanatana Dharma which for us is nationalism. This Hindu nation was born with the Sanatana Dharma, with it it moves and with it it grows. When the Sanatana Dharma declines, then the nation declines, and if the Sanatana Dharma were capable of perishing, with the Sanatana Dharma it would perish.
>
> This is the message that I have to speak to you.

In one stroke, an entire civilization's philosophy, theology, culture and ideals had been presented to the nation that was once again stirring from darkest inertia. As if the gospel had been spoken or the lotus *sutra* passed down with a single gesture to the humblest and the simplest of his people.

2.

Sri Aurobindo and the Indian Literary Awakening

The Indian literary renaissance is not over. It has barely begun. If we look back at its golden age when it produced some of the greatest works of world literature, we identify not a single author but several, including the Vedic *rishis*, Valmiki, Ved Vyasa, and an illustrious line of poets, philosophers, critics, grammarians, linguists, and commentators in its thousand languages and dialects. We also note a tremendous culture of self-development and refinement without which no renaissance is possible.

It is my opinion that India will return to a greater literary output with increased puissance, self-confidence, impact on world culture and literature, and wideness of scale and reach. That the veins of its golden riches are yet overflowing and opulent. Sri Aurobindo in a unique way created new lines of development and thought on a broad scale and initiated a movement of adherence to the genius of India among our writers, poets and thinkers while being forward-looking and modern. He emphasized the need for discovering our sanskriti and living by it. He is not the cause of our renaissance – no one person can ever be, nor is that my thesis

– but he is a representative man, embodying the dawn of a new age of *kavya* and *sahitya* for India.

Sri Aurobindo transformed our outlook and understanding of Indian spirituality, including its two salient darshanas, Vedanta and Tantra, and showed us that spirituality is not an ossified state but a dynamic ever-evolving enlargement, deepening and heightening. He stood up for India and advocated a *swarajya* not only in self-government and polity but also in our articulation and expressions of our most unique identity.

It may be argued that his influence was minuscule and scant and that most Indians barely knew him when he was alive. But the evidence is to the contrary. For literary influences are subtle movements in the subterranean body of any society and artesian springs may burst after long years of waiting. It seems to me that his contribution towards India's transformation is finally being recognized and will be seen in full display over the years to come.

He must be credited for anticipating several movements in literature, including *The Future Poetry*, the limitations of translation, research in linguistics, and phonology of languages in India and their close relationship with other European languages and a return of Indian writers to our own themes, motifs, and symbology.

Whether he contributed as a central figure in India's decisive turn to *swarajya* is no longer a matter of debate due to advances in our research and the extensive material available that confirms so. It seems to me that his presence at a crucial time of India's struggle to discover its own identity made it possible for her to begin looking at her own *svadharma* and *svabhava*[91].

Sri Aurobindo lived many lives in one, as a prophet, a visionary, a littérateur par excellence, a nationalist, cultural and educational innovator, scholar, and yogi. But when we just look at his literary contributions, here too we find that he lived many lives in one: as a poet, philosopher, aphorist, playwright, writer of essays, stories and letters, translator, linguist, and critic.

His contribution to the translation of our *srutis*, the Vedas and Upanishads and the Gita, turned India from Sankara's Universal Illusionism to his own Universal Realism in Vedanta. He brought together a unique synthesis of Vedanta and Tantra in an integral and practical system and darshana. His contribution towards the spiritual resurgence of India is monumental and seismic, which is the key reason why India is free in principle from foreign domination in thought, art, and literature and free to create its own destiny.

When we look at the European Renaissance, we come across the revitalizing of spirit across its societies, nation-units, and cultures. Leonardo Da Vinci was a central figure who epitomized the power of invention, beauty of mind, body and spirit, and incredible curiosity and joy of exploration of multiple fields of human endeavor, as Walter Isaacson has shown in his biography *Leonardo Da Vinci*. By him bearing the flame of human ingenuity in various avatars as painter and sculptor, engineer and biologist, architect and astronomer, a new possibility was created for earth in the next stage of its evolution. To me, Sri Aurobindo seems to be a

[91] *Svabhava* literally means "own-being" or "own-becoming". It is the intrinsic nature, essential nature or essence of beings. (Taken from Wikipedia)

similar incarnation of an ancient wisdom finding new body in modern times.

It is also instructive to see how Sri Aurobindo interacted with other great literary figures of his age even while in seclusion, advanced them, and supported them in the shared ideals they had. He worked ceaselessly for fundamental solutions to the challenges that India faced in its march towards self-sufficiency and self-reliance. This perhaps is his greatest contribution, his indisputable love for India manifest in everything he did, as he aspired for the highest flowering of its inherent genius. To me, he is the brightest confirmation that the spirit of India is alive and has lost none of its original vitality. And is ready for another awakened age after shedding the dead and dry exoskeleton of the past in its metamorphosis.

Suggested Reading

1. Amal Kiran *Talks on Poetry*
2. Bryan Magee *The Story of Philosophy: The Essential Guide to the History of Western Philosophy*
3. *Complete Works of Sri Aurobindo*
4. *Complete Works of the Mother*
5. Ezra Pound *ABC of Reading*
6. Harold Bloom *All his books*
7. Samuel Taylor *Coleridge Selected poems and prose*
8. Stephen Law *The Great Philosophers: The Lives and Ideas of History's Greatest Thinkers*
9. TS Eliot *Selected Essays*
10. T.Z. Lavine *From Socrates to Sartre: The Philosophic Quest*
11. Walter Kaufman *Nietzsche: Philosopher, Psychologist, Antichrist*

Index

A

Abbey Theater. *See* Irish Dramatic Society
Abrahamic theology, 81, 82
Abstract thinking and mathematics, 67–68
Absurdist Theater, 261
Accent in English, 158, 163, 167, 215, 219, 221, 313, 328, 330, 331, 338
Accentual meter, 329
Accentual principle, 328
Adharmik, 19
Advaita Vedanta, 37
Advent, 6
'Aedh Tells of the Rose in his Heart,' 240
"Affective exuberance of sound," 226
'A God's Labor,' 125–129, 168
  comparison with Shelley's poem, 125–126
  expressions of self-giving love, 128–129
  focused on spiritual journey, 127, 128
  focused on yogic sadhana, 127–128
  sweet and still lines from, 125
Ahmedabad trial of Gandhi, 357
Alcaics, 123, 153–154, 158
  of 'Jivanmukta,' 340
  of 'Ocean Oneness,' 341
Alienation, 86, 89
Allegory of Cave, 68
'Anahata.' *See* 'Chaitya purusha'
Analects of Confucious, 278

Anandamaya, 67
Anapestic meter, 332
Ancient Hindu concept of ages, 51
Ancient India, 20–22, 24, 36, 45, 50, 67, 126, 222, 313
Ancient writings of Vedas, 232
Andromeda, 257, 259
A New Earth, 55
Anglo-Saxon harmonies of English, 173
'An Image,' 156–158, 164, 219
Anirvacaniya. *See* indescribable
Annihilation, 115
Anticipation, 74, 96, 114
Antony, Mark, 360
Aphorisms, 22–23, 271–279, 346. *See also* Sri Aurobindo
  aphoristic prose, 276
  books of, 278
  colloquy at Kurukshetra, 275
  concision of, 274
  on divine love, 274
  empirical test of, 275
  esoteric, 278–279
  exile of Krishna in *Brindavan,* 275
  on God and Divine, 272–273, 277
  life and crucifixion of Christ, 275
  on nature, 271–272
  parables of God's, 273
  siege of Troy, 275
  style of, 276
  On Thoughts and Aphorisms, 271
Aporia, 98–99
'Apparuit,' 151–152
Archer, William, 321
Argumentative Indian, The, 309
Arjuna, 19–20, 284, 285, 360
Art of Aphorism, The, 275

Art of Reading Poetry, The, 264
Arya, 29, 249, 276
Asiatic immensities, 17
Assonances, 132, 196, 215, 247, 304, 313
A Theory of Aphorism—From Confucius to Twitter, 274
At the Existentialist Café, 44–45

B

'Baji Prabhou,' 174–178, 219, 235
  comparison with national poems, 176—177
  difficulty in writing, 174, 175
  fierce patriotism depicted in, 174, 177, 202–204
  integrity and perfection, 176
  landscape of, 201–202
  sublime theme, 204
Bakewell, Sarah, 44
Bande Mataram, 243
Barfield, Owen, 265, 299
Bauls, 15, 144
'Because Thou Art,' 227
Beckett, Samuel, 8, 16, 135, 261
Beerbohm, Max, 279
Being and Nothingness, 57
Being and Time, 22, 103, 104
"Being," Sri Aurobindo's description of, 22
Bengali renaissance, 246
Berlin, Isaiah, 123
Bhagavad Gita, 19, 21–22, 46, 109, 144
Bhakti-marga, 15
Bharatavarsha, 15
Bhartrihari, 301
Bhashya
  definition of, 283
  Essays on the Gita, 284–286

stances, 283
Bible, 164, 169, 195, 267, 330, 333
Binaries, 95
Blank verse, 9, 27, 122, 123, 171, 174–175, 179, 195, 219–220, 221, 256
development of, 210–211, 235
disadvantages of, 213
Eliot's views on, 212–213
escaping shackles of past in, 201
requirements of recovering, 214–216
Blood-consciousness, 58
Bloom, Harold, 7–8, 135, 185, 217, 264, 310
Bondage, 69
Bottomley, Gordon, 309
Brahma-gyani, 365
Brahman, 38, 117
Indian conception of, 65
understanding of, 93
Buber, Martin
attempt to bring God into equation of I-Thou, 114–115
Ich and Du (I and Thou) and, 114
I-Thou relationship and, 113–114
vedantic realization, 115–116
Buddha, 63, 99
Buddhism, 77–78, 103
Buddhist view of life, 77
'Burnt Norton,' 42

C

Caesura, 177, 196, 215
Canonical literature, 276
Canonical writers, 7–8
'Cantos, The,' 148
Catullan Hendecasyllables, 171

Catullus, Gaius, 149
Chaitanya, 262
'Chaitya purusha,' 126
Chaupais in Hindi, 328
Chitta. *See* Consciousness
Christ, 49, 65, 83, 128, 143, 229, 275
Christianity, 113
Classical meters, 327–328, 332
Classical poetry, 155, 158
Classical rhythm, 340
Classic and the Romantic in Literature, The, 254
Classic, definition of, 123
Cocq, Rhoda P. le, 49, 61–62, 104
Coleridge, 171, 179, 314
Colloquy at Kurukshetra, 275
Colonialism of geography, 78
Community, 19–20, 58, 68, 86
Comparative philology, 299
Compassion, 57, 106, 128
Composition of Four Quartets, The, 188
Conception of God, 277
Consciousness, 11, 38, 41, 45–47, 54–59, 56, 57–58, 60, 63, 72–73, 82, 88–89, 94, 98, 102–103, 107, 111, 137, 146, 178, 215, 241, 258, 263–265, 264–265, 267, 274, 278, 286, 299, 320, 353
  concept of intentionality, 46–47
  Husserl's pursuit to study, 45–46
Consciousness-Force, 87
Contemplative piety, 143
Creative demiurge, 354
Creative Evolution, 50
Cuckold, 8
Cummings, E.E., 148

D

Dactylic, 158, 164, 169, 331–332, 335
Dactylic meters, 333
Dactyls, 130–131, 148–149, 153, 155, 158, 164, 171, 189–190, 330, 337–338
Darshana, 19, 20, 29, 36–37, 40, 46–48, 95, 108, 122–123, 258, 264, 286, 292–293, 324, 368
Darshanik, 18, 40, 47, 79, 97, 101, 217–218
Dasein, 102–103
Deconstruction, 20, 40, 96, 99, 102
De-identification process, 99
Derrida, a Biography, 95, 99
Derrida, Jacques, 6, 95–97, 99, 102, 115
Descartes, 45, 55, 80, 103, 349
'Descent,' 5, 147–152, 219, 339–340, 341
Descriptive phenomenology, 45
Devotional poetry, 220, 224
  'Because Thou Art,' 227
  categories of, 224–225
  'Collar, The,' 227–228
  'Golden Light, The,' 228
  'Jordan I,' 229
  'Love (III)', 226–227
  secular's views on, 225–226
  strictures against, 230
  'Word of the Silence, The,' 229–230
Devotional poets, 224–230
Dharma, 19, 30–31, 57, 232–233, 284–285, 294, 298, 313, 315, 323, 359, 361, 364, 365
Dhyana, 47, 102, 266
Diachrony, 97
diCesare, Mario A, 228

Divine, 20, 24, 64–65, 81, 83, 88–89, 117, 143, 161, 190, 193, 204, 225–227, 241, 267, 272–273, 275, 285, 297, 346, 358, 363
Divine Hearing, The, 142–146
Divine Lila, 65
Divine Word, 238
Divinity, 72, 117
Doha in Hindi, 32–328
Donne, John, 145–146, 220, 224, 254, 264
'Do not go gentle into the good night,' 153
Doors of Perception, The, 111
Douglas, David, 330
Dramas, 17, 125, 217–218, 221, 252, 257, 261–263, 276, 309, 322–326
"Dramatic Romance," 249
Drishta, 40–41
Dryden, John, 230, 288, 314
Dubliners, 353
Dukkha samsara, 19
Dun Emer Press, 232

E

Ear, 36, 80, 144, 164, 213, 219, 234, 312, 329, 332, 335
Earth Has a Soul, The, 50
Eastern darshana, 47, 109
Eastern philosophy, 78
Education system of Thomas Babington Macaulay, 232, 247–248
Ego, 41, 45, 55, 57, 113
Einstein, Albert, 68, 82, 86, 146
Elegiacs, 168, 327, 340
'Elegy Written in a Country Churchyard,' 159
Eliot, T.S., 7, 42, 102, 122–123, 130, 147, 151, 153, 156, 166, 168, 181, 185, 187–188, 196, 203–204, 210,

212, 214, 215, 224, 225, 235, 256, 257, 288, 291, 312, 314–315, 317, 336, 348
critical review of Milton, 214
on "dissociated sensibility" of Milton, 204
on good writing, 349
on Herbert's authenticity, 225
memorial lectures on Yeats, 241
on Pound's translation, 291
thrilled at stripping away of adjectives, 203
Elizabethan drama, 224, 257, 304–305
Emerson, 218, 347–348
Empson, William, 314
Emptiness, 99, 139, 271
"Encumbrance," 291, 348
English foot *vs.* Greek foot, 330
'English Hexameter Verse with a Specimen,' 157, 167, 330
English literary development, 23
English literature, 9, 106, 125, 141, 217, 225, 231, 309, 316, 324
English poetry, 23, 122–123, 148, 158, 164, 166, 182, 186, 206, 219–220, 225, 310, 313, 315, 317, 328, 336, 341
challenge of writing long poems in, 166
Sri Aurobindo's contributions to, 219–220
English poetry criticism, 309–312
by Bloom, 311
by Bottomley, 309
Celtic and Indian poets, emergence of, 315
Chaucer's work, 313
Coleridge's work, 314
by Eliot, 312–314, 317
by Empson, 314
historical dimension to, 317
Milton's work, 314

by Nuttall, 314
richness and power of expression, 315
Romantic revolution, 314
Shakespeare's work, 313
by Sri Aurobindo, 310–312, 315–317
vital crudeness, 316
Wordsworth's work, 314
English prosody, 219, 221, 242, 247, 327, 338
English quantitative verse, 336
English quantity, 337
English verse, 17, 23, 123, 167–169, 216, 219, 230, 234, 315, 327, 330, 341
history of, 23
innovations in, 341
newer trends in, 234–235
quantitative meter potential value to, 327
true unit of, 167
Epic poetry, 163
Esoteric mysticism, 225
Essays, 58, 62, 102, 167–168, 192, 214, 233, 241, 254, 257, 264–265, 271, 275, 284, 293, 302, 312, 319, 328, 331, 346–348, 351, 353–354
Essays on the Gita, 17, 21, 284–286, 293, 346
Essential Husserl, The, 47
Eternal life, 42
Eternally unchanging principle, 94
Eternal recurrence, 51
Eternal stability and eternal change, 66
Ethics, 42, 53, 68, 71, 78, 286, 290, 321–322
Etymology, 97, 292, 296
European mysticism, 94
European mythos, 258
European philosophical tradition, general characterization of, 67
Exile of Krishna, in *Brindavan,* 275

Existence-Consciousness-Bliss, 97–98
Existentialism, 22, 56–57, 59, 64, 102
Experience and intellect, 98
Eyeless in Gaza, 106–108, 274

F

Farnaby, William Asquith, 110
Fire, 340
  Heraclitus's concept of, 62
  Sri Aurobindo's concept of, 64
Fitzgerald, Edward, 287
Form poetry, 153
Foundations of Indian Culture, The, 24, 321
Fourth Brandenburg, 110
Fragments, 61–63, 90, 157, 185, 200, 279, 301
Freedom of speech, 81
Free verse, 153–154, 168–169, 332, 336–337
Free will, 74–75, 81, 84
French verse, 147
Frost, Robert, 154, 229
Future Poetry, The, 23, 218, 234, 245, 309–311, 324

G

Gardner, Helen, 188
Genius, 12, 15, 29, 35, 39, 42, 48, 135, 160, 204, 215, 219, 221, 244, 313–315, 330, 341, 350, 369
George Herbert and the Seventeenth- Century Religious Poets, 228
Ghose, Aurobindo. *See* Sri Aurobindo
Gita, 9, 17, 21, 29, 126, 232, 266, 283–285, 286, 291, 293, 296, 301, 346, 347, 360
  bhashya of, 246
  Sri Aurobindo's commentary on, 218

translations and interpretations of, 232
'Gita Govinda,' 322
Gnostic being, 87–88
Gnostic communities, 86–87
Gnostic individual, 87–88
God, 50–51, 60, 63, 65, 73, 80–84, 81–83, 89, 114–115, 117, 125, 127, 129, 143, 150, 161, 164, 168, 170, 187–191, 193, 199, 206, 208, 229, 241, 250–252, 254, 267, 272–275, 277, 279, 314, 323, 334, 346, 359, 363, 364
of Abrahamic religions, 50
anthropomorphic, 89
existence, realization of, 73
priori definition, 115
Sri Aurobindo's concept of, 50–51
Gödel, Kurt, 39
Gopnik, Adam, 275
Gray, Thomas, 159, 314
Great Philosophers, The, 76, 80
Great Tradition, The, 7
Greek, 29, 61–64, 66, 86, 154, 157, 218, 221, 295, 299, 304, 313, 327–330, 336
Latin and Sanskrit, linguistic connections among, 299
and Latin models of prosody, 330

H

Hamlet, 335
Hammer-stroke of stress, 329
Hankins, Luke, 224, 228
Harmony, 15, 19, 48, 57, 61, 87, 124, 154, 234, 251, 259, 264, 265, 288, 304, 305, 346
Haunting verse, 183–186
Hedgehog and the Fox, The, 256
Hegel, 6, 44, 58, 81, 85–89, 104

on anthropomorphic God, 89
and gnostic being, 87–88
individualistic conception of liberation, 86
philosophy of history, 85–86
Heidegger, Martin, 6, 22, 46, 50, 58, 62, 79, 101–105
approach to being, 102
approach to verse, 104–105
association with Nazism, 101
Being and Time, 103, 104
closeness to Indic roots, 104
critiqued Sartre's statement, 102
impressed by Buddhism, 103
on joy and serenity, 105
rejecting Husserl's intentionality of consciousness, 102
turned to poetry, 104
Hemingway, Ernest, 16–17, 148, 174, 348
Hemingway House in Florida Keys, 16
Hendecasyllables, 149, 171, 327, 340–341
'Heraclitus' (essay), 61
Heraclitus of Ephesus, 6, 22, 61–65, 90, 278
condemnation of idol worship, 63
cryptic statements, 62
as destroyer, 64–65
on dry soul, 63
on fire, 62
on nature, 64
on unity of being, 62–63
on unity of opposites, 62–63
Herbert, George, 145, 220, 224
authenticity of, 225
'Collar, The,' 227–228
'Golden Light, The,' 228
'Jordan I,' 229
'Love (III)', 226–227
Hero and the Nymph, The, 218

Heumer, Wolfgang, 220
'He Wishes for the Cloths of Heaven,' 236
Hexameter, 157, 164, 166–167, 169, 213, 330, 340
Hexametric verse in English, 330
'Higher Mind,' 73
Hindi, 247, 327–328, 330, 352
Hindu drama *vs.* Elizabethan drama, 304–305
Hinduism, 15, 77, 297, 358
'Hollow Men,' 336
Holy Quran, 145
Holy Trinity, concept of, 83
Hopkins, Gerald Manley, 224, 225
Hui, Andrew, 274, 277
Humanity, 15, 21, 23, 27, 72, 78, 108–109, 127, 219, 267, 275, 315–317, 358, 361
Human Potential Movement, 108
Human thralldom, 68–69
Husserl, Edmund, 44–47, 45, 50, 58–59, 67, 69, 75, 79, 102
  approach to phenomenology, 44–45
  concept of intentionality, 46
  influence on western philosophy, 46–47
  pursuit to study consciousness, 45–46
Huxley, Aldous, 6, 57, 78–79, 82, 108–109, 274
  contributions to English literature, 106, 111
  on 'dark peace,' 108
  influenced by Murphy, 108
  novel of, 106–108
'Hyperion,' 200, 205

I

Iambic-anapestic lines, 333
Iambs, 332
Ich and Du (I and Thou), 114–115, 117

Idol worship, 64
Idylls of the Occult, The, 353
'I-It' relationship, 113
'Ilion,' 163–169
  basis for writing, 163
  dactylic and trochaic intonation, 164
  naturalness of verse of, 163–164
  sustained intensity, 165–166
'Image, An,' 157, 219, 341
Imagery, 7, 140, 151, 158, 172, 181, 208, 210, 222, 287, 288, 303, 305
'Image, The,' 338–339
Impersonality, 348
Impersonal silence, sense of, 230
Inanimate rock, 77
"Incompleteness theorems," 39
'Incorruptibles,' 99–100
Indescribable, 41
India and the Future, 321
Indian Contribution to English Literature, The, 309
Indian darshana
  lines of, 20
  realization of existence of God, 73
  shoonya poetic description in, 58
Indian English poetry, 122–123
Indian literary renaissance, 366–369
Indian literature, 8, 29, 321–324
  Dravidian languages, 323
  'Gita Govinda,' 322
  historical development, 324
  oceanic mass of, 322
  philosophy, 323
  'Rama Charita Manas,' 322
  Ramayana and Mahabharata, 323
  salient features of, 321

Sanskrit language, 322
Sanskrit literature, 322, 324
songs, 323
Upanishads, 323
Vedas, 323
Indian mythology, 232, 258
Indian myths of creation, 140
Indian philosophy, 17, 298, 321
Indian seerhood, ancient ideal of, 23
Indian spirituality, 18, 20, 21, 284–285, 367
Indic approach of unifying words, 97–98
Indic drama, 304–305
Indic literature, 16, 323
encyclopedic task of putting together, 16
metamorphosis of, 300
subtle body of, 16
Indic narrative, 19
Individual, development of, 47
Individual existence, categorization of, 113
Individual growth, 86
Individualism, 86
Individualistic conception of liberation, 86–87
Individual perfection, 86
'In Horis Aeternum,' 188
Innovations, 148, 158, 195, 341
in English verse, 341
examples of, 331–333
Integral philosophy, 46
Intellect, 35, 61, 98, 106, 257
Intense unified movement, 332
Intentionality, concept of, 46
Intentional phenomenology, 46
In the Lives of the Poets, 143–144
In the Moonlight, 159–162
beginning of, 159

philosophic debate in, 159–160
pungency and metaphysical wit, 161
Intonation, 123, 124, 331, 335
Intuitive illumined states of poetry, 235
Ionesco, Eugene, 109
Irish culture, 231
Irish Dramatic Society, 232
Irish Literary Revival, 231
Irish spirituality, 231
Isha Upanishads, 26, 237, 291, 293
essay on, 94
translation, 301
Islamic poetry, 287

J

Jeffares, A. Norman, 232
Jeffers, Robinson, 178
Jesus, guidance of, 334
Jivanmukta, 5, 153, 155, 219, 340
Johnson, Ben, 221, 256
Johnson, Samuel, 17, 143, 144, 145, 230, 345, 347–348
Joyce, James, 16, 82, 231, 351, 353, 365
Judgment, 73–74, 81, 101–102, 145, 179, 238, 317, 348
Julius Caesar, 360
Jung, Carl Gustav, 50

K

Kala, 86, 358
Kalidasa, 26, 218, 301, 303–305, 322, 324
Kant, Emmanuel, 6, 22, 44, 46, 71, 78, 349
comparison with Sri Aurbindo, 71
faith in philosophy of, 73
on free will, 74

Platonic world of noumenon, 75
"priori" knowledge of mind, 72–73
Transcendental Idealism, 71–72
universal ethical principle, 72
Kantian revolution, 78
Kapila, Sage, 46, 63
Karma kanda, 297–298
Karnad, Girish, 244
Keats, John, 81, 175, 179, 195, 205, 208, 211, 314, 318
appreciation of Milton, 211
on dominion of poetry, 226
epistle to his brothers, 318
'Hyperion,' 200–201
Kena Upanishad, 36, 265, 293, 301
King, Martin Luther, 117
Kiran, Amal, 337–338
Knowledge, 1, 12, 20, 28, 37, 38, 46, 47, 72, 73, 107, 109, 110, 165, 240, 295, 296, 319, 334
Krishna, Lord, 21
Krishnamurti, J., 51, 99, 109, 114, 115, 200

L

'Lake Isle of Innisfree, The,' 235
Language, 17, 30, 31, 36, 39–40, 84, 95, 97, 106, 122–123, 202, 204, 210, 215, 217, 218, 220–222, 247, 255, 258, 291, 296, 299, 300, 302, 305, 311, 312, 316, 320, 328, 329, 331, 333, 337, 341, 345, 357
Lawrence, D.H., 23, 25, 58, 146, 174, 202, 265, 318
Law, Stephen, 76, 77
Learning Organization, 320
'Le Cygne,' 153
Lessing, Gotthold Ephraim, 81–82
Letters, 25, 37, 38, 54, 126, 188, 201, 208, 211, 233–234, 243, 262, 266, 304, 318–320, 346, 353, 368

Letter-writing, 318–320
Life and crucifixion of Christ, 275
Life Divine, The, 9, 17, 18, 20, 82, 84, 87, 108, 218, 246, 256, 258, 286, 292, 293, 296, 346, 347
Light verse. *See* Nonsense poetry
Linguistic and comparative philology
  aporia, 98–99
  deconstruction, 99
  etymology of Sanskrit sounds, 97
  Indic approach of unifying words, 97–98
  oppositions, 98
Linguistics, 30, 97, 241, 292, 293, 318, 367
Literary criticism, 29, 121, 141, 218, 302, 309–312, 315, 350
Literary imperialism, 300
Literary landscape of India
  Himalayan stretch of, 15
  regional literatures, 15
Literature, 1, 8, 15, 16, 23, 25, 27–29, 31, 82, 104, 121–122, 148, 228, 232, 244, 254–255, 258, 289, 294, 301, 309–311, 316, 318–319, 321, 322, 346, 354, 366–368, 373
  aesthetic and moral function of, 8
  purpose of writing, 228–229
'Little Gidding,' 349
Logopoeia, 230
Logos, 62, 65, 292
'Love (III)', 226–227
'Love and Death,' 195, 197–198
Love and Guilt, 226–227
Low, Anthony, 224–225
Ludwig Wittgenstein, The Duty of Genius by, 35, 42
"Luminous bliss," 110
Luminous divine energy, 62
Lyrical Manifesto, 327

M

Macrocosm, 15
Magee, Bryan, 58, 77, 78
Mahabharata, 15, 321, 323
Mahavakya, 273, 278
Maitra, Sisir Kumar, 6
Mallarmé, Stéphane, 147
Mandukya Upanishad, 238–239
Manomaya. *See* mind
Mantra, 23, 97, 104, 264–267, 297, 311–312, 315
Marlowe, 205, 221, 222, 256, 259, 313
Marlowe's drama, 259
Mason, Emma, 226, 230
Mathematics, 39–40, 66, 78, 114
    and abstract thinking, 67–68
Matter, 61, 63, 80, 82–84, 87, 101, 103, 108, 127, 161, 205, 208, 221, 259, 275, 285, 352, 358, 367
Maugham, Somerset, 351
Maya, concept of, 19
McLuhan, Marshall, 257
Meditation, 9, 47, 102, 111, 189, 224, 228, 266, 275, 302
Meeting of East and West in Sri Aurobindo's Philosophy, 6
Meghduta, 303
Melopoeia, 157
Memory, 42, 74, 86, 96, 144, 146, 184, 318
Mental awareness, 58, 59
Mental mastery, 277
Merleau-Ponty, 59
Meta-fiction, 352
Metamorphosis, 8
Metaphysical anti-realism, 99
Metaphysical poetry, 225
Metaphysical statement, 102

Metaphysics, 35, 40, 44, 56, 71, 78, 82, 193, 283, 285–286, 290, 296, 348
Metronome, 110
Micro-essays, 346
Micro-models of empirical inquiry, 278
Miller, Henry, 109
Mill, John Stuart, 278
'Milton,' 154
Miltonic vital energy and Tennysonian false simplicity, difference between, 200
Milton, John, 123, 137, 145, 154, 175, 179, 195, 197–199, 201–205, 207, 209–217, 211, 212, 220, 238, 261, 264, 310, 314, 348
  challenge to future poet, 195, 216
  dedication to life's purpose, 205
  Eliot's essay on, 214
  mighty wall of, 195
  oppressive art of, 202
  'Paradise Lost,' 198–199
  success of, 204–205
Mimesis, 8
Mind, 67, 69, 71
  as one level of consciousness, 73
  "priori" knowledge of, 72–73
  sensory data to, 73
  time in, 74
Mirabai, poetry of, 128
Mishra, Manoj K., 256
Mistral, Gabriela, 218
Moby Dick, 8
Modernist poetry, 23, 202, 310
Modernist verse, 167
Modern linguistic analysis, 95–97
Modern medicine, conundrum of, 114
Modern metaphysics and thought, 323–324

Modern verse, reasons for deterioration of, 154
Modulations, 196, 215, 329
Monism, 84
Monk, Ray, 35
Monotheism, 291
Montefiore, Simon Sebag, 358
Morality plays, 250–251
'Morte d'Arthur,' 200
Movements, 16, 20, 23, 41, 45, 54, 56, 63–64, 85, 93–94, 109–111, 188, 232, 244, 257, 259, 331, 351, 352, 365, 366, 367
Mueller, Max, 115, 295, 300, 301
Murphy, Michael, 108–109
'Musa Spiritus,' 219, 238
Music, 28, 110, 142, 168, 172, 184, 219, 235, 244, 247, 263, 265, 322, 331, 332
Mystical experience, 67, 187, 221, 225, 279, 340
Mystical works of Sri Aurobindo, 236

N

Nada Brahman, 266
Naidu, Sarojini, 122
Nandy, Pritish, 244
Narayan, R.K., 351
Nationalism, 28, 30, 358, 365
National renaissance, 246
Nature, 39, 47, 48, 50, 57, 59, 63, 64, 73, 77, 82, 83, 84, 87, 88, 90, 105, 131, 132, 175, 213, 224, 225, 255, 272, 278, 285, 311, 354, 368
Natya Shastra, 304
Nazism, Heidegger's association with, 101
"Near death experience," 10
"Negative capability," concept of, 318
Neruda, Pablo, 138, 247

New Ways in English Literature, 313
Nietzsche, Friedrich, 48–52
  conception of Supermind, 49
  descendants, 50
  opposition to Darwinian model, 49
  transformation of philosophy, 49–51
'Night by the Sea,' 236–237
'Nirvana,' 39, 130–133, 220
  first and second lines, 131
  octet, 132
  rhyme scheme, 130, 132–133
  sestet, 132
  structure, 130
Noncommercial art, 256
Nonsense poetry, 134
  challenges of writing, 135
  purpose of, 135
Nothingness, 58
Noumenal world, 76–77
Noumenon, 75
Nuttall, A.D., 314

O

Occident, 22
'Ocean Oneness,' 341
Omar Khayyam, 287
Omond, Thomas Stewart, 157, 167, 330–335, 341–342
On Nature, 90
'On Quantitative Meter' on, 327–342
On Thoughts and Aphorisms, 271
Ontology, 42, 50, 53, 58, 101, 103, 292
'On Translating Kalidasa,' 303–304
Oppositions, 85, 95, 96, 98
Orchestral harmonies, 157

Order of Time, The, 74
Orient, 22
Osho Rajneesh, 62

P

Pandemonium, 211
Panpsychism, 83
Pantheism, 83, 143
'Paradise Lost,' 212
  Keats admiring, 208–209
  opening scene of, 206
Parallel subliminal movement, 334
Paramahansa, Ramakrishna, 20
Paranjapc, Paranjape, 222
Parmenides, 90
Parmenides of Elea, 80, 90–94
  as deterministic, 92
  and Heraclitus, 90
  as mystic, 90–91
Pater, Walter, 184
Patient–provider engagement, 113
Peace, 74
Pensees, 273
Perception, 36, 41, 59, 79, 111, 130, 234, 239
Perennial Philosophy, 108–109
Perfect society, 89
Perseus the Deliverer, 257–260
Peters, Benoit, 95
Phantom Hour, The, 352–353
Phenomena, 45–46, 50, 58
Phenomenology, 44–47, 67
Phenomenology of Perception, 59
Philosopher King concept, 68

Philosophy, 2, 6, 7, 12, 18, 20, 29, 31, 35–36, 40, 47, 49, 50, 53–54, 61, 64–65, 68–69, 73, 75, 77, 81, 86, 89–91, 95, 100, 102–104, 121, 220, 231, 278, 286, 287, 289, 290, 292, 296, 302, 317–318, 322, 323, 345, 348, 364, 371, 373
as "disease, a word-game," 40
eastern, 22, 40, 47, 78, 310
sankhya, 45, 46, 54, 74
western, 22, 39, 43, 44, 46, 47, 59, 69, 71, 74, 75, 77, 78, 79, 80, 93, 94, 95, 371
Philosophy of Composition, The, 351
'Philosophy of the Upanishads,' 58
Phonemes, 332
Physical awareness, 59–60
Plato, 6, 44, 66–70, 77, 90, 347
ideal of perfect place, 66–67
mathematical approach of, 67–68
Philosopher King concept, 68
Platonic world of noumenon, 75
Platonism, criticism of, 96
Platonistic hierarchies, 96
Plays by Shakespeare, 259
Plays by Sri Aurobindo
in Elizabethan model, 259
foreignness of symbols in, 258
Indian mythology and symbols in, 258
Perseus the Deliverer, 257–260
'Savitri' as, 261–263
Viziers of Bassora, The, 249–256
Plotinus, 22, 66
Poe, Edgar Allan, 351
'Poem as Devotional Practice, The,' 224
Poems and Ballads, 171
Poetic Diction: A Study in *Meaning,* 265, 299
Poetry of Mirabai, 128

Poetry of Sri Aurobindo, 232
after withdrawal from political life, 241
'A God's Labor,' 125–129, 168
comparison with Shelley's poem, 125–126
expressions of self-giving love, 128–129
focused on spiritual journey, 127, 128
focused on yogic sadhana, 127–128
sweet and still lines from, 125
'An Image,' 156–158
'Baji Prabhou,' 174–178, 235
comparison with national poems, 176—177
difficulty in writing, 174, 175
fierce patriotism depicted in, 174, 177, 202–204
integrity and perfection, 176
landscape of, 201–202
sublime theme, 204
contributions to English poetry, 219–220
'Descent,' 147–152
comparison with sapphics by Swinburne, 149–150
sapphics in, 148, 152
devotional and religious, 220
Divine Hearing, The, 142–146
Future Poetry, The, 234
harmony and intonation, 123, 124
'Ilion,' 163–169
basis for writing, 163
dactylic and trochaic intonation, 164
naturalness of verse of, 163–164
sustained intensity, 165–166
importance of studying, 121–123
'In Horis Aeternum,' 188
intuitive illumined states of, 235
Jivanmukta, 155
'Love and Death,' 195, 197–198
In the Moonlight, 159–162

beginning of, 159
philosophic debate in, 159–160
pungency and metaphysical wit, 161
Musa Spiritus', 238
'Nirvana,' 130–133, 220
first and second lines, 131
octet, 132
rhyme scheme, 130, 132–133
sestet, 132
structure, 130
nonsense poetry/light verse, 134
challenges of writing, 135
purpose of, 135
'On Quantitative Meter' on, 327–342
refining, 161–162
Rose of God, 187–194, 240–241
'Savitri,' 123, 237
'Sea at Night, The,' 236
Self's Infinity, The, 136–138
'Shiva,' 140–141
spiritual, 224
'Thought the Paraclete,' 170–173
'Urvasie,' 180–182, 195–197, 305
Vigil of Thaliard, The, 183–186
vision and clarity of perception, 235
on yogic experiences, 123
Point Counterpoint, 108
Pondicherry, India, 17
Popper, Karl, 141
Possibility of a Poetic Drama, The, 257
Pound, Ezra, 102, 211, 287, 298, 336–337
Prakriti, 45, 94
Pranamaya. *See* Vital
Prayers and Meditations, 302
Pre-reflective consciousness, 54–55, 57

Prières et Méditations, 301–302
Priori knowledge
of mind, 72–73
of time, 74
Prose of Sri Aurobindo, 345–350
aspects of, 345
categories of, 345–346
criticism of, 347–348
gadya, 349
luminous, 348
masterpieces of, 347
perfection and impersonality of, 347
Prosody, 158, 173, 219, 221, 226, 242, 247, 327, 338
'Psyche,' 126
Public debate and discourse, 309
Pudding, 338
Pure awareness. *See* Purusha
Purusha, 45, 55, 63, 74, 88, 94
"Putrescent" and "pismires," 161

Q

Quantitative hexameter, 9, 122, 157, 163, 169, 327, 331, 338
Quantitative intonation, 335
Quantitative meters, 140–141, 157, 302
adapted in English, need for, 331
cardinal errors with attempts linked with, 329
classical, 337
definition of, 327
examples in Bible, 330–331
fixed by natural cadences of language, 333
hexameter, 330
and modulations, 329
reasons for failure in adopting, 328

  stress along with, 329
  theory on, 140, 329, 331

R

Radhakrishnan, S., 35
Radical Thinkers: Heidegger and Sri Aurobindo, The, 61–62, 104
Ragas, 263, 266
Ramakrishna Mission, 20
Ramayana, 7, 15, 321, 323
Rationality and knowledge, 73
Records of Yoga, 111
Religion, 28, 49, 51, 54, 78, 89, 143, 145, 254, 272, 323, 324, 357, 358, 359, 361, 363, 364, 365
Religious poetry, 220
Religious verse, 143, 145
Res ipsa loquitur, 339
Rhythm, 130–131, 148–151, 155, 157–158, 164, 167–168, 177, 181, 183, 186, 188, 189, 193, 196, 204, 206, 210, 212, 213, 220, 234, 247, 265, 287, 292, 302, 311, 312, 319–320, 327–330, 332, 334
  classical, 340
  inspired, 235, 264
  masculine, 177
  Sanskrit, 26
Ringers in the Tower: Studies in Romantic Tradition, The, 185
Rolland, Romain, 219
Root sounds, 97
Rose of God, 187–194, 240–241
Rossetti, Christina, 224
'Rubaiyat,' 287
Russel, Bertrand, 67

S

Samadhi, 47
Sanatana Dharma, 19, 28, 50–51, 298, 361
Sankhya, 20, 22, 46, 94
Sankhya philosophy, 54–55, 74
Sannyasa, 18–19
Sanskrit chhanda, 173
Sanskrit meters, 173
Sanskrit sounds, 97
Sapphics, 123, 148–149, 158, 327, 328, 339, 340, 341
Sartre, Jean-Paul, 6, 50, 53–59, 102, 351, 371
  desire for popularity, 54
  on ego, 55
  existentialism of, 56, 57
  intellectual development stages of, 58
  on pre-reflective consciousness, 54–55, 57
  sympathy towards Marxism, 56–57
Sat-Chit-Ananda, 65, 93, 97–98, 103, 190, 297. *See also* Truth-Existence-Bliss
'Savitri,' 9, 123, 207–208, 219, 220, 237
  adoration of divine mother, 211–212
  criticism by modernist critics, 210
  as play, 261–263
  quiet and intense pain described in, 209–210
  radical shift in protagonist awareness, 238
  rhythm and 'metrical phrase' of, 213–214
  statement about composition of, 10
Scansion, 131, 219, 328, 329, 337, 338
Schism, 89, 95
School of Aurobindonian poetry
  characteristics of, 319–320
  growth of disciples, 320
"Schools of resentment," 7
Schopenhauer, Arthur, 76–79

disagrement with Kant's philosophy, 76, 77
undifferentiated noumenon of, 78
world as "will and representation," 77
'Sea at Night, The,' 236
Secret of the Vedas, The, 296
Secular philosophy, 17
Seer, 1, 24, 27, 36, 40, 98, 101, 116, 267, 299
Selected Poems, 288
Self and Spirit, 87–88
self-consciousness, 57
Self's Infinity, The, 136–138
Sen, Amartya, 309
Sermon on the Mount, opening verses of, 334
Shakespeare, William, 8, 137, 152, 167–168, 179, 213, 220, 223, 238, 256, 259, 264, 305, 310, 313, 333, 347, 360
achievement of, 217
Heumer's views on works of, 220
language creativity, 221, 222
plays by, 259
plays of, 218
similes of, 220
Sri Aurobindo's comparison with, 217
success as dramatist, 221
Wittgenstein's views on works of, 220–221
Shaw, Bernard, 50, 69, 257, 262, 276, 277, 299, 347–348
'Shiva,' 140–141
Shlesha, 17
Shocking Image, The, 228
short story, 9, 246, 348, 351, 353
Siege of Troy, 275
Sight. *See* Darshana
Silence, 37, 38, 40, 54, 94, 136, 160, 169, 202, 207, 210, 222, 229, 230, 246
'Society for the Protection of Religion,' 357

Socrates, 58, 86, 90
Soliloquy, 335
Soma-rasa, 297
Song Celestial, The, 284
'Song of the Broad- Axe,' 332–333
Sonnets, 9, 146, 153, 162, 171, 220, 221, 227, 229
  'Nirvana,' 130–133
  rhyme scheme, 130, 146
  Self's Infinity, The, 136–138
  structure, 130, 146
Sound-music, 222
Space and time, 72–73, 76
Spatio-temporal world, 80
Speeches that Changed the World, 358
Speech pattern review, 333
Spinoza, Baruch, 80–84
  aspiration of, 84
  conception of world as single unitary substance, 80
  exoteric thought process, 80
  on freedom of speech, 81
  on free will, 81
  on God, 81, 82
Spirit and matter, 83–84
Spiritual and cultural renaissance, in Bengal, 20
Spiritual calling, Indian response to, 18–19
Spiritual devotion, 224
Spiritual evolution, 109
Spirituality, 19, 25, 111, 137, 143, 245, 259, 285, 286, 315, 323, 324, 346, 367
Spiritual philosophy, 17
Spiritual poetry, 143–146, 224
Spondees in English, 330
Sri Aurobindo, 95. *See also* Aphorisms; Plays by Sri Aurobindo; Poetry of Sri Aurobindo; Prose of Sri Aurobindo

achievements as poet, 122–123
arrest by British, 243
books, 17
comparison with Kant, 71
concept of God, 50–51
as critic, 241
on desire for popularity to philosopher, 54
dramas of, 217–218
experience of watching thoughts, 45
as greatest literary figure, 16
integral philosophy, 46, 58
on limits of thought, 41
literary masterworks, 5
nirvana experience, 38–39
as philosopher, 18, 35
integrator of disparate lines, 95
reaction to request for article on metaphysics, 35
physical awareness discovery, 59–60
prose of, 17
reversing lifelong opposition to British, 101
solution of gnostic community of highly evolved beings, 68
supra-ethics, system of, 72
thought, foundations of, 6
views on Heraclitus's work, 64–65
views on philosophy, 36
vision of Übermensch, 48–49
yogic experience, 37–38
Sri Aurobindo, the Poet, 233
Sri Krishna, 19, 21, 29, 46, 49, 95, 116, 117, 266, 284–286, 285, 360
Srotrasya srotram, 265
Stanza, options to scan, 338
'Statues, The,' 17
Sthairya, 112

Stories, 346–347, 351
  beginning and ending of, 352
  Idylls of the Occult, The, 353
  Phantom Hour, The, 352–353
  short, 351
Story of Philosophy, The, 89
St Paul, 334–335
Strife and contradiction, 62
Structuralism, 40
Studies in Classic American Literature, 23
Suffering, 77
Superconscious planes, 58
Super-language, 222
Superstitions, 64
Supra-ethics, system of, 72
Supramental Manifestation, The, 246, 298
Swamy, Purohit, 238, 239
Swarajya, 358
Swinburne, Algernon, 148–151, 171, 328
Syllables, 132, 149, 155, 171, 172, 196, 265, 329, 330, 331, 337, 338
Symbol Dawn, The, 207–208
Synchrony, 97, 99
Synthesis of Yoga, The, 17, 20

T

Tagore, Rabindranath, 8, 18
  achievements of, 244
  comparison with Sri Aurobindo, 246
  English poetry, 122
  lyricism and spirituality of, 245
  paintings of, 244
  respect for Sri Aurobindo, 243
  translations of, 247

visit to Pondicherry, 245–246
Talks on Poetry, 337
Tathastu, 358
Tat of Vedanta, 91
'Temple, The,' 225
Tennyson, Alfred, 154, 171, 175, 179, 195, 202, 215, 314, 328, 330, 333
'Morte d'Arthur,' 200
'Ulysses,' 199–200
Thomas, Dylan, 153
Thoughts and Aphorisms, 279
'Thought the Paraclete,' 170–173, 340–341
Thou, realization of, 116–117
Time and space, 72–73
Times Literary Supplement (London), 219
Tirukkural, 299
Tolle, Eckhart, 42, 55
Tractatus, 276, 348
Tractatus Logico-Philsophicus, 40
Transcendental idealism, 71–72
Transcreators, 287
Translation
challenges, 291–292
Gita, 301
global reach of, 247
ideal, 287–288
Kalidasa and Bhartrihari, 301
literary imperialism and, 300
meaning of, 287
"metaphrase" or "paraphrase," 288
Prières et Méditations, 301–302
Selected Poems, 288
theory of translating cultures, 289–290
threefold approach to, 300–301
Tirukkural, 299

Translator's Invisibility: A History of Translation, The, 288
as transplant, 288–289
Upanishads, 238–240, 290–293, 301
Vikramorvasie, 303–305
Translations of Vedas, 294, 298
Rig Veda, 295–297
threefold approach to, 300–301
Transliterators, 287
Trochaic-dactylic meter, 333
Trochee-dactyl rhythms, 333
Trochees, 332
Truth-Consciousness-Bliss, 49, 93, 297
Truth-Existence-Bliss, 50

U

'Ulysses,' 199–200
Unifications, 97–98
Unified field theory, 68
Unitarian principle, 108
Unity, 20, 22, 57, 61, 81, 93, 106, 107, 113, 167, 225, 313
of being, 62–63
of opposites, 62–63
spiritual, 277
Universe, 22, 61, 80, 82, 86, 88, 90, 93, 94, 116, 133, 169, 217, 230, 273, 279, 291, 332
Unsentimental non-sententious verse, 202
Upanishadic sound, 238
Upanishads, 15, 67, 76, 77, 83, 115, 144, 208, 218, 232, 238, 266, 290–293, 291, 292, 296, 301, 312, 321, 322, 323
'Urvasie,' 180–182, 195–197, 305
Uttara Mimansa, 298
Uttarpara speech, 357–365

as eloquent discourse, 361–362
laid out in front of people, 360–361
message of Gita in, 361
personal element in, 362–363
significance for Indian, 357
significance for world of future, 359–360

V

Vaughan, Henry, 224
Vedanta, 18–20, 29, 41, 46, 47, 82–83, 87, 90, 93, 98–99, 109, 111, 115, 264, 278, 298, 367
basic postulate of, 90
indescribable, 41
wisdom of, 278
words, 41
Vedantic method of pursuing, 102
Vedantic monism of Brahman, 98
Vedas, 18, 28, 60, 64, 144, 208, 218, 232, 246, 292–299, 301, 316, 321, 322, 323
secret of, 246
translation of, 60, 218
Vedic gods, 298
Vedic India, 64
Vedic rishis, 94
Venuti, Lawrence, 288
Vigil of Thaliard, The, 183–186
Vigyanamaya, 67
Vikramorvasie, 303–305
Vipassana, 45
Vital, 67, 108, 225
Vital awareness, 58
Vivekananda, Swami, 20
Viziers of Bassora, The, 218, 249–256
caustic towards other cultures, 253–254

deep purpose of, 251
delightful lines of, 254
as farce, 251–252
history of, 249
mission to buy slave-girl, 252–253
as morality play, 250–251
precursors of, 254
romantic mold, 254–255
story of, 249–250
Vowel
in English, 337
in Hindi, 327

W

Waller, Edmund, 143
War, 24, 25, 62, 63, 177, 218
Watson, Francis, 233
WB Yeats: A New Biography, 232
Western canon, 7–8
Western Canon: The Books and School of the Ages, The, 7
Western philosophy, 22, 39, 42–43, 44, 46, 47, 59, 69, 71, 74, 75, 77, 78, 79, 80, 93, 94, 95, 371
What Really Matters: Searching for Wisdom in America, 108–109
Whitehead, Alfred North, 67
Whitman, Walt, 23–24, 27, 157, 164–165, 196, 211, 265, 327, 332
Wilde, Oscar, 135, 252, 254, 347, 348, 376
Wittgenstein, Ludwig, 35, 56, 75, 93, 220, 310
contribution to modern thought, 42–43
on ethics and aesthetics, 42
on limits of thought, 41
on logical system, 39–40
on silence, 40

Tractatus, 276
understanding of time and eternity, 42
views on philosophy, 35–37
'Word of the Silence, The,' 229–230
Wordsworth, William, 224, 327
World as "will and representation," 77

Y

Yajna, 297
Yeats, William Butler, 16, 17, 27, 179, 181, 187, 190, 193, 196, 212, 242, 247, 315
artistry of, 237
association with Irish Dramatic Society, 232
as critic, 241
half-lit subliminal shades of, 235
home in Gaelic occult, 237
'Lake Isle of Innisfree, The,' 235
luminous high-romanticism of, 236
as master of incantation, 240
parallelism with Sri Aurobindo, 231
as poet of Celtic twilights, 231
spirituality of, 233
and Sri Aurobindo, difference between works of, 235–242
Sri Aurobindo's views on works of, 233–234
translation works of, 238–240
Yoga, 7, 9, 17, 20, 25, 35, 46, 67, 67, 74, 111, 112, 114, 137, 218, 264, 266, 276, 276, 298, 301, 318, 346, 347, 363
Yogi, 46, 47, 73, 111, 130, 149, 251, 286, 320, 358, 368
Yogic experience, 37, 108, 123, 137
Yogic sadhana, 127
Yogi Emperor, Indian ideal of, 68

Z

Zeno of Elea's paradoxes, 93–94
Zohar, 80

About the Author

Pariksith Singh is a poet, writer, entrepreneur and healer. His life, work and literature are uniquely personalized expressions of his spiritual journey and unfolding realization. One can sense a constant striving towards deeper and wider truth in all that he is and does.

Pariksith's creativity spans from literature, philosophy and science to politics, business and entrepreneurship. He writes widely and deeply on all matters that he feels are relevant to contemporary human civilization. His concern, though all this, remains only one — the articulation of the deeper and the wider.

Pariksith published his first work, *The Shoreless River*, in 2005. In 2008, his works, *Riddles for Pesky Teenagers* and his first Hindi poems, *Chhuti Ke Din*, were published. In 2019, *Kshitijon Ke Paar*, a collection of Hindi poems, and selections from *Radha's Geet*, a series of mystical devotional poems in English, were published.

There was a Girl I Loved Once, a collection of his English mystical-symbolical poetry, was published in 2018. *Swayam Ka Ghuspaithiya*, a collection of his symbolical Hindi poetry, was also published in 2018.

Besides his prolific poetry, Pariksith also writes medical literature. *Health Care Primer*, a series of books on medical practices, is being published every year from 2018. *Grow Your Medical Practice* is another of his published books on medical practice and entrepreneurship. In 2021, he has published *MRA Made Simple* and *Compliance Made Simple*.

Pariksith presently lives in Florida, US, with his wife and four children and practices medicine while running a healthcare business.